Woman as Mediatrix

Recent Titles in
Contributions in Women's Studies

The Ottoman Lady: A Social History from 1718 to 1918
Fanny Davis

Leading the Way: Amy Morris Homans and The Beginnings of
Professional Education for Women
Betty Spears

The Politics of the Feminist Novel
Judi M. Roller

Radiant Daughters: Fictional American Women
Thelma J. Shinn

New World, New Roles: A Documentary History of Women in
Pre-Industrial America
Sylvia R. Frey and Marian J. Morton

Gender, Ideology, and Action: Historical Perspectives on Women's
Public Lives
Janet Sharistanian, editor

American Women and Political Participation: Impacts of Work, Generation,
and Feminism
Karen Beckwith

The American Victorian Woman: The Myth and the Reality
Mabel Collins Donnelly

Gender and Destiny: Women Writers and the Holocaust
Marlene E. Heinemann

Nineteenth-Century Women Writers of the English-Speaking World
Rhoda B. Nathan, editor

Women's Rights in France
Dorothy McBride Stetson

Charity, Challenge, and Change: Religious Dimensions of the
Mid-Nineteenth Century Women's Movement in Germany
Catherine M. Prelinger

Woman as Mediatrix

Essays on Nineteenth-Century European Women Writers

Edited by
Avriel H. Goldberger

Prepared under the auspices of Hofstra University

Contributions in Women's Studies, Number 73

Greenwood Press
New York . Westport, Connecticut . London

Library of Congress Cataloging-in-Publication Data

Woman as mediatrix.

(Contributions in women's studies, ISSN 0147-104X ;
no. 73)
"Prepared under the auspices of Hofstra University."
Bibliography: p.
Includes index.
1. Women authors, European—19th century—Biography.
2. European literature—19th century—History and
criticism.   3. European literature—Women authors—
History and criticism.   4. Feminists—Europe—Biography.
I. Goldberger, Avriel H.   II. Hofstra University.
III. Series.
PN471.W55   1987   809'.89287   86-14236
ISBN 0-313-25515-6 (lib. bdg. : alk. paper)

Library of Congress Catalog Card Number: 86-14236
ISBN: 0-313-25515-6
ISSN: 0147-104X

First published in 1987

Greenwood Press, Inc.
88 Post Road West, Westport, Connecticut 06881

Printed in the United States of America

The paper used in this book complies with the
Permanent Paper Standard issued by the National
Information Standards Organization (Z39.48-1984).

10 9 8 7 6 5 4 3 2 1

Copyright Acknowledgment

Permission to reproduce material from the following source is
gratefully acknowledged.

Sofya Kovalevskaya, *A Russian Childhood* (New York: Springer-Verlag,
1978). Translated, edited and introduced by Beatrice Stillman.
© 1978 by Beatrice Stillman.

Contents

Introduction

Germaine Brée

For several years now, Hofstra University's Cultural Center has successfully organized and hosted a series of conferences on topics germane to the intellectual climate of our time. One of these conferences was the widely attended November, 1980, Conference on Nineteenth-Century Women Writers. It drew participants not only from colleges and universities throughout the United States but also from France and England. In 1980 women's studies had been developing vigorously, and Hofstra was one of its active centers with, among other contributions, its strong sponsorship of George Sand studies. The 1980 conference was thus able to program some fifty papers by established scholars, most of them women. The present volume contains a selection of fifteen of these papers, chosen with great care to give it a coherent framework, hence the absence of the great English novelists—Austen, the Brontës and George Eliot—and of Emily Dickinson, who were not absent from the conference program and are represented in a companion volume (Rhoda Nathan, ed., *Nineteenth-Century Women Writers of the English-Speaking World*, Greenwood Press, 1986).

It takes much thought on the part of an editor to draw such a frame from the papers themselves, where none had been pre-imposed. There are a few papers that are, as it were, self-contained, whose tie to the others is merely that they refer to a nineteenth-century woman writer; they offer solid contributions to literary history: Julia Frey's well-documented account of the puppet theatre at Nohant, Alex Szogyi's sensitive presentation of Sand's role in the creation of the best of Musset's plays, *Lorenzaccio*, Ruth Joeres' description of the career of the poet Louise Otto as an advocate of liberalism and Maruta Ray's account of the strange discrepancies in the critical evaluation of Annette von Droste-Hülshoff's "Die Judenbuche."

As we roam through Europe and over the years, what questions might one not raise concerning French, English, German, Swedish, Russian and American women writers, so numerous and so different in their social and cultural backgrounds? They are women whose lives in fact range over two centuries: Germaine de Staël was born in 1766 and Juliette Adam died in 1936, although to be sure, *she* was a centenarian! Very little seems to link the stolid Frederika Bremer, Sweden's "first feminist," to the two beautiful and fascinating Korvin-Krukovskaia sisters, of the Russian intelligentsia, whose adventures ending in an involvement in the revolutionary violence of the French commune Isabelle Naginski relates. What connection, if any, do these "rebels" have with the arch-conservative Juliette Adam except that they were feminists and lived in the nineteenth century?

Chapter 1 draws the parameters of an inquiry which brings the other chapters into focus. Marie-Claire Hoock-Demarle starts from the premise that, different as they are, women in the nineteenth century do share a common new experience: the industrial revolution deeply affected the structure of all European countries and from period to period will modify a thoughtful woman's perception of her role, rights and place in the society. Her approach is dialectical, taking three well-known figures—Mary Wollstonecraft, the precursor, Bettina von Arnim and Flora Tristan—and analyzing the process whereby, under the impact of social change, each takes a further step away from the dominant image of the ideal woman toward an ever more active involvement in socio-political activities. They glimpse, she feels, that a new economic society will require a "new woman" and attempt to identify themselves in relation to that image. Her chapter furnishes an excellent example of socio-cultural history to which Doris Starr Guilloton's brisk presentation of the German situation belongs. Her "representative women"—Rahel Varnhagen and the Countess Hahn-Hahn—are seen more concretely in their relations with two well-defined literary groups—the "Romantics" and the members of "young Germany." Dealing with the same process of change, but in literary terms, Madelyn Gutwirth traces the changes in the sensibility and awareness of young Germaine Necker, at first a fervent admirer of Rousseau's image of

woman as the "angel in the house." As she herself becomes Madame
de Staël, so Rousseau's Julie steps aside making way for that assertive
feminine genius Corinne, who most flatly refuses to be either consigned to the household or condemned to virginity.

We approach here what appears to be a dichotomy in the feminine
search for a new role and identity. On the one hand new aspirations
may take the form of a passionate response to fictional figures that
symbolize a woman's desires. So Margaret Fuller, dreaming herself
into the role of the "Yankee Corinna," is deftly described by her able
biographer, Paula Blanchard; on the other hand we discover a deep-
ening feminine sensitivity to social problems. Staël and Sand in this
respect provide a double model for women—in fiction and in reality—
hence no doubt their immense prestige. But that ideal has its counterpart, which shows up the limits that differences in culture may place
in the path of the most determined feminine "humanist." As amusing
as they are revealing are the articles in which Patricia Thomson, Marie-
Jacques Hoog and Eve Sourian trace the boundaries and conflicts in
literary sophistication and social prejudice characteristic of these writers: Sand's ambivalence toward the English, Staël's immovable attachment to Paris society and its ways, her contempt for the social life in
all other European countries. Most entertaining is Marie-Jacques Hoog's
analysis of the wonderful Frances Trollope, who managed to reconcile
her deep adherence to middle-class British proprieties and her enthusiasm for George Sand by serenely drawing an opaque veil over the
improprieties, moral and literary, that Sand, just as serenely, had committed. Most intriguing is the combination in Juliette Adam of the
themes of feminism and its practice with espousal of the most reactionary political stance.

Thus, great travellers that they were, and writers of memoirs and
novels, these women present a mirror to us through which we see
them better than they could see themselves in relation to their society.
We measure the courage they needed to break some of the taboos of
the time. Two types of rebellion emerge, both social: the deliberate
personal rebellion against sexual and cultural constraints; the less colorful
but perhaps more effective effort to bring about social reforms. But
only rarely, it would seem, is either conducive to literary fame. Staël
and Sand, exceptionally, seem better than most others to have found
their own—so different—literary voices. As these women pass before
our eyes, we in turn become aware of the sometimes ironic affection

and complicity with which they are treated, even in such short works. There is much food for thought in these chapters but even more in the network of cross-references that they bring to light. "To be continued," one thinks as one closes the volume, and this is a real tribute to editor and scholars alike.

Woman as Mediatrix

1

The Nineteenth Century: Insights of Contemporary Women Writers

Marie-Claire Hoock-Demarle

> For women have sat indoors all these millions of years, so that by this
> time the very walls are permeated by their creative force, which has,
> indeed, so over-charged the capacity of bricks and mortar that it must
> needs harness itself to pens and brushes and business and politics. But
> this creative power differs greatly from the creative power of men.
>
> Virginia Woolf, *A Room of One's Own*, Hogarth Press, 1931.

Throughout the ages women had turned their hand to writing, with
novels, diaries and letters claiming pride of place as their chosen medium. But for the most part the literature they produced, spontaneous
in its inspiration, was essentially sporadic and short lived and personal
in its approach. It is therefore curious to see, between 1750 and 1850,
a different kind of literature emerging from the pens of women writers, one that was both more specific in its form and more deeply rooted
in reality in its content. The assertion of a female viewpoint was bound
to be a slow process, with pitfalls along the way. It has seemed interesting to retrace the development of some of these early writings, apparently unconnected geographically, socially or even chronologically.

From what was initially a mere observation of fact—progressive
industrialization in the West and simultaneously the increasing number
of commentaries by women on the subject—we go on to ask ourselves
whether there was a growth of awareness on the part of women in
particular and, if so, whether it brought with it a new mode of literary
expression, one that was specific to women.

In an attempt to answer these questions, which cast women adrift from their traditionally accepted position of confinement to the family circle, we have chosen to discuss the work of three writers from different backgrounds—Mary Wollstonecraft, who was English and whose works we shall consider only cursorily; the German writer Bettina Brentano-von Arnim and the French writer Flora Tristan. It is possible, despite their differences, to discern some logical sequence in the questions they raised and in the answers provided to the initial question: why, precisely during this period, did women turn to social comment in their writing?

The reason for our referring to the figure and role of Mary Wollstonecraft in introducing this study is that her work, in particular *A Vindication of the Rights of Women*, published in 1792, gave those who came after her a point of departure for their own investigations.[1] Chronologically, Mary Wollstonecraft was a daughter of the eighteenth century, but intellectually she belonged to that pivotal generation whose ideas spilled over and indeed continued into the nineteenth century. With her, and after her, the image of women changed.

Mary Wollstonecraft's whole approach is that of a contemporary of the French Revolution, with its excesses but also with the merit of clearly stating the major issues of concern to contemporary women writers—the role of education by and for women, the right to work, women's place in society—all palpable claims, which from then on were to be inseparable from the question of recognition of equality of the sexes.

The difficult position of this pioneering figure was, however, discernible in what she wrote, which was marked by her constant effort to assert herself as a woman in a man's society. Her portrayal of herself as a creature of reason made her forget at times the woman that she was and the women around her, with the result that a strange paradox emerges from her book—the woman of the future is seen, to use her own expression, as a "masculinated woman." To be sure, reason and equality emerge victorious, but that victory obscures the trap into which she has fallen and, when all is said and done, prevents the author of the *Vindication* from inventing her own personal language. Mary Wollstonecraft thus remains a figure of reference, one who brought herself to ask the questions that others would attempt to answer.

A generation later, the position of women in relation to contemporary society was different. For many women, being accepted into society no longer represented a hazardous course to a distant goal. Such was the case of Bettina Brentano-von Arnim, who was born into the wealthy merchant class whose fortunes had been made amid the vicissitudes of the revolutionary and post-revolutionary period. Like many women of her generation, Bettina von Arnim successively moved in and held sway over various social circles, from the eighteenth-century salon to the Romantic movement and the political circle she gathered around her in Berlin from 1835 on.[2] The issue at stake, therefore, was no longer so much to wage a battle for women's autonomy in a man's society as to safeguard the individual, of either sex, in a world increasingly threatened by the mass movements unknown to the previous generation.

Von Arnim's work is a comment on her age and a deliberate attempt to record the struggle waged in her time by the individual, by women and by the writer; and it revolves entirely around the concept of the individual, progressing from a sometimes complacent autobiographical portrait to an ever more down-to-earth grasp of the social phenomena of her age. What may appear to be a step backwards from the theories of Mary Wollstonecraft is, in fact, evidence of a more radically feminist approach. Women are no longer seen as beings endowed with faculties of reason, social creatures, but as individuals in their own right. Von Arnim took up the fight where Mary Wollstonecraft let herself become submerged in generalities. The demand for equal rights for men and women is here surpassed by the burning issue of the day, the identity of men and women alike.[3] Women have a part to play in this process. Von Arnim, personally conscious as she was of the importance in her life of her own female forbears, believed that women have an essential quality, namely energy.[4] It gives them a twin role in the history of that period. First, in the midst of the breakdown of society they are the custodians of the established values of family, education and human dignity. But they are also the opponents of any form of hypocrisy and intrigue. Von Arnim's positive heroes are, on the one hand, the great criminals of history[5] and, on the other hand, Goethe's mother, Frau Ray, a figure shaped by the enlightened spirit of the eighteenth century, who does not let herself be taken in by either princes or priests.[6]

Von Arnim's chance in history was to have witnessed the confrontation between the individual and the world around him or her, to have proved capable of denouncing the burden of social issues on every human being. Between that new entity, the mid-century urban environment, and the woman writer, a new relationship was growing up and was reflected in "social writings." In a work entitled *This Book Belongs to the King*, published in 1843 and then a year later in a "Book of the Poor," unpublished for reasons of censorship, von Arnim recounted a phenomenon that made a tardy appearance in Germany but spread rapidly—industrialization and its corollary, urban poverty and the emergence of the "artificial poor." The Berlin Vogtland, with its 2,500 workers' families, is one of the most striking examples—although by no means the only one—of these "poor colonies" living on the outskirts of urban centers.[7] But von Arnim's approach was a very personal one; she did not merely reflect on the poverty of the working class but was struck more deeply by the isolation and uprooting of the masses, with the disruption of families, deterioration of human relations and breakdown of kinship ties as a result of the rural exodus. Paradoxically, overcrowding led to isolation, just as the spirit of competition that now dominated the notion of work led to distrust. Caught up in the constant battle for his daily subsistance, the Vogtland industrial worker was threatened with the loss of those qualities that had made him a human being in his own right in his family, his work and his contacts with those around him. Von Arnim related this irreversible process of dehumanization. These beings, victims of industry, competition and the inability to adapt to their times, are objects—objects of charity, of pressure and of exchange if they should prove unprofitable. What else in fact was that relegation of the individual to the rank of an object but what Marx, in other terms, was beginning to describe broadly as alienation?[8] We are in fact touching here on one of the fundamental characteristics of women's social comment. Now that the central issues were no longer being dealt with on a theoretical, abstract plane, the question of the impact of women's views, their immediate effect, was posed in different terms. Von Arnim's book was reprinted several times in her lifetime, and the chapter on the Vogtland was even translated into French in the periodical *La Voix des femmes* (*Women's Voices*), March, 1848. That it met with such a response among the general public was evidence of its significant influence on the incipient awareness of that precise fact that the neglect, indeed the contempt, in which von Arnim's social writings have been held, is due less to their content than to the fact that they were written by a woman.[9]

But there is more to it than that. With von Arnim's social writings, we witness the birth of a new kind of literature. Abandoning autobiography, a genre that she treated in a manner very much her own, she embarked on an entirely new approach, and a remarkable one. Her "Book of the Poor" represented the findings of a survey conducted on the basis of criteria that, though still rudimentary, even then were to yield positive results: correspondents *in situ*, use of the press to request information, complex survey grids, consultation with reputed medical practitioners, jurists, and so on. It was a collective endeavor, with von Arnim merely assuming a role of organizer and editor.[10] There is clearly a transition from pure literature to social writing and, in approach, from fiction to a documentary account. Underlying the human being's "intrinsic genius," which has too often obscured all else, there is, then, an inescapable logic and a steadfast belief in the identity of the individual. But the individuals are threatened on all sides, by urban overcrowding and the ever swifter pace of life, by the destruction of their systems of values and the disappearance of the whole network of relationships by which they previously defined themselves. It is the survival of the individual that von Arnim is defending, and her plea takes her from an analysis of her own specific position as a woman, a writer and an individual—also threatened—to an analysis of a mass phenomenon. It is an unbroken itinerary from her discovery, then affirmation, of her own identity, to her demand for recognition of the identity of all human beings.

In contrast with Mary Wollstonecraft, von Arnim's approach did not ultimately deepen the rift between women and the society in which they lived. Between women, still excluded by the mid-nineteenth century middle class, and factory workers alienated by industry, a new community of purpose grew up, bringing to light the existence of two focal points of resistance that were destined to draw closer and closer together.[11] What was new was that the accounts written by women, about everyday life and experience, more visual than abstract and deeply rooted in contemporary reality, were a contributing factor in that rapprochement. Moving further and further away from literary imaginings and Utopian schemes, hostile to any form of systematization, they became a medium of communication between individuals threatened with losing their identity—workers in the towns and women in society.

Neither Mary Wollstonecraft nor Bettina Brentano-von Arnim had yet, however, taken the decisive step of using her writing as a means of direct action. Yet would Flora Tristan's commitment, which led her to stand up to the taboos of English society and the obstacles she met with on her "Tour de France," have been possible if the way had not been prepared by her predecessors? Flora Tristan's tribute to Mary Wollstonecraft in her *Promenades dans Londres* is a significant admission of the debt she owed her.[12] It is true that the social question was becoming more acute, that Flora Tristan travelled more widely than her two predecessors and that the comparisons she was able to draw from her experience lent her testimony greater meaning and depth, since her analysis took in both the contemporary scene—in France— and the consequences of the recent past—in England. Her works tell of a phenomenon that in the space of a few generations had become the "Social Question"—an ineluctable, omnipresent, worldwide phenomenon.[13]

So England, from which Mary Wollstonecraft had turned aside to survey the scene of the continent, again became the focus of attention for women writers and was to be a constant source of fascination to the budding sociologists of the time.[14] But it was not merely to retrace the origins of the phenomenon. The England and especially the London of the mid-nineteenth century epitomized all the upheavals that industrialization could bring in its wake: the sprawling monster of a city with its socially excluded groups, the disintegration of its social fabric, prostitution, robbery, physical and moral decline—but also the Chartist movement, the early schools run along the lines advocated by Owen and the beginnings of a workers' co-operative movement.[15]

Five years apart, in two very different cities, two women were to record the situation as they saw it—Flora Tristan with "La Paroisse Saint-Gilles" in London and von Arnim with the "Vogtland" in Berlin. At first sight their approach seems remarkably similar—visits *in situ*, questions, descriptions of living and working conditions and of family and human relations. But their surveys of the working-class environment differed in many respects. It is true that some of the differences were due to the actual nature of the object of the survey, in that the older established English type of manufacturing industry was distinct from the cottage industry pattern, which still prevailed in the

Vogtland.[16] The main difference, however, seems to lie in the writers themselves and their approach, showing how swift was their ability to adjust to the scale and consequences of the phenomenon of industrialization. Whereas von Arnim's typology merely gives a picture of young and old struggling to face up to adversity and safeguard their human dignity, Flora Tristan was pitiless in her portrayal of the "rank stupidity," apathy and degeneration of the working-class world.[17] Her observation of the social situation led her to adopt a far more radical position than von Arnim, and it is unmistakably the class struggle that she is predicting here.[18]

With her *Tour de France* (1843–44) it is no longer a question of merely observing but of sacrificing herself to carry her message into the remotest provincial towns of France. With the transition from chronicle to message, the written word had become a direct means of action and commitment.

Although Flora Tristan's writings were addressed to men and women alike, she never overlooked the specific role of women. Like von Arnim and Mary Wollstonecraft, Flora Tristan founded her faith in a new society on two inseparable elements, women and education. Because she was aware that her words must be followed by deeds, she spoke to women of their exploitation in forthright terms. In the *Promenades dans Londres*, she had retraced the scourge of prostitution in London with remarkable courage and clear-sightedness. She discovered that prostitution was everywhere, in Lyons as in London, in the street and in the workshop.[19] Her strength lay in demonstrating that prostitution was not merely a corollary but an integral part of the system. The vicious circle of unemployment and prostitution had become the price to be paid in relations between the exploiter and the exploited. On entering the production process, a woman—"the proletarian of proletarians," to use Flora Tristan's expression—had perhaps won some kind of equality, but it was a negative form of equality that would ultimately mean a deterioration of her status as a human being. Yet, in the course of her travels, Flora Tristan was to discover that women had a greater potential for revolt than men.[20] Pragmatism and energy were qualities she encountered daily and ones that she skillfully made use of to broadcast her message.[21]

In Flora Tristan's eyes, women also had a vital part to play as educators for the world of tomorrow. Here, too, the English model, beginning with a reading of the *Vindication,* was decisive. In a chap-

ter of the *Promenades dans Londres* dealing with infants' schools,
Flora Tristan pleaded the case for public, egalitarian, compulsory education. The supreme aim of equal education for all was to prepare
women for corporate life, the basis of any new society.[22] It is evident
that Flora Tristan was reflecting here one of the key ideas of the Utopian socialism of her generation. The blueprint for education was the
master plan for society as a whole and went beyond mere faith in the
power of education. While freely developing his or her personal faculties, the individual is socialized from an early age. That is the foundation on which the new society must be built, as opposed to a process
of accommodation within an established social order, ostensibly in the
name of reason and of the individual.

Flora Tristan's travels throughout provincial France also alerted her
to a contradiction that was to fuel her plea for women's emancipation.
Despite the ignorance in which women were kept by virtue of the
social system, they "had a primary role in educating children."[23] All
that was needed was for them to be made aware of the importance of
that role, and with their natural energy, they would overcome the obstacle of ignorance inflicted on them not by nature but by society.
Indeed, the voice of Flora Tristan was heard, since the women cam-
paigners of 1848 were to draw their leitmotif of an "Association of
socialist men and women teachers" from her appeal.[24]

Thus through their own education and that which they were subsequently to dispense, women were seen by Flora Tristan as the center
of the social movement and no longer just of society as such. Her
position, placing equal emphasis on the emancipation and the social
role of women, is clearly summed up in her affirmation that "she must
be recognized as a social individual."[25] There is nothing contradictory
in her statement. "We must emancipate ourselves before we can
emancipate others."[26]

It can be seen, despite the varying degree of emphasis in our treatment of their work, that the writings of these three women differ primarily in the questions raised and the manner in which they are resolved—the author's conception of women, her relationship to herself
and the specificity of her literary approach. It is perhaps on this latter
point that the differences are most striking. Mary Wollstonecraft's work
reveals a degree of compliance with a given model that, though seeking to emancipate, remains in the sphere of the general and the ideal.
Bettina Brentano-von Arnim, refusing, in the name of individual iden-

tity, a dichotomy of the sexes, invented a style that reflected intimately her own personal experience. But as social reality impinged on her consciousness and she turned from autobiography to documentary observation and social inquiry, her writing, a woman's view of her epoch, acquired its social significance. With Flora Tristan, writing became an act of faith, and women were given their voice in society.

There is nonetheless an underlying continuity in their works. In all three cases, the role of women is forcefully affirmed. Mary Wollstonecraft's contribution to this was decisive, speaking as she did as a woman to other women, even if her ideas were not always new.[27] Flora Tristan was prompted by very much the same concerns in seeking to make women aware of the importance of their role.

Similarly, the problem of female identity is a recurrent theme. Out of Mary Wollstonecraft's demand for civic identity was born von Arnim's emphasis on individual identity and Flora Tristan's claim for social identity.

The basic difference among the three approaches is in fact due more than anything to the changes that occurred during the period from 1750 to 1850. Being women in 1790 or in 1840 was a different matter. For Mary Wollstonecraft, the aim was primarily to raise women to equal status with men, while Flora Tristan, writing in 1840, was concerned with working women, and although some degree of equality did exist, it was an equality pervaded by poverty and degradation. Could the emancipation of women be reduced to the emancipation of the "bee at work?"[28] This is where von Arnim's ideas come into their own. Without the emancipation of the individual, saving him or her from being alienated through work, the process would be irreversible.

Although three very personal approaches to the same question are presented here, they reveal an underlying continuity, whether deliberate or fortuitous. For they provide the first evidence of the expression of a specifically female point of view, the way in which women both surveyed the contemporary scene and reflected on the role of a new kind of woman in a new kind of society.

NOTES

1. Mary Wollstonecraft, *A Vindication of the Rights of Women* (London: J. Johnson, 1792). New edition 1891 by Mrs. Henry Fawcet. Reprinted by the Norton Library, New York, 1967.

Daughter of a modest landowner ruined by the agrarian reforms, Mary Wollstonecraft (1759–97) led an unsettled existence hardly conducive to a regular education. With her sisters she started a school in the suburbs of London and then travelled through Portugal, France and Norway. Deeply affected by her relationship with Imlay (she attempted suicide in 1792), she eventually linked her fate to that bitterest opponent of the institution of marriage, the philosopher Godwin. She was to die giving birth to a daughter, the future Mary Shelley, author of *Frankenstein*.

Mary Wollstonecraft's work was known to von Arnim, for it is listed in the (unpublished) catalogue of the library at Wiepersdorf, the von Arnim's country residence. See *Goethe-Schiller Archiv* (Weimar Lfd 1123). Flora Tristan, for her part, paid a double tribute to her predecessor, citing her as a source at the beginning of her *Promenades dans Londres* (Paris: Maspero, 1978) and speaking highly of her in her chapter on English women in the same work (chap. 17).

2. Bettina Brentano-von Arnim (1785–1859) was born in Frankfurt into a wealthy Italian merchant family, the Brentanos. She spent her young years between the ancient Imperial free city and the district of Offenbach, the home of her grandmother, Sophie von La Roche, who had herself been a distinguished woman of letters in her day. Introduced by her brother, the poet Clemens Brentano, into the group of Romantics known as the Heidelberg group, in 1811 she married the Prussian poet and aristocrat Achim von Arnim, whom she bore seven children. She did not embark upon her literary career until 1835, four years after the death of von Arnim and three years after that of Goethe, her relations with whom have been subject to various interpretations.

3. During the years preceding the 1848 revolution, von Arnim was to assert her position in the singular political climate of the Prussian *Vormarz*. See von Arnim's use of the neuter "es" to describe herself in her "Goethe's Correspondence with a Child" (*das Kind*, 1835) in Bettina von Arnim, *Werke und Briefe* (Gustav Konrad, Koln: Bartmann-Verlag, 1959), Band 2.

4. Von Arnim's grandmother, Sophie von La Roche, was a talented novelist, and Lotte in Goethe's *Werther* was modelled partly on her mother, Maximiliane.

5. The criminal as a "positive hero." See von Arnim, *Werke und Briefe*, Band 3/4, p. 182. It is a theme taken up by Flora Tristan in *Tour de France*, vol. II (Paris: F. Maspero, 1980), p. 209, and by Eric Hobsbawn, *Primitive Rebels* (New York: Norton Library, 1965).

6. "Dies Buch gehort dem König" (1843); *Werke und Briefe*, Band 3/4. "Das Armenbuch," written in 1844 and published in the *Jahrbuch des freies deutschen Hochstift*, ed. W. Vortriede (Frankfurt, 1961), p. 497ff. Reprinted by Insel-Verlag, Frankfurt, 1981.

7. See in particular Friedrich Engels, *Die Lage der arbeitenden Klasse in England* (Leipzig: O. Wigand, 1845).

8. On the meetings between Marx and Bettina von Arnim (especially at Kreuznach in 1843), see G. Meyer-Heppner, "Das Bettina von Arnim Archiv," in *Sinn and Form*, vol. II (Berlin: Rutten und Loening, 1954), p. 594ff.

9. Cf. how the critics have reacted to von Arnim's work—from Engels (who makes no mention of her) to Carl Schmitt, *Politische Romantik* (Berlin: Duncker und Humblot, 1968), p. 193, n. 1, not to mention the *Allgemeine Deutsche Biographie*, which expresses regret that a woman should indulge in political considerations of this ilk!

10. M. C. Hoock-Demarle, "Les Ecrits sociaux de Bettina von Arnim ou les débuts de l'enquête sociale dans le Vormarx prussien," in *Le Mouvement social*, no. 110 (Paris: Les Editions ouvrières; January 1980).

11. A. Bebel, *Die Frau und der Sozialismus* (Zurich: Volksbuchhandlung, 1891); J. Stuart Mill, *The Subjection of Women* (1869).

12. Flora Tristan (1803–44). An illegitimate child, she never lost the feeling of being an "outcast." After a difficult childhood and a disastrous marriage, she fled her troubled existence, travelling in England (1826, 1831, 1837 and 1839) and in Peru. She won renown with accounts of her travels, "Pérégrinations d'une Paria," published in 1838; her first socially committed works were her *Promenades dans Londres* (1839) and her pamphlet "L'Union ouvrière" (1843). Her journal, "Le Tour de France," 1843–44, was not published until 1973. Notes by J. L. Puech (Paris: La Tête des feuilles); republished in 1980 (Paris: Maspero, collection: *La Découverte*, introd. S. Michaud). Of Mary Wollstonecraft's book, Flora Tristan was to write: "This is an imperishable work."

13. As a true follower of Saint-Simon, Flora Tristan was not opposed to industry as such but to the uses to which it was put.

14. See the journal of G. d'Eichthal published in England under the title *A French Sociologist Looks at Britain: Gustave D'Eichthal and British Society in 1828*, Trans. Barrie M. Retcliffe and W. H. Chalonner (Manchester: Manchester Union Press, 1977). On the other works of the period concerning England, see F. Bédarida, Introduction aux *Promenades dans Londres* (Paris: Maspero, 1978), pp. 14–15.

15. See the chapter on Owen that Flora Tristan did not include in the first edition of her *Promenades dans Londres*, p. 358ff., and her reflections on the Chartist movement and the "Workingmen's Association" (chap. 5 of the *Promenades*).

16. On industry in London, see F. Bédarida, "Londres au milieu du XIXème siècle," *Annales XXIII*, E.S.C. (Economies, Sociétés, Civilisations) no. 2 (March 1968).

17. "No, unless it has been SEEN it is impossible to conceive of such

ghastly poverty, such debasement, more total degradation of the human being!''
(*Promenades*, p. 192.) Also quoted in the *Tour de France*: "Truly the stupidity of the workers is capable of disheartening, deterring, repulsing the most
ardent spirit'' (*Tour*, p. 34.)

18. ''Proletarians, my purpose is to expose the great social drama that England will be playing out before the eyes of the world, to prepare you for the
great events of the terrible struggle that is beginning to be waged between the
proletariat and nobility of this country'' (*Promenades*, p. 53).

19. ''An article should be written about charge-hands. They are an ignoble
species; they exploit the workers and especially the women among them, demanding that they become their mistresses on pain of being given no work''
(*Tour*, p. 225).

20. ''I noticed more deeply-marked faces, more signs of physical exhaustion in the room where the men were (all factory workers) than in the women's
room. What is the reason for that? For proletarian women have far more physical labour and mental strain to endure than men. But the thing is that women
have greater moral strength'' (*Tour* I: 122).

21. ''I have been approached by women from modest backgrounds. . . .
I explained to them that there was no keeping politics out of anything, even
their cooking pot. And they understood perfectly well'' (*Tour*, p. 133).

22. ''Establish infants' schools, and, as if by magic, you will transform
both the child and the worker's household. The child will learn day by day to
live in association with others'' (*Promenades*, p. 244).

23. ''The first thing to be done is to educate women, because it is they
who are responsible for bringing up their children, whether male or female.''
''Union ouvrière,'' in D. Desanti, *Flora Tristan, vie et oeuvre mêlées* (Paris:
Union générale d'éditions 10/18, 1973), p. 415.

24. This was an association founded by Pauline Roland. On the development of the feminist movement in France, see M. Albistur and D. Armogathe,
Histoire du féminisme français, 2 vols. (Paris: des Femmes, 1977).

25. Desanti, ''Union ouvrière,'' p. 420.

26. Karl Marx, *The Jewish Question* (1843).

27. At the same time in Germany, an eloquent little book by Theodor Gottlieb von Hippel was published on the same theme, *Uber die burgerliche Verbesserung der Weiber* (Berlin: Sammtiche Werke, 1828), Band VI. First re-
printing, Frankfurt: Syndikat-Verlag, 1977.

28. An expression used by A. Bebel, *Die Frau und der Sozialismus*. The
same theme is taken up by the German philosopher Ernst Bloch, ''Kampf ums
neue Weib,'' *Prinzip Hoffnung*, Teil IV (Frankfurt/Main: Suhrkamp, 1959),
p. 687ff.

2

Woman as Mediatrix: From Jean-Jacques Rousseau to Germaine de Staël

Madelyn Gutwirth

"Take Julie from the world and nature will mean nothing to me."[1] Rousseau wrote this curious sentence concerning the fictional heroine he was in the process of creating into the margin of his letter to Voltaire of August 18, 1756, on Providence. The murderous Lisbon earthquake of All Saint's Day, 1755, had claimed 40,000 lives in what appeared to mere human understanding to be the most gratuitous of events. In response to it, Voltaire had written his *Poem on the Lisbon Disaster*. In Popean accents fueled by his deep dismay, he asked in anguish,

> And will you say as you survey the throng
> Of victims, God's revenge is taken for their wrongs?

The Enlightenment's complacency concerning the essential goodness of creation had been cruelly shaken by this reminder of nature's indifference to our sense of good and evil. Rousseau, ever Voltaire's antagonist, soon came forward to refute such negative theses with his defense of the wisdom of Providence.[2] This marginal note concerning his Julie marks the first we ever hear of her: as far as we can know it, the absolute onset of her conception.[3]

Julie, then, his archetype of the good woman, from the very first stands in Rousseau's mind as the unifying factor in the creation. As Paul Hoffmann confirms, "the function of woman [for Rousseau] is that of restoration, of conservation, not one of invention nor of creation.''[4] In a world deprived of spiritual wholeness by the evils of society, woman alone—a being, as Rousseau sees it, more natural and essentially unchanging than man, therefore intemporal, not caught in the wattle of events, of history, wars, hatreds and economic strife— possesses the capacity to restore men to spiritual wholeness, to a sense of the goodness of Providence, to metaphysical order.

The sentence that the author Rousseau had written in his letter reappears in the novel in the words that Julie's lover Saint-Preux addresses to her: "Without you, nature means nothing to me" (I, ix). Before we write off Rousseau's Julie in the terms by no means unwarranted that Nancy Miller (inspired by Simone de Beauvoir) has enunciated, as a mere emblem of man's apotheosis, we first need to reassimilate the impact of so influential a heroine.[5] Indeed, we have fully to recognize that the reason women so adored the novel and its author was precisely for his having given so huge a place to women in his cosmogony. For certainly, *La Nouvelle Héloïse* is not unique because it places the power of love at its center: it astonished because it made the beloved woman's very being, including her physical passion, her biological destiny, her ideas, her manners and her acts, an exemplar of all human comportment.

Probably Rousseau had it in mind in his *Héloïse* to correct our sense of Peter Abélard's failure of spiritual love toward the remarkable and chastening example to men of the steadfast Héloïse. We make this surmise from Julie's reproaches to her lover once she is separated from him: "Sensual man, will you never know how to love?" and "Thankless one! What can you delight in when you are alone to feel pleasure?"(P. 213) To these taunts Saint-Preux makes the responding pledge, "It is you I adored when first I became susceptible to true beauty; you are the one I will never cease to adore even after my death . . . " Saint-Preux's passion, unlike the unhappy scholastic's, will never falter. But if he is, like Abélard, Julie's tutor and elder at the outset, he soon dwindles into the role of respectful adorer, near acolyte.

What arrests Saint-Preux in Julie from the start is essential to underline here: it is her "touching fusion of so lively a sensibility with an unalterable gentleness; it is her tender pity for the ills of others; the soundness of mind and exquisite taste that draw their purity from that of her soul; the charms of her sentiment, far more than those of her person; it is these that I adore in you" he writes (P. 6). If her personal graces make her irresistible to her lover before they have sexual congress, these powers seem to him to be only enhanced by the totality of her abandonment to love.

In his novel Rousseau embraces the Platonism inherent in courtliness, but according to a Genevan rather than a Florentine pattern. If Dante and Petrarch are smitten with the transcendent beauty of those juveniles, Beatrice and Laura, the Protestant will make his Saint-Preux respond even more powerfully to the realities of Julie's moral, ethical and religious being than to her beauty. In this sense, Rousseau is a mere literalist who needs to spell out in detail the rectifications his beloved brings to the nature of things as compared with his more allusive courtly forebears. But however he refashions it, he continues the courtly tradition of the excellence and perfection of the lady. The myth of the weaker sex's control over the stronger is sustained in Saint-Preux's posture of postulant to the beloved. He will confess to her, for example, that

you know how to love better than I. Yes, my Julie, it is you who give me my life and my being; surely I adore you with all the powers of my soul: but yours is the more loving one; love has penetrated it more deeply; it can be seen and felt; it is love that enlivens your graces, that rules your discourse, that gives your eyes their gentle perceptiveness, your voice its touching accents; this it is that lets you communicate by your mere presence directly with other hearts, without their perceiving your own heart's gentle commotion. How far I am from that enchanting state that is complete unto itself! (P. 276)[6]

Into man, Saint-Preux, a being incomplete, Julie infuses like God himself into Adam by her "gentle breath" a "new soul." Although Julie may well call Saint-Preux her "master," her "apostle," the worship that pervades the novel is of her being, her powers.

It is in fact she who structures all value. Such authority does she possess over his soul that Saint-Preux finds her "more divine than human." Faced with her scornful scrutiny he finds himself driven to becoming what she esteems. "Know how to suffer misfortune," she upbraids him, "and be a man. Remain, if I dare say so, the lover Julie chose to love" (p. 189). In the wake of their separation and of her forced marriage to her father's friend M. de Wolmar, although Julie takes on the yoke of husbandly leadership in worldly affairs, her spiritual authority remains undimmed, as her loving cousin Claire testifies: "My Julie, you were made to reign. Your authority is the most total of all those I know: it impresses itself even upon the will'' (P. 390).[7] Saint-Preux and Claire together share a feeling of subjection to Julie, a worship of her. What they worship in her is not her supreme goodness and mercy alone but her vivifying effect upon their lives, and as Saint-Preux writes, in her arms he rediscovers warmth and life, and he veritably scintillates with joy as he enfolds her in his.

Yet, despite these near-primal powers, Julie is not merely an earth mother. If the heart is, for Rousseau and for Saint-Preux, the sole organ of truth, the source from which we intuit the true relationships that obtain among things, Julie's heart, being best is also wisest, her judgment the most complete. Hence it is she who preaches tirelessly (but alas, not to tireless readers!) concerning virtue, education, domestic management and faith to her amazed lover and erstwhile schoolmaster. Her priggishness is intrinsic to this schoolmistressy role, and it is more than probable that any female novelist of the age who ever allowed her heroine similar excesses would have been mocked to dust for pretentiousness and presumption. Rousseau, however, does not flinch from making his delicious heroine utter sentences such as: ''It is in gilded chambers that the schoolboy goes to acquire the manners of the world, but the wise man learns to unlock their mysteries in the cottages of the poor'' (p. 282), nor would a female novelist lightly have had Julie write in so withering a vein as this to her lover: ''Your letter is, like your life, sublime and servile, full of strength and of childishness. Dear philosopher, will you never cease to be a child?'' (P. 675) In addition to her assumption of superiority, Julie, in very occasional lapses from her perpetual earnestness, is even allowed a smidgen of wit.

But even universally wise as she is, and deserving of the homage of all humankind, Julie belongs to a sex assigned severely restricted, though enormously crucial, tasks. For all her sagacity, intelligence of social dynamics and cultured ability to quote Cato and Petrarch, she is no better than a baby nurse and lacks the requisite wisdom to ''form men.'' The Rousseau who sees in woman a ruling genius for gentleness, directness and the will to please tries to make of his Julie not only a wise and agreeable companion but also a quintessential consoling angel, a soother of injury, a restorer of faith, the good mother.[8] Woman as *anima* is the centerpiece of female nature in Rousseau's canon: Julie is the animating center of her domain of Clarens. By virtue of her role as gardener/theorist she may be said to be the place's native poet and presiding genius, for in the sexual division of labor established between Wolmar and his spouse, his part is that of reason, hers of soul; "il m'éclaire et je l'anime," she proclaims. ("He enlightens me; I animate him.")

Assigned the part of sufferer for humankind, Julie testifies inexhaustibly to her capacity for surviving distress and for experiencing vicariously the sufferings of others, especially in the sexual domain. "You become only the more dear to me," she tells her lover, "in forcing me to hate myself." The force of her masochism is such that it impels her to ask of Saint-Preux that he leave to her the pains of love and keep for himself only its pleasures (p. 111). Here is the traditional delegation to the female partner of the weight of conscience, felt as too painful to be borne equally by both partners in life. Accordingly, Julie experiences sexual guilt far more steadfastly and acutely than does her lover: it becomes a permanent feature of her life as she strives to live down her early "fault" in a subsequent life of virtue, for her isolated instance of willful sexual impulse creates what is felt by her to be an unbearable contrast with her apparent public stainlessness as pure matron. The entire weight of Christian morality is therefore intolerably in her charge, as well as the well-being of all who come near her.

Despite Julie's preachy self-righteousness, she unfailingly strikes postures of modest retiringness, virtually withdrawing into a domesticity and a privacy that preserve her from the incursions of her own will and energy. It is notable that, confirming her role as unifying force, Julie may not hate: her lover notifies her that if she should become capable of hating something, he would become capable of ceasing to love her. But Rousseau seems unconscious of this paradox: the discord between Julie's posture as meek, weak woman—"I am nothing but the gardener's servant" (p. 111)—and her overexplicit, haranguing, excessively vital tone is never resolved in the novel.

Rounding out her quintessential representation as the female in a Jungian polarity, Julie is a universal seductress whose person is endowed with an irresistible power to make all who look upon her love her. But indissociable from this appeal of hers is her personal enthusiasm not alone for virtue but for life itself, which tends to make her a human rather than merely a female model. In this novel, which breaks out against Rousseau's own prejudices (expressed elsewhere within it) to a realm beyond sex—and paradoxically through its espousal of sexuality—a pre-Marcusean note is struck. "L'âme a-t-elle un sexe?" ("Does the soul have a sex?) it asks, as it asserts unflinchingly the sexual nature of both sexes. In affirming the right to passion of women as well as of men, Rousseau links this right, confusedly, to be sure, to a Utopian ideal conducive particularly to women, of a society of "tenderness and peace," as opposed to that historical world he so hated, dominated by power and opinion. Although Rousseau tried to compose it so as not to threaten what he viewed as the natural dominance of men over women, his *Nouvelle Héloïse* remains a lyrical prose-poem in praise of the power of love to enhance every domain of life. Woman, for him, is in this work not only the mediatrix to, but whether he willed it so or not, the exemplar of his alternative order.

It comes as no surprise, then, that women loved this novel, which promised to reconcile them with themselves, to herald a new style of love and to demand a gentler world in exchange for the repressive and friendless one they knew.[9] The broad appeal of the work came from its skillful counterbalancing of moralism with its defense of the rights of passion. In fact, within its pages the reproving and virtuous camouflage merely enhances the explosive charm of free sexual impulse. But of course there were many who resisted this kind of charm. Germaine de Staël's mother, Suzanne Necker, was one of their number, especially as she was moved to consider its effects on the sensibilities of her young and passionate daughter. In fact, their differing valuation of the *Nouvelle Héloïse* was one of numerous apples of discord between mother and daughter. Madame Necker, although she was otherwise rather an admirer of Rousseau, thought his novel a "bad book," dangerous and immoral, an "edifice of virtue built on a foundation of vice."[10] The terms of her daughter's disagreement with her (which are part of her first published work, an essay on Rousseau) are striking in their delineation of the paradox in the creation of Julie alluded to above.

Although Rousseau tried to prevent women from taking part in public affairs, from playing a notable role, how he had the gift of pleasing them in speaking of them! Ah! If he wished to deprive them of some rights foreign to their fate, how fully he granted all those that will forever be their portion! If he wished to lessen their influence on men's deliberations, how fully he consecrated their rule over men's happiness! If he forced them to descend from a usurped throne, how he set them back upon the throne to which nature destined them! If he is indignant with them when they strive to resemble men, how he adores them when they appear to him with all the charms, weaknesses, virtues and errors of their sex! Finally, he believes in love; his pardon is granted: what does it matter to women that his reason quarrels with their powers, when his heart surrenders to them? What does it matter to those whom nature has endowed with a tender soul if they are robbed of the false honor of governing the one they love? No, it is far sweeter to feel his superiority, to admire him, to believe him a thousand times above them, to depend upon him because they adore him; to submit to him voluntarily, to abase all at his feet; to themselves give the example and to demand no other return than that of the heart which they have made themselves deserving of in loving.[11]

It is plain that seeing as clearly as she did the repressive implications of the image of Julie for women of her own participatory nature, Germaine Necker yet chose to espouse Rousseau's emotional structuring of sexual relations rather than face the conflict between the sexes inherent in resistance to it. For what Rousseau advocates is a total, brutal repression of women's rights in the extra-domestic realm, combined with a proffered supremacy in the affective, domestic realm. It is no wonder she seizes upon and appropriates the latter. But it was not possible to still the inward revolt of one so nearly conscious of repression.

Jean Roussel rightly claims that Germaine de Staël's novels recapitulate *La Nouvelle Héloïse* but that the author can preserve the positive dimension of the book only with great difficulty.[12] Roussel finds Julie to be sustained by a profound lyricism lacking in Staël's Delphine and Corinne who are, for him, merely heroines of generosity. He recognizes, however, that Delphine has affinities as a redemptress to Julie. Staël enthusiastically embraced Rousseau's Julie cult, with all its repressive features, even to the point of decrying the reasoning and preaching of Julie as unfeminine and inappropriate echoes of Rousseau's own voice, which detract from the "charm of self-abandonment that a true heroine should display."[13] But Staël was eventually to refashion Julie's powers of goodness and generosity into strengths which empower human nature to take up the moral challenge to resist the strong and to protect the weak.[14] While apparently internalizing the Rousseau polarization, she seeks within it the psychic powers and emotional justification for launching her own revolt.

For even as she struggled to set forth in her heroines models of a profoundly appealing mediating femininity after Julie's example, Staël's inner reservations prevented her from achieving a similarly selfless effect. The passage from the *Letters* cited above reveals to our scrutiny that Staël had perceived all too precisely what Rousseau wished to repress in woman: participation in public life, playing a notable role, having rights, exerting influence on the affairs of the world, resembling men in power, sitting on a throne. Aside from the unreasoned repression of individual female powers of intellect and energy inherent in Rousseau's stance, Germaine de Staël, as a woman not happily married, is undoubtedly troubled by its lack of adequacy as a normative conception of woman. Like that fascinatingly clairvoyant sufferer named Henriette who wrote to Rousseau in desperation that she agreed with him concerning women's role, but that no one would marry her and so where was she to find validation for her life,[15] Staël knows, even as she burns with desire to maintain the primacy of love in woman's life, that Julie's example could never be her ideal, either.[16] If she continues to search for female validation through the couple, as time goes on she reveals more and more boldly her own previously repressed doubts about the sublime Julie as we see in the new composites that are her own heroines.

The depiction of Delphine, first, reveals to us the characteristic Staëlian juggling act designed to conciliate a host of irreconcilable contraries: this disarming protagonist combines

various graces, so many that they would appear to belong to entirely different orders of being. Expressions always well chosen and an ever natural manner, gaiety of spirit and melancholy of feelings, exaltation and simplicity, discipline and energy! an adorable mixture of genius and candor, gentleness and strength! having to the same degree all that the deepest thinkers might be impelled to admire, and all that the most ordinary of people might find agreeable if they have a modicum of goodness and are fond of meeting with such touching traits in the loftiest yet most relaxed, most enchanting yet simplest of forms.[17]

Proud, yet unpretentious, Delphine moves away from Julie in her trend toward independence and freedom of thought and in her androgynous blend of qualities. It is scarcely a surprise that so exemplary a paragon should be seen not so much as mediatrix to her lover, as he will be to her.

Léonce exclaims when first he meets her:

How enthusiastically she speaks of virtue! She loves it above all the beauties of moral nature; she breathes in goodness as if it were fresh air, as the only air breathable to a generous soul. But if the reaches of her mind give her independence, her nature is in need of support; her glance has something in it that is sensitive and frail and seems to beg for help . . . ; her soul is not fashioned to withstand the storms of life. Ah, my friend, how happy will that man be whom she chooses as the protector of her destiny, whom she will elevate to her level, who will defend her against the wickedness of men.[18]

In an astonishing transfiguration of Saint-Preux's adoration of Julie's power to bring him to the realization of the highest good, we find Léonce addressing to Delphine, perverting them, the words that Milton's Eve speaks to Adam: "God is thy law, thou mine." Here Staël indulges in the very turnabout of the sexes that Rousseau had striven in vain to keep in check by his insistence on hierarchies and the separation of sexual spheres. If Julie is celestial, Delphine is positively empyrean. But Delphine takes Staël as far as obeisance to the Julie model, with its moral hypocrises, allowed her to go. In fact, this heroine plays the roles both of Saint-Preux, as independent lover and interloper in the marital triangle, *and* of Julie, mediatrix and priestess to a vague realm of value. The novelty of *Delphine* lies in her being sacrificed for both of her roles: as sinful exceptional woman and as innocently loving woman in a wickedly loveless world.

Staël's supreme novel, *Corinne*, reveals the most arresting set of contrasts between Julie and this most evolved and realized of her heroines. But before going on to them, one basic parallel must be emphasized. Like *La Nouvelle Héloïse*, and nearly all of the literature of love, *Corinne or Italy* reaffirms the absolute primacy of couplehood, even as it breaks out to assert the right to female singularity. The tale, interlarded with travelogue, is of a self-made poetess born to an English lord and his Italian wife. The novel introduces us to her at her spectacular crowning with the laurel of Petrarch and Tasso. This is its pinnacle, for as she leaves the scene of her glory, Corinne meets Oswald, Lord Nelvil, with whom she will fall in love. Nelvil's deep conservatism, which creates doubts within him concerning Corinne even as he becomes enchanted with her, is buttressed by her revelation of her origins, which damn her in his eyes. Intending to return, he yet leaves her in Italy and never comes back to her. She sickens and loses the power to create. When finally, married to her half-sister, Oswald returns and attempts to see her again, she fades and dies. It is not erroneous to say that she dies of his failure to sustain their union. So love, not her gift, is the highest good for Corinne, but even within this context we perceive an evolution we might have predicted from the demonstrated conflict expressed in Mme de Staël's tortured praise of Rousseau's idea of love and women. Here is a description of Corinne and Oswald's way of relating to each other.

There existed between Oswald and Corinne a singular and all-powerful sympathy; their tastes were not all the same, their opinions rarely jibed, yet nonetheless deep in their souls there were similar mysteries, emotions that sprang from the same source; in sum, there was a somewhat secret resemblance between them that presupposed at base a single nature, although external circumstances had modified it differently.[19]

The couple here is not a courtly one but an egalitarian one. Both Oswald and Corinne have moments of worship, one of the other, but the paradigm of their relationship is the balance scale. Rather than the absolute disparity between male and female nature posited so much of the time by Rousseau, Corinne and Oswald share "a single nature."[20] Germaine de Staël's concept of emotional parity moves closer to that of Romanticism, with its search for secret essences shared by lovers. Where Rousseau had sought to make the idyll of domestic duty the center of his novel, Staël has winnowed out of it, to become the core of her own the fatal passion of lovers. Domesticity, enthroned by Rousseau, is made to appear dull and destructive alongside Corinne's vigor and talent. The self-sacrificing side of Julie is cast aside (until the ending), leaving only the remnant of her right to love as heritage to Corinne.

In fact, for an author as smitten as Mme de Staël had been with Julie (she would weep whenever she read the account of her death) she reconstructs Rousseau's mediatrix to the world in decidedly unforeseen ways. The retiring and intimate woman whose virtue is to be seen and felt only by her intimate circle here reappears as a public figure. If Julie is an angel, Corinne is a "celestial being shrouded by clouds." Whereas Julie lives in obscurity and dependence, Corinne is as independent and as celebrated as human society can make one. Julie will write that "real talent, true genius has a certain simplicity that makes it less unquiet, less mobile, less apt to show itself than an overt and false talent that is taken for true, but is only a vain anxiety to shine'' (p. 521).[21] True talent should remain quiet amidst the throng, she warns. Talents are not necessary to really good people. It goes without saying that Rousseau would have held that they are least necessary of all to women. Throwing off this implicit moral reproach decisively, Germaine de Staël gives her Corinne not some few talents, merely, but all of them: genius. ''Long live Corinne! Long live genius!'' cry the crowds at her approach. Oswald hears people saying that hers is the most touching voice in all of Italy, that she plays tragedy formidably well, that she dances like a nymph, sketches remarkably, that no one has ever written verse so fine as hers, that her conversation is full of grace and eloquence. Yet we see that moral Julie's impress is still upon her, mitigating her sense of victory, for though she is happy to be admired, she is timid before the plaudits of the multitude and seems to ''ask its forgiveness for her triumph.'' A hangover of female guilt undermines her. In fact, like Delphine's, her very talents make her especially vulnerable, so that in the midst of all this celebration it seemed to Oswald that ''Corinne had begged, by her glances, for the protection of a lover, a protection which no woman, no matter how superior can do without; and he thought that it would be sweet to be the support of one whose sensibility alone made her need it.''[22] Oswald's role will be in fact, like Léonce's, that of inspiritor to Corinne: ''his presence,'' says the narrator, ''animated Corinne and inspired her with the desire to be amiable.''[23]

But surely the most shocking shift of all from the Julie model lies in the displacement of female mediation from private happiness not merely to the public sphere but to the realm of transcendence. For Corinne is woman endowed with a special power of revelation to humanity. As she considers how love has reduced her, she laments the world's loss. ''Had I been happy,'' she writes, ''if the heart's fevers had not consumed me, I would have been capable of an elevated contemplation of human destiny and found new connections with nature and with heaven.''[24] Corinne's calling to be mediatrix to humankind founders on the shoal of her lover's need to maintain the traditional hierarchy of Rousseau's Clarens deep in the Northumberland hills where he marries the gentle, tractable Lucile. In the opposition Corinne expresses to her own Northumberland origins we read an outright rejection of that life of retirement that Rousseau had raised to ideal status, but which Corinne describes as a living death, in which the sole means of distinguishing one day from the last is, as she writes, "by the date on the calendar and by the effects of the years, which finally became imprinted on the women's faces, as if they had lived during that time."[25]

The rebellion implicit in the Corinne image as against that of Julie is again visible in Staël's insistence on Corinne's gaiety, as against Julie's nearly unvarying solemnity. Staël would free her heroine to be capable of laughter, insists on her mobility as a woman of all the moods. Yet she cannot quite convince us that Corinne's is real laughter, even as she portrays Gozzi's spoof, *La Figlia dell'aria*, to perfection. The domination of destiny inherent in laughter was never part of Julie's portion, but Mme de Staël lays claim to it, if somewhat awkwardly, for her Corinne.

An analogous and capital contrast is the place ascribed in the two works to the role of the aesthetic in life. We know how Rousseau despised it, and Julie and Wolmar especially proscribe art from their utopia, preferring infinitely the attractively functional to the beautiful, a too-seductive category to their taste. Germaine de Staël, against the preferences of Rousseau and her own Genevan parents' upbringing, flings her Corinne into a near religion of art's transcendent value.

Clearly, biological motherhood, though not rejected in *Corinne*, is no longer the normative female fate, any more than is marriage. It would scarely have escaped Mme de Staël that when Julie dies at age thirty, she claims to have fulfilled all that life has to offer her, having lived a great passion, fulfilled her domestic career, and given two sons to the world that she had reared up to the point in their lives when it is no longer appropriate that mothers influence their sons. But the *symbolic* maternal or connective role of Julie within her circle is seized upon by Staël who makes of her Corinne a universal connective. Agape is the highest level of love for both, but in this domain Corinne may be said to out-Julie Julie.

Madame de Wolmar had told her lover that all the charm of the society in which they lived came of "that openness of heart that harmonizes all feelings and all thoughts and which making everyone feel as he must, all show themselves as they are."[26] All who come within Julie's purview feel an increase in authenticity, in a sense of self, in their relationships to others. Her openness of heart, the wholeness with which she embraces the traditional female portion is given as Julie's genius. While rejecting the narrow theater in which it is expressed,

Corinne continues to be inspired by Julie's example as if it were the representation of what is most sublime in female nature. She interiorizes this female portion and becomes what her panegyrist in the novel, *Castel-Forte*, calls

the link among all her friends; she is the movement, the interest in our lives; we count on her goodness; we are proud of her genius; . . . when foreigners insult this country . . . we tell them:—Look at Corinne.—Yes, we would follow in her footsteps, we would be men as she is woman, if men could, like women, create a world in their own hearts, and if our genius, necessarily dependent upon social relations and external circumstances, could light its way solely from the flame of poetry.[27]

As Corinne attempts to elevate the cult of female sensibility to such a pitch that it enters the wider society, she does so clearly by using the Julie paradigm. It is in fact as if Germaine de Staël has stripped Rousseau's great intuition of its timidity and hypocrisy and applied the vision inherent in his novel of what women had it within them to contribute not to the narrow theater of intimacy, but to all of life, to the wider culture. In Corinne's presence, as in Julie's, nature seems more complete. Providence is no longer an empty term. But whereas Julie is the mediatrix to man, his complement and his sometime ideal, the megalomaniacal Corinne has the gall to make a candid bid to become in her own person and not as part of a couple, an exemplar of human perfection, for the expanded significance lent her capacity for love, her power of sympathetic imagination, Corinne's "flame of poetry."

The fate of such heroines is necessarily death. Julie, having served out her function cannot forever retain her powers of seduction; so she is discarded, dying in touching martyrdom to mother love, apotheosized forever in Book VI of *La Nouvelle Héloïse*. Her sexual degradation, as Nancy Miller has written, had been followed by amelioration, and she expires conveniently before sexual temptation can again deprive her of her exemplarity.[28] Her power of mediation over male destiny is exhausted with her youth. We cannot help but suspect that a fear of her excessively influential presence is expressed in the abrupt disposition made of her. Indeed, Saint-Preux had written to her not long before her death a far different assessment of Julie's sex than that relentlessly pacific one given lip service in the rest of the novel:

Women! Women! dear and fatal objects whom nature ornamented to torment us, who punish us when we approach you, whose hatred and love are equally harmful and whom we can neither seek out nor flee with impunity! . . . Beauty, charm, attractiveness, sympathy, divine reality or incredible specter, abyss of sorrow and of sensuality! Beauty more terrible to mortals than the element from which you were born, unhappy is he who gives himself to your deceptive calm! It is you who produce the tempests that torment humankind. (P. 664)[29]

Rousseau thus gives away the falseness at the core of his novel, the willed suppression of this negative pole that woman, a being destructive at the core, is for Saint-Preux, for the sake of creating a bogus myth of wholly constructive female mediative power.

Corinne, too, is of necessity a novel with blinders. In rejecting all that is not positive in female nature Mme de Staël not only presents her heroine as "as good as" Julie but even deprives her of that open sensuality which Rousseau had accorded to *his* wish fulfillment to make her more enticing. Seizing upon Julie's apparent elements of self-realization—her erudition, her fullness in the expression of her ideas—as if these things gave license to a portrait of a fuller female humanity, Staël incorporated them into her Corinne. But her heroine's death is a sort of enactment, an intuitive mime of Saint-Preux's statement concerning the negativity of woman. The Oswald who fears Corinne as an exceptional being—that is, as a woman untamed—even as he comes to love her, rejects her power to mediate his personal destiny. Corinne's lack of apotheosis, the unrelieved bitterness and sadness that shroud the final pages of the novel, testify to a bitter recognition that female power, beyond the realm of the couple, although transcendentally valuable and capable of transforming the world, is doomed by male terror to fail of its redemptive potential.

The women novelists who scrutinize *Corinne* in pain and wonderment adduce different lessons from her example. Sand's Consuelo is virtually alone to choose genius and then in the realm of performance only. Dorothea Brooke tries desperately to repress her own intelligence and yet let it serve the world (like Corinne) but via the domestic circle (like Julie). But that the women novelists who follow attempt to affirm female goodness and the positive power of female mediation as against a silent screen of belief in female evil, it would be difficult to deny. The sexual Manichaeism of the nineteenth-century novel has roots in this conflict, visible in the struggle of women characters as diverse as the Shirley of Charlotte Brontë or the Miriam of Henry James' *Tragic Muse*.

Enticed by Rousseau into believing that they could have power over culture as purely private persons, that they could thereby be the world's glue and maintain a sense of purpose in the cosmos, most women, like Germaine de Staël were powerless to resist so literally seductive a lure. But she alone, using her Corinne as a counter-model to Julie, tried to transform the halo of love surrounding women into a diadem, the kind of crown granted not to selfless generosity but as a reward for great deeds. She really believed what Rousseau merely fantasized: that the repressed spiritual powers of women could effectively change the world.

NOTES

1. Cited by René Pomeau in his introduction to Garnier edition of *Julie, ou la Nouvelle Héloïse* (Paris: Garnier, 1960), p. iv. It is this edition that will be subsequently referred to throughout. Translations are my own. Subsequent references to the text will appear in the body of the chapter.

2. Voltaire, *Lettre sur la Providence* (1756).

3. The autobiographical origins of both Julie and Claire have been relentlessly sought out: Rousseau's *Maman*, Madame de Warens is thought to be their *fons et origo*. As English Showalter has written, "Both the novel and the *Confessions* are nourished . . . by a nostalgic dream of happiness, and obsessed by the recurrent nightmare of its loss." As yet unpublished communication by Showalter on the chronology of *La Nouvelle Héloïse*, presented at a meeting of the Northeast Modern Language Association (NEMLA), 1980. For a probing of the roots of these characterizations in Rousseau's psychic life, I refer readers to Ronald Grimsley's *Jean-Jacques Rousseau: A Study of Self-awareness* (Cardiff: University of Wales Press, 1961); to Jean Guéhenno's massive biography, *Jean-Jacques Rousseau*, trans. by John and Doreen Weightman, 2 vols. (London: Routledge and Kegan Paul/New York: Columbia University Press, 1966); and to Lester Crocker's *Jean-Jacques Rousseau*, 2 vols. (New York: Macmillan, 1968–73).

4. Paul Hoffmann, *La Femme dans la pensée des lumières* (Strasbourg: Association des Publications près les Universités de Strasbourg, 1977), p. 359.

5. See Nancy Miller, "Exquisite Cadavers: Women in Eighteenth Century Fiction" (Review of Pierre Fauchery's *La Destinée féminine dans la roman européen du dix-huitième siècle, 1713-1807*), *Diacritics* (Winter, 1975), 40.

6. Julie's strong domineering presence in the novel, where she is "queen

of the cosmos at Clarens'' (p. 276), has also been discussed by Victor Wexler in an important essay, ''Made for Man's Delight: Rousseau as Antifeminist,'' *American Historical Review* 81 (April, 1976), 266-91. Wexler argues that Rousseau's fear of women's sexual power over men impelled him to assign to them the role of regulators of passion. (He cites Wolfgang Lederer's book *The Fear of Women* [New York: Harcourt Brace, 1967], as I have also had occasion to do elsewhere, in support of his argument.) It was this fear, rather than mere condescension, Wexler believes, that made Rousseau seek to reinforce the division of society into separate sexual spheres. Wexler's argument is powerful and impressive. The only question it does not quite answer is how much was conscious and how much less than conscious in Rousseau's apprehensions. Did he *know* he feared? Or did he fear to know?

7. Marlene Le Gates has noted concerning Julie in her essay ''The Cult of Womanhood in Eighteenth-Century Thought'': ''it is remarkable that the family, religion, and the state are now identified with woman rather than seen as being threatened by her.'' Le Gates concluded that in the novels of both Richardson and Rousseau ''the drama of the aggressive male checked by the virtuous woman is paradoxically a reaffirmation of the patriarchal authority of the family.'' *Eighteenth-Century Studies* 10 (Fall, 1976), 30-31.

8. Pomeau, Introduction, xxxiv.

9. Ibid., xxiv.

10. See Suzanne Necker, *Mélanges*, 3 vols. (Paris: Charles Pougens, 1798), III: 105. As cited by Jean Roussel, *Jean-Jacques Rousseau en France après la Révolution* (Paris: A. Colin, 1972), 323.

11. Madame de Staël, *Lettres sur le caractère et les écrits de Jean-Jacques Rousseau*, Lettre I. (All references to works by Madame de Staël refer to part or chapter since so many editions are now in use.)

12. Roussel, *Jean-Jacques Rousseau*, p. 345.

13. Staël is critical of Julie's moralism. If she concedes that in the letter on duelling Rousseau has done well to ''make Julie speak as he himself would have spoken,'' she adds in her very next paragraph, ''I must nonetheless confess that it often displeases me to perceive Rousseau in Julie; I would prefer to find in her a man's ideas, but not his character.'' She reproves Julie for her sermons and her lack of modesty and argues that it is right that it be because Claire urges her to do so that Julie hides her affair with Saint-Preux. Julie should herself be incapable of withholding ''le charme de l'abandon.'' See Lettre II.

14. See Staël's, ''Seconde préface'' to *Delphine* (Paris: 1802).

15. Hoffmann, *La Femme*, pp. 444-45. Rousseau was apparently flabbergasted, nonplussed by her plea and unable to make a coherent reply. He could envisage no extra-domestic, merely human solution to her existential dilemma. See Rousseau's *Correspondance générale*, No. 2076, Vol. XI, p. 60.

16. Roussel, *Jean-Jacques Rousseau*, p. 352.

17. Madame de Staël, *Delphine*, I, xxiv.

18. We see here the play of resemblances to and departures from the essential nature of woman as Staël saw her in the Rousseau letter, where no note of superiority or independence was allowed to intrude. But Delphine still is a Julie: of both it can be said, "C'est par l'âme, l'âme seule, qu'elles sont distinguées" (*Delphine Lettre* II).

19. Madame de Staël, *Corinne* (Paris: 1807), XV, ii.

20. Saint-Preux writes entrancedly of his entry into Julie's gyneceum, her cosy consecration of her belief, which he shares, that too intimate and protracted commerce between the two sexes never produces anything but evil. (*N.H.*, IV: x). The novel itself, reflecting so many scenes of intense conversation, excursions, rambles, in all of which both men and women take part, certainly seems to give evidence in troubling contradiction to this stance.

21. This is a frequent theme of Rousseau's.

22. Madame de Staël, *Corinne* (Paris, 1807), II: i.

23. Ibid.

24. Ibid., VIII: v.

25. Ibid., XIV: i.

26. It is interesting to reflect that an ambivalence toward marriage (present also in *Delphine*) which we find in *Corinne* as its heroine fails to force Oswald to a decision concerning it, preferring their present state to an uncertain future one, is expressed already by a woman in *La Nouvelle Héloïse*. Rousseau projects this position in his depiction of Claire's situation: she well enumerates marriage's many drawbacks to her (VI: ii).

27. Madame de Staël, *Corinne*, II: ii.

28. "Female Sexuality and Narrative Structure," *Signs*, I,3 (2) (Spring, 1976), 609-38.

29. This text is the doublet of the "Vers sur la femme," J. J. Rousseau, *Oeuvres Complètes*, 4 vols. (Paris: Pléiade, 1961), 2, pp. 1160-61). No author I know of so fully exhibits as does Rousseau, lays so bare, that complex of feelings combining anxiety with distrust, attraction with need, that men feel for women. He grapples with and confesses what others conceal. For a subtler view of the dynamics of such fears of women than Lederer's (see *supra* Note 6), I refer readers to Karen Horney's discussion of this male psychic paradigm printed in her *Feminine Psychology* (New York: Norton, 1967), pp. 107-18.

3

Germaine de Staël and the Position of Women in France, England, and Germany

Eve Sourian

Because of her Swiss origins; her travels in England, Germany, Italy, Russia and Sweden; and her varied interests, Germaine de Staël can be considered European. Yet it was neither London, Weimar, Berlin nor Vienna that mattered to her, but only Paris. The only life this "European," so notably interested in both Germany and England, could conceive of, was life in Paris, the only place where a woman could be happy.

Germaine de Staël required love, Paris and power; as she wrote to her father from Weimar in 1804: "One of these three things is necessary to fill the heart and mind, and to keep active. Lacking one of them, the figurative pleasure to be had from everything else becomes in fact painful. What do you think of this real portrait of my intimate self?"[1]

For her, "to be occupied with politics is religion, ethics and poetry all at once." She added: "Love, supreme power of the heart, which embraces poetry, heroism, and religion!"[2] For love and politics go hand in hand and are only possible in Paris.

Chateaubriand did not understand this desperate nostalgia for Paris. When she told him she would die if she could not see *la rue du Bac*, he wondered what it was: "this miserable fate of enjoying glory, leisure, and tranquility in an opulent retreat in sight of the Alps, compared with thousands of victims without bread, without name, without aid, banished to all the corners of Europe."[3]

Napoleon, however, shrewdly understood Germaine de Staël. He knew perfectly well that she could not refrain from politics, for they had the same sense of what it was. As he said, "To speak of literature, of ethics, of the arts, of everything under the sun, is to engage in politics!" He also knew that Paris was the ideal place for its practice. As he said to Auguste de Staël, who had interceded on his mother's behalf in December, 1807:

If I allow her to return to Paris, she will do foolish things. She will make inroads among my entourage; she will make me lose Garat. Was it not she who cost me the *Tribunat*? You must understand that Paris is my home, and I don't want anyone living here except those who love me. . . . Let her go wherever else she likes—Rome, Naples, Vienna, Berlin, Milan, even to London to spread her libels. Who but your mother would be so unhappy at having been granted all of Europe![4]

After all, Napoleon had said, scathingly, "Women must keep to their knitting!"[5] He feared women and the power they exercised in the salons and as early as 1797 had written to his friend Fabre de l'Aude: "Everything I hear about that one leads me to think of her as a frequenter of salons who goes and comes and tries to attach herself everywhere, wants to be something; and since her skirts prevent her from taking things over directly, she tries to gain authority by ruses."[6]

In fact, it should be remembered that women in Paris did have power, especially through their salons. The salon of the young wife of the Swedish ambassador on the eve of the Revolution was in the tradition of her mother's. The politicians, however, had succeeded the philosophers. Talleyrand, Narbonne, Condorcet, Siéyès, Brissot, the Lameth brothers, Malouet, Barnare, were the most illustrious figures; later came Moreau, Daunou, Barras. Germaine de Staël was thus at the very heart of political life.

There was also the power concentrated at Auteuil and opposed to Napoleon, in the salon of Mme Helvetius, continued in 1800 by Sophie de Condorcet, who gathered about her such liberal "ideologues" as Cabanis, Tracy, Daunou, and subsequently all the republican intellectuals, all those opposing the *Tribunat* and *l'Institut*.

Irritated, Napoleon confronted Sophie de Condorcet: "I don't like women mixing in politics," and she answered, "You are quite right, General, but in a country where their heads get cut off, it is natural for them to wish to know why."[7]

Germaine de Staël certainly intended to influence her time through her writing as well as through her eloquent conversation and her friends. Away from Paris, from her *rue du Bac*, she no longer felt alive, for she no longer had power. To be away from Paris was to be bored and lonely, for she could not imagine social life except in Paris; all that remained to her was that paltry substitute—Europe.

She would discover Italy, and especially Germany and England, but only with her eyes still fixed in the direction of Paris. None of these countries succeeded in replacing Paris. For her it was the center of the world, but it most especially represented a social life in which she, as a woman, was accepted as an equal and, particularly, could play a role. Once in foreign parts she discovered what the other emigrés had discovered before her—the absence of the spirit of conversation, the abrupt end of truly sophisticated social life. Away from Paris, the requisite ingredients simply did not exist all together. Where else were to be had all at once a highly centralized government, freedom of expression, the presence of women on an equal footing and flexible class distinctions, notably in the face of intelligence? In the Parisian salon there were no social barriers to sex and intelligence.

What insured the glory of the French salon was severely lacking in Germany. Still feudal, Germany had no great center to serve as a cultural rallying point. Weimar was too small; Berlin was too "Frenchified," since Frederick II ignored German literature; in Vienna society was almost exclusively made up of foreigners—often speaking French.

"In Germany, society is the court; in France it was everyone who could prove equal to it," according to Staël.[8] Her impression of social life in Berlin was negative. She wrote to Goethe: "It is a country which does not strike the imagination at all; society is set up in Prussian fashion, and the women here must be astonished to find themselves aged, since they continue to say and do exactly the same things for over sixty consecutive years."[9]

While the great charm of conversation in France came from the very fact of the presence of women in the literary and philosophical salons, in Germany men and women were systematically separated, and the general rule was to exclude women from men's dinners. There were exceptions, however, such as the salons of Rahel . . . Radziwill. Furthermore, men were hardly disposed for the life of the salon: "The military state gives them a certain roughness which inspires in them a need not to bother themselves about women.''[10] She found furthermore that since there were relatively few men, they were spoiled, having neither ''anxiety, nor any need to please.''[11] As for military men on leave, they came to Berlin especially to dance and to gamble.

All of these limitations applied to Viennese society as well, which was not frequented by the more intelligent of the men. ''One finds only women, and one is astonished by the wit they do display, in spite of the kind of life they lead.''[12]

In general, Germaine de Staël's opinion of German men was rather unfavorable. No court could attract or retain all these nobles at loose ends or develop in them a taste for society. The German nobility, she found, had no means of worthily occupying themselves. ''Physical activity only serves to develop moral indolence. Spiritual force is transformed into roughness. The day is spent in vulgar exercises and amusements—horses, hunting, feasts, which would be proper as relaxation but which are sottish as occupations.''[13]

She pitied German women and understood why they sought refuge in the idealized world of poetry: ''I cannot imagine how they can place their love anywhere but in the realm of the ideal, since there is nothing more real than these men whom they are obliged to marry.'' Even so, she was critical of their sentimentality: ''this obligatory enthusiasm for the moon, the forests, the countryside and for solitude . . . these troubled nerves, these mannered voices, these looks which aspire to be looked at.''[14]

Such sentimentality, moreover, seemed to her to endanger the social order. Suprisingly, we have the author of *Corinne* herself, criticising romantic German mores and defending society. ''Love'' she wrote, ''is a religion in Germany, but a poetical religion, too easily tolerant of everything that sensibility excuses.''[15] Each follows his inclination, noted Staël, with stupefaction, observing the conjugal complications of the brothers Schlegel and of Schelling: ''the good nature of the men and women causes them to accept these facile ruptures entirely without bitterness.''[16] She was touched, however, by the fact that ''the Germans believe themselves to be more committed by affection than by duty.''[17] Their strong sense of loyalty makes love less dangerous to the happiness of women, in contrast to the complacency of the French, exemplified by the Vicomte de Valmont in *Les Liaisons dangereuses*.[18] Still, these same Frenchmen have a sense of social order: they respect "positive obligations," whereas the Germans "out of a sense of honor . . . are especially faithful to promises *not* insured by law." Staël, however, affirmed that legal guarantees are more important to social order.[19]

Such an affirmation by the author of *Delphine* is not really surprising but in fact is characteristic of Germaine de Ştaël. She respected marriage, not conceiving happiness to be possible for women otherwise even though her own marriage was a failure. Her individuality remained, in spite of everything, subordinate to the rules of society. Anarchy was, after all, repugnant to this Frenchwoman of the end of the eighteenth century, a believer in the power of laws and of institutions.

Staël did not hold Germany up to France as a political model. The country she admired was England, whose constitution guaranteed liberty to its citizens. What was the status of women in that country?

The true character of a woman is to be known and admired in those countries which are free. Domestic life inspires all of the virtues in women. . . . In England, a woman of the people feels rapport with the Queen, who has looked after her husband and raised her children, just as religion and morality requires of all wives and mothers.[20]

Women in England seem to be in striking contrast with Frenchwomen. The arbitrary *Ancien Régime* in France did not encourage women to withdraw into domestic life but rather to exercise all their means of seduction to attain influence and to secure positions for their friends. "In a country where the women are at the center of all intrigues, since it is favor which determines everything, the mores of the ranking class have nothing in common with those of the rest of the nation, and no fellow feeling can be established between the salons and the country."[21]

The literature of a nation reflects its character and institutions, and Staël attributed the success of the English novel as a genre to Englishwomen:

Up to now, love has been the subject of these types of novels. In England, the existence of women is the principal cause of the inexhaustible fecundity of the English writers in this genre. The relationships between men and women are infinitely multiplied through sensibility and refinement.[22]

According to Staël, "England is the country in the world where women are most truly loved."[23] For Englishwomen, the *home* is everything. Yet their education is superior to that of women in other countries, notably to that of Italian women, raised in convents.[24]

Still, Germaine de Staël could not have lived in England. According to Sir James Mackintosh, "She admired the English, in the midst of whom she could not have lived."[25] Women in England had little place in the life of society and were "accustomed to remain silent in the company of men, where politics are concerned;"[26] furthermore, women had no active personal existence; thus "they live all the more intensely in the objects of their affection."[27] England, then, was not for Staël, any more than Germany. "Since the happiness of the English is founded on domestic life, it would not be suitable for their women to create by choice social circles composed of a certain number of people constantly interacting with each other."[28]

By inclination, she needed to live in society, and from temperament she had a need to shine. What could have been more contrary to such a nature than this country where, with the men having an active life, "women must stay in the shadows."[29]

In spite of all her willingness to admire England, then, Germaine de Staël could not have lived there. Boredom, the suffocating constraints of social etiquette, the glacial reserve of English salons—none of this suited her. Indeed, in *Delphine*, she had attacked the tyranny exercised by society over superior beings, but this same tyranny held even more sway in England. She had experienced it herself in 1793 during her stay at Juniper Hall among her emigré friends Talleyrand, Montmorency, Lally-Tollendal, Malouet, Jaucourt, Madame de la Châtre, the Chevalier d'Arblay and the handsome Narbonne, whom she adored. She had taken a liking to Fanny Burney, and the two women writers understood each other very well until the day Fanny renounced the friendship. She had received a letter from her father warning her that she was compromising herself by frequenting the daughter of the revolutionary minister Necker and the lover of Narbonne. Fanny Burney's obedience to her father's letter and to social prejudice was to their friendship what the letter of Oswald in *Corinne* was to love. Oswald had sacrificed his love to the social prejudice expressed by his father, indeed just as Gibbon had done when he renounced marrying Suzanne Curchod, the future Madame Necker, since an Englishman could only marry an Englishwoman. Wounded in her friendship, Germaine de Staël exclaimed: "But is a woman under guardianship during her entire life in this country?[30] Moreover, Horace Walpole, who had received Germaine and her parents seventeen years before, had refused to receive the group of emigrés at Strawberry Hill because he disapproved of unmarried couples.

In spite of her glorious reception in London in 1813, on her third and last visit, she did not feel happy in England. As she wrote to August Schlegel: "I am devastated by spleen, though everyone is very good to me. . . . My life is in pain."[31]

Returning to Paris on May 12, 1814, she at last reopened her salon. Faithful to the principles of 1789, she continued to play as important a political role as she had before her exile. In a sense, Napoleon had treated her as an equal by exiling her, having thus recognized her power and admitted his apprehension of her.

In feudal Germany there had been no political role for a woman to play. In constitutional middle-class England, politics were reserved for men. In Restoration France, however, there was still room for salons and their influence—notwithstanding the enduring patriarchal stamp of the Napoleonic Code.

NOTES

1. Gabriel-Paul Othenin d'Haussonville, *Madame de Staël et L'Allemagne* (Paris: Calmann-Levy, 1928), p. 62.

2. J. Christopher Herold, *Germaine Necker de Staël* (Paris: Plon, 1962), p. 59.

3. François-René de Chateaubriand, *Mémoires d'Outre-Tombe*, 4 vols. (Paris: le Club français du livre, 1969), II: 197.

4. Louis de Villefasse and Jeanine Boissounousse, *L'Opposition à Napoléon* (Paris: Flammarion, 1969), pp. 298–99.

5. Ibid., p. 299.

6. Ibid., p. 80.

7. Ibid., p. 155.

8. Madame de Staël, *De l'Allemagne* 2 vols. (Paris: Hachette, 1958), I: 170.

9. Staël, "Briefe der Frau von Staël an Goethe," *Goethe Jahrbuch* 8, no. 187, 5–6.

10. Staël, *De l'Allemagne*, I: 238.

11. Ibid., I: 239.

12. Ibid., I: 134.

13. Ibid., I: 66.

14. Ibid., IV: 360:

15. Ibid., I: 68.

16. Ibid., I: 69.

17. Ibid., I: 80.

18. Ibid., I: 83.

19. Ibid.

20. This and all succeeding references to Madame de Staël's works are to the *Oeuvres complètes* 3 vols. (1861; rpt. Genève: Slatkine, 1967). *Considérations sur la Révolution Française*, III: 326.

21. Ibid.

22. Staël, *De la Littérature*, O.C. I: 267.

23. Ibid.

24. Staël, *Considérations sur la Révolution Française*, O.C. III: 305.

25. Sir James Mackintosh, *Memoirs of the Life of the Right Hon. Sir James Mackintosh* 2 vols. (Boston: Little, Brown, 1853), I: 406.

26. Staël *Considérations sur la Révolution Française*, O.C. III: 140.

27. Ibid., III: 308.

28. Ibid., III: 7.

29. Staël, *Corinne, ou l'Italie*, O.C. I: 305.

30. Madame d'Arblay (Frances Burney), *Diary and Letters of Madame d'Arblay*: 5 vols. (London: Bickers and Son, 1842–1846), V: 414.

31. Paul Usteri et Eugène Ritter, *Lettres inédites de Madame de Staël à Henri Meister* (Paris: Hachette, 1904), pp. 268–270.

4

Corinne and the "Yankee Corinna": Madame de Staël and Margaret Fuller

Paula Blanchard

Margaret Fuller began to read Mme de Staël in 1826, when she was sixteen. Her friend Lydia Maria Child read with her. By then Staël was dead, but the Boston historian George Bancroft was keeping her memory alive with dinner-party stories of his visit with her in the last weeks of her life. Bancroft was one of the half-dozen young men who brought Europe suddenly nearer to Massachusetts in the 1820's, and it may have been through his friendship with Child that the two young women first became interested in Staël. At any rate, they found in her an important model, a woman who had actually forced the male literary world to acknowledge her as an equal, though at the cost of a heavy barrage of vilification and ridicule. I would like to look at what sort of model she was for Fuller, focusing on her novel *Corinne* and its conflicted image of womanhood.

Ten years after Fuller and Child read *Corinne* together, Child wrote a biography of Staël. It is admiring, even laudatory, and is still a useful introduction, despite Child's insistence that Staël never strayed from the path of Christian virtue. For students of Margaret Fuller it is full of resemblances made all the more fascinating because Fuller consciously modeled herself on Staël, and one wonders how much Child's description is grounded in her observations of Fuller. Besides the obvious parallel of intelligence, one is struck by the extreme (and even picturesque) sensibility of both women; the high value they placed on candor in personal relationships; their awkwardness and nearsightedness as girls; their love of flamboyant dress; their insatiable need for reassurance from their friends; their ambivalent, deep attachment to their fathers and their political liberalism, for which both risked their personal safety and even their lives.

Particularly notable is the amount and kind of ridicule both were subjected to. Their opinions were often not attacked directly but through the medium of their sexuality. Margaret Fuller was accused both of being mannish and of knowing more about subjects like prostitution than any decent spinster had a right to know. Staël was verbally abused by the press both during the Revolution and under Napoleon. In this she was not alone: Madelyn Gutwirth, in her recent study of Staël, points out that any woman who tried to rise above anonymity in France was subjected to the same violently misogynist attacks. "Harlot" was one of the milder terms applied to Staël, but her enemies would sneer, almost in the same breath, that she was unsexed. Even friends like Benjamin Constant and Lord Byron were not above this sort of insult. Napoleon circulated an obscene rumor, said to have originated with one of her ex-lovers, that she had some kind of sexual deformity.[1]

Staël's novels *Delphine* and *Corinne* both portray gifted women who are destroyed by their love for relatively limited, conventional men. Written as cries of defiance against the social oppression of women, they both succeeded in arousing public sympathy. But the image of womanhood in both books is deeply traditional, in that both heroines choose to renounce their independence for the sake of love. It is in *Corinne*, the later novel, that the conflict between the two is most thoroughly explored. Here the heroine is not only gifted but spectacularly gifted so there is no doubt what her renunciation costs. She is described as an *improvisatrice*, gifted in all the arts but especially in poetry and drama. And she does not confine her talents to the drawing room but performs in public and is publicly acclaimed at the Capitol in Rome. The book describes in agonizing detail the choice she is forced to make between creative freedom and her love of Oswald Lord Nelvil, a Scottish nobleman; he in return vacillates between offering her a life of stifling domesticity in Scotland and offering her nothing at all. Eventually, he marries her thoroughly conventional English half-sister, and Corinne dies of a broken heart.

For all its absurdities of plot and the exasperating indecision of hero and heroine, *Corinne* was important as an early, sympathetic portrait of a free woman and an exploration of the emotional cost of freedom. Staël wanted it understood as social criticism, and she depicted the

Italian setting in a particular way to make her point. Italy here is an ideal society, where a woman may love and create freely. Britain—which Staël admired in many respects—is seen as a repressive society, and it is Nelvil's blind allegiance to his country, its social order, and the memory of his dead father that prevents his remaining in Italy with Corinne.

But he is also prevented by male pride, and throughout the novel the conflict in both characters is presented in psychological as well as social terms. In her narrator's voice, Staël explains his reservations:

However distinguished a man may be, he rarely feels unqualified pleasure in the superiority of a woman. If he does not love her, his self-esteem takes offence; if he does, his heart is oppressed by it. Beside Corinne, Oswald was rather intoxicated than happy: the admiration she excited increased his passion, without giving stability to his intents. She was a phenomenon every day new; but the very wonder she inspired seemed to lessen his hopes of domestic tranquility. She was, notwithstanding, so gentle, so easy to live with, that she might have been beloved for her lowliest attributes, independent of all others; yet it was by these others that she had become remarkable. Lord Nelvil [*sic*], with all his advantages, thought himself beneath her, and doubted the duration of their attachment. In vain did she make herself his slave: the conqueror was too much in awe of his captive queen to enjoy his realm in peace.[2]

Corinne herself can argue strongly for her independence, which she has won through hardship and risk:

Are not great thoughts and generous feelings debts due to the world, from all who are capable of paying them? Ought not every woman, like every man, to follow the bent of her own talents? Must we imitate the instinct of the bees, whose every succeeding swarm copies the last, without improvement or variety? No, Oswald; pardon the pride of your Corinne, I believed myself intended for a different career.

But she has only been describing the magnificent gift she is willing to offer him:

If it pleased you to pass your days in the heart of Scotland, I should be happy to live and die with you; but far from abjuring the imagination, it would teach me the better to enjoy nature, and the further the empire of my mind extended, the more glory should I feel in declaring you its lord.[3]

For the reader, it is no more possible to imagine Corinne communing with nature in the heart of Scotland, deprived of the public that gives life to her talent, than it is to imagine Staël herself in the same position. Nature held no charms for her; Napoleon could hardly have devised a crueler punishment than exiling her from Paris. The social obstacles, genuine though they are, serve to mask the fact that Nelvil could not under any circumstances remain in Italy and be continually "in awe" of his "queen." Corinne cannot really follow him to Scotland, nor can she give him up. But forced to choose between independence and dependence, she chooses dependence.

This is a false resolution, though, and rather than leave her heroine stuck with it, Staël has her die of a broken heart. As Gutwirth points out, the ending is an expression of Staël's anger, a way of saying to the world, "Look what you do to your brilliant, creative women."[4] At the same time, the entire book is an expression of Staël's own conviction that "women owe fealty in love."[5]

So the legacy Madame de Staël passed on to Margaret Fuller, along with her celebration of German and French Romanticism, was the whole vexed question of how a gifted woman could relate to men and particularly how she coud reconcile her needs for independence and dependence. The very sensibility cultivated by Romanticism exacerbated the problem. Margaret Fuller's admiration of Staël was well known, and she was called the "Yankee Corinna" in a tone that was not always complimentary. Even the circumstantial parallels are striking: There is the family with one cold, demanding parent and one warmer one, though in Fuller's family it was the father who was cold. There is the rigorous education administered by this cold parent and abruptly changed in early adolescence, though in Fuller's case it shifted toward the cultivation of social acceptability rather than sensibility. There is the politically active, liberal home where the child mixed with the brightest people of her time and place, and there is the irony of seeing this liberalism applied to almost everyone except women. Like Staël, Fuller achieved intellectual dominance while longing for a relationship that would allow her some emotional dependence. Like her—and also because of her—she visualized Italy as a society that offered more emotional freedom to women than her own. Like her she tended to fall in love with men younger than herself (Ward, Nathan, Ossoli).

But Staël lived out her search for the ideal relationship in a series of liaisons that left her always heartbroken and sometimes humiliated.

Fuller, born in a country that would not tolerate such behavior in women, understood and excused it in George Sand and Mary Wollstonecraft and by implication in Madame de Staël, though she did not mention her by name: "such beings as these, rich in genius, of most tender sympathies, capable of high virtue and a chastened harmony, ought not to find themselves, by birth, in a place so narrow, that, in breaking bonds, they become outlaws." [6] Finding herself in exactly such a place, she forearmed herself against Corinne's disastrous choice and put aside all hope of marriage. She resolved to lead a single—and perforce a chaste—life. But she was remarkable for her ability to acknowledge that this was an artificial choice. She did not need to deny her own need to be dependent as well as independent. She once wrote to a friend:

From a very early age I have felt that I was not born to the common womanly lot. I knew I should never find a being who could keep the key of my character; that there would be none on whom I could always lean, from whom I could always learn; that I should be a pilgrim and sojourner on earth, and that the birds and foxes would be surer of a place to lay the head than I. [7]

But she wrote such statements only to close friends and her own journal, maintaining in public the stance of a completely independent being. She came near to following Corinne's example only once, in her relationship with James Nathan. Then she allowed herself to express a passivity that was startlingly at odds with her public image:

I am with you as never with any other one, I like to be quite still and have you the actor and the voice. You have enough life for both; you will indulge me in this dear repose. [8]

I have felt a strong attraction to you, almost ever since we first met, the attraction of a wandering spirit towards a breast, broad enough and strong enough for a rest, when it wants to furl the wings. [9]

But Nathan was neither broad enough nor strong enough to provide rest for Margaret Fuller. By sheer force of love and illusion, she was making him into someone he was not, just as Corinne had with Nelvil.

Some time earlier, in a less vulnerable mood, she had written her own version of *Corinne*. The story "Mariana" is often cited in connection with Fuller's experience at boarding school. The ending of the story is pure fantasy and is not so well known as the beginning. The heroine, Mariana, is described as an "improvisatrice," in a direct allusion to Staël's novel.[10] Like Staël, Fuller has her heroine fall in love with a man (Sylvain) not her equal. She is blind to the disparity for some time: "loving so much, she imagined all the rest." When she does realize she has made him into someone he is not, she is "too deeply in love to leave him." She marries him and finds he wants nothing more of her than to oversee his home and leave him in peace. For his sake she tries to enter society but finds it every bit as stultifying as English society in *Corinne*, as German society in *Germany*, and as Groton, Massachusetts, society had been to Margaret Fuller. She looks for consolation in "other relationships"—presumably all platonic. But as Fuller herself often did, she overwhelms those she chooses for friends by the power of her mind and the intensity of her emotional needs. Eventually, like Delphine and Corinne, she takes the only way out that is left and dies. At the end of the story Fuller blames Mariana's fate on the imperfect state of society. If Mariana had been a man, she points out, "many resources would have presented themselves. . . . He would have been called by life, and not permitted to be quite wrecked through the affections only. But such women as Mariana are often lost, unless they meet some man of sufficiently great soul to prize them."[11]

As an alternative to Mariana and Corinne, Fuller offers in *Woman in the Nineteenth Century* the example of Miranda. Educated by an enlightened father who, unlike Fuller's and Staël's, "cherished no sentimental reverence for Woman," Miranda is a model of self-reliance. She is welcomed by men as an intellectual equal: "The world was free to her, and she lived freely in it." She has achieved "an outward serenity and an inward peace." But she is clearly celibate:

She was fortunate in a total absence of those charms which might have drawn to her bewildering flatteries, and in a strong electric nature, which repelled those who did not belong to her, and attracted those who did. With men and women her relations were noble,—affectionate without passion, intellectual without coldness.[12]

As a model of intellectual self-reliance Miranda is both admirable and believable, but other women could hardly have found her total absence of sexuality either comforting or realistic. In effect she is a Transcendental nun, without admitting even to those inner conflicts that nuns themselves must struggle with. In Mariana and Miranda, Fuller has created two characters from the opposite sides of herself which she was unable to integrate—at least until, years after writing both pieces, she met Ossoli. To avoid the fate of a Mariana or a Corinne, she seems to say, a gifted woman should become a Miranda.

She did not expect that most women would be permanently celibate. She did urge them to free themselves from their excessive intellectual dependence by separating themselves from men for a time, at least until they had achieved a firm sense of identity. Celibacy, she wrote, was "the great fact of the time," though she hoped the time would change, partly as a result of her book. Meanwhile, "Union is only possible to those who are units. . . . It is a vulgar error that love, *a* love, to Woman is her whole existence." [13] Once most women had learned to think and exist without men, she expected they would be able to enter marriage as it then existed and be reasonably happy despite its restrictions. But for unusually gifted, dominant women like herself marriage was a trap. Love itself undermined one's judgment, so that if there were those "great-souled men" around who could cherish a Mariana or a Corinne, it might be impossible to tell them from the Nelvils and the Sylvains. The gifted woman had far better remain resolutely self-sufficient.

Without being a clinician, one can guess that for both Fuller and Staël the strain of having to demonstrate publicly that women could be as strong and creative as men exaggerated their need to "owe fealty" in love until it became a real danger to their integrity. The luxury of a momentary dependence from which one recovers and goes on, the give-and-take of dependence and independence between men and women, was not something they could easily imagine or achieve. Staël tried to achieve it, but her relationships always foundered. Both women carried the burden not only of their own independence but also that of all women.

Both had lost strong fathers whose support of their careers had been mixed, at best; indeed, Staël wrote *Corinne* while she was still mourning the death of her father. Both women had to suffer insults specifically directed at their sexuality. The powerful minds and personalities of both threatened the male integrity of the men around them. Nelvil's reservations about Corinne's superiority are typical even of the liberal men of the day. Fuller saw no man around her who seemed capable of loving a woman who ventured out of the domestic circle. Emerson, the most philosophically advanced man she knew, visibly shrank from such a notion. Both women keenly felt the isolation this imposed on them, and Gutwirth's words about Staël could equally be applied to Fuller: "Caught in a struggle between the will to be free, to be her own unorthodox self, and a will to be loved, to be yielding, gentle, moral, like those women traditionally given fealty by men, she had found herself an ever-aberrant being."[14]

So it could be argued that for these exceptionally strong women the temptation to sacrifice their independence for the sake of being loved by a man was greater than for most women. *Corinne* and "Mariana" are recognitions of the attraction and dangers of such a sacrifice. Written as protests against a particular social order, they also bear witness to the more persistent difficulty of balancing independence and dependence between the sexes and to the weariness both women felt at always having to be first at the barricades.

NOTES

1. Madelyn Gutwirth, *Madame de Staël, Novelist: The Emergence of the Artist as Woman* (Urbana: University of Illinois Press, 1978), pp. 96–98, 286–88.

2. Madame de Staël, *Corinne, or Italy*, trans. Isabel Hill (Philadelphia: Henry Cary Baird, 1854), p. 123.

3. Ibid., p. 241.

4. Gutwirth, *Madame de Staël*, pp. 256–57.

5. Ibid., p. 249.

6. Margaret Fuller, *Woman in the Nineteenth Century* (New York: Norton, 1971), p. 75.

7. Margaret Fuller, *Memoirs of Margaret Fuller Ossoli*, ed. Ralph Waldo Emerson, William Henry Channing, and James Freeman Clarke, 2 vols. in one (New York: Burt Franklin, 1972), I: 98–99.

8. Margaret Fuller, *Love-Letters of Margaret Fuller, 1845–46* (New York: D. Appleton, 1903), Letter XVII.

9. Ibid., Letter XIX.

10. Perry Miller, ed., *Margaret Fuller: American Romantic* (Ithaca, N.Y.: Cornell University Press, 1963), p. 18.

11. Ibid., pp. 16–23.

12. Fuller, *Woman*, pp. 38–39.

13. Ibid., pp. 119, 177.

14. Gutwirth, *Madame de Staël*, p. 157.

5

George Sand's View of the English

Patricia Thomson

Most readers of the letters of George Sand are surprised by her obduracy in refusing warm invitations to visit England when she was at the height of her fame. These invitations were pressed upon her, in the 1840's and 1850's, not only by such admirers as Macready, Lewes and Mazzini but by close friends like Pauline Viardot and Charlotte Marliani. There was a lot of coming and going between the two countries in that period, and in addition, London was the refuge for many of the exiles with whom Sand had worked so closely in the Revolution. She continued to keep in touch with them but always by letter, from across the Channel.

The excuses she makes about lack of money, family responsibilities, inopportune timing and so on convince at first reading, but with reiteration they sound lame. George Sand had a way of getting around obstacles if she really wanted to. Giussepe Mazzini, puzzled by her attitude, attempted to analyze it in a letter of 1845 to Emila Hawkes:

I have done all that I could to persuade her to a trip to England: but I have my doubts about the result. She cannot afford to travel now and when she has got over her difficulties she seems bent on another journey to Italy. . . . England is still viewed in a strange light: partly true but exaggerated: it is still . . . the land of Aristocracy and utilitarianism.[1]

"Aristocracy" and "utilitarianism"—these terms may well be described as *idées reçues* about England and not peculiar to George Sand.

But she was open minded enough about other things, and one may ask why a lifelong admirer of Byron, Shakespeare, and Scott could cling so obstinately to this stereotyping of the nation and should again and again single out as exceptions, as "peu Anglais que possible" (little English as possible), all the Englishmen and women she met and approved of? Why was it that she was so reluctant to cross the Channel, thereby running the risk herself of the epithet *insulaire*, which came so trippingly to her pen in her allusions to the English?

These questions are not easy to answer nor is her stance easy to define. A full investigation would have to take into account not only the remarks made in her letters—as Thelma Jurgrau has done in her valuable resume of the English references in the *Correspondence*[2]—but also her autobiographical works, her use of English characters in her fiction and their literary precedents, if any. It is important, too, *when* she conceived her views. George Sand's pronouncements, in *Histoire de ma Vie*, on the English character, morals and physiognomy stand out from her lively and loving re-creation of the young girl's impressions as the generalizations of a woman of fifty. She intersperses her comments on English pride and coldness, controlled passions and prudery, with recollections of the girls and nuns that testify to their warmth, friendliness and openness. Such juxtapositions should have made anyone, less settled in her prejudices, question their truth, but there is no doubt that early influences had been strong enough to give Sand complete confidence in herself as an authority on things English.

These influences were exerted in the two and a quarter years—often talked of by Sand as three years—that she spent in Paris at an English convent school, *le Couvent des Dames Augustines Anglaises*. This period in Aurore Dupin's adolescence was enormously important for her as a break in the emotional tug-of-war between her plebian mother and her aristocratic grandmother, in her words "a neutral territory . . . a sort of breathing space" and also as a revelation to her of what religious conversion could mean. Biographers have tended to concentrate on these two aspects and to confine the English legacy to the acquisition of charming manners or to a lifelong preference for tea. But she herself did not underestimate the effect. She later wrote: "I did not know that I was perhaps truly entering the world in crossing the threshold of the cloister, that there I might acquire connections, habits of mind, even ideas which would fix me, as it were, in the class from which I had wanted to break away.''[3]

That world was, in fact, no ''neutral territory.'' It not only catered to the noble and wealthy but was also overpoweringly English. In her autobiography George Sand recalled how stunned and shocked she felt— this thirteen-year-old ''peasant from Berry'' as she significantly describes herself—on entering this foreign country—in fact, this part of the British empire: next door was the Scots college, four doors off the Irish seminary, and all the nuns were either English, Scots or Irish, as well as two-thirds of the boarders, tenants and some of the visiting priests. For some hours each day English was the only language spoken, and even the epitaphs on the graves in the cloister were written in English. She summed up: ''All was English in that house, the past and the present, and when the iron gate had shut behind one, the sensation was of having crossed the Channel.[4]

In reading *Histoire de ma Vie* it is very easy to underestimate this fact, mainly because the nuns are referred to as Soeur Agathe, Soeur Hélène, Soeur Eugénie and so on. But if instead we substitute their English names and birthplaces and also those of her friends, many of the escapades and experiences of Aurore (nicknamed ''Madcap'') sound as if they could have come out of an English school story—of japes in the dorm and classroom, midnight feasts and nocturnal scrambles over the roofs. The roll call of the staff is impressive: the Reverend Mother—the headmistress Miss Canning; Miss Stoning from Oxfordshire; Miss Finchet from Lancashire; Miss Bishop from Warwickshire; Miss Fairbanks, Miss Jones, Miss Spiring. Aurore had French friends as well as English, but two of her ''best friends'' were English, and George Sand punctiliously catalogued many more. Even the cat was called Whisky.

This was surely very considerable immersion in England and English ways for a young, impressionable girl. It should be remembered that she was genuinely cloistered: she had practically no outings and had no holidays at home to allow her to recapture her Berry background. At the same time, she associated the convent with all the things her grandmother approved of and her mother scorned—dignity, reserve, serious application to study, etiquette and good manners. One of the first letters she received from her grandmother stressed the importance not only of a good carriage in dancing but of learning English. She wrote: "Pray do not neglect your English. You will soon master it and one day you will be glad of it, we have so many links with that country that it's shameful not to know their language when they know ours so well."[5]

Surrounded by nuns who spoke French badly or not at all, Aurore had no such illusions but she soon learned enough English to chatter with her friends, to eavesdrop to her satisfaction and eventually even to comprehend the dialect of the Scots lay-sisters.[6] But at the same time, her patriotism was roused by being in a minority of French pupils, and in the convent war games she led her own small band in the role of generalissimo of the French army, a Bonapartist against English Royalists. André Maurois quotes the scribbles from her notebook where, even as she praises equally her French and English friends—"Anna de Wismes is a little darling! Isabella Affleck is charming!"—she goes on to denounce the nation: "Down with the English! Death to the English dogs! Long live France! I do not like Wellington!"[7] It is easy to see where George Sand's conviction was bred that England was a nation of aristocrats; one need look no further than the convent, her fashionable English finishing school, that symbol of "the class from which I had wanted to break away."

A vital feature of that life was her relationship with one of the nuns, Alicia-Mary Spiring. As is well known, Aurore temporarily resolved the passionate conflict that had torn her apart for so long between her two "mothers" by audaciously seeking adoption as her "fille" ("daughter") by a third—the best and cleverest nun, with the most beautiful eyes, Madame Alicia. A quarter of a century later Sand movingly sings the praises of her chosen mother; at last she had found someone wise and serene, who loved her, who scolded the "diable incarné" ("devil incarnate") firmly but without acrimony, who laughed with her and who had faith in her. Long after Aurore Dupin had become Aurore Dudevant—indeed, until just before she became George Sand—she continued to write to her and to visit her when she was in Paris. "She was my ideal, my sainted love, my chosen mother."[8] It is clear that Sand always cherished the thought of Madame Alicia as half-French, half-English: "Born in France of a French mother, brought up in France, she was more French than English, and the mixture of the best in the two races produced a perfect being—she had the dignity of the British without their inflexibility.[9]

She was, in fact, an Englishwoman on both sides whose mother did

not speak a word of French. It is perhaps as well that the young Aurore was ignorant of this, for the blending of the two nationalities
meant a great deal to her, as her fiction shows.

In the years that followed her abrupt and reluctant departure from
the convent in 1820, she tried to keep up with her friends, but her
lament, that she lost her English quickly, is borne out by her letters.
Scraps of pidgin English continue to ornament them for some time:
"J'ai vu Louise there is some time ago"; "je kisse ta soeur"; "un
homme precious"; "une lazyness d'esprit." Certain words stick a little longer—the ones she must have heard most often on the lips of her
teachers—words like "nonsense" and "dearest child." [10] But she never
lost her sense of knowing, if not English—the English—and for the
rest of her life continued to draw on impressions formed at school. It
is not really surprising that George Sand was reluctant in later life to
visit England, a real England, which she would have found an alien
country and one whose language she no longer knew. In doing so she
would have run the risk of losing her long-valued sense of familiarity
with English customs and characteristics. It is always humiliating and
disappointing after one has made capital out of an experience—and I
think we may assume that George Sand had done so over the years—
to admit that one is not as much of an expert as one has given the
impression of being. Aurore Dupin "crossed the Channel" once when
she was thirteen, and she got enough out of that extended stay to draw
on for her writing life.

Sand corresponded with Madame Alicia until 1830, and only a year
later she used the convent as copy for the novel *Rose et Blanche*, in
which she collaborated with Jules Sandeau. One can scarcely say that
she immortalized it, but in their liveliness the convent scenes are all
that save the book from deserved oblivion.

On the whole, Sand sticks very closely to her sources. Rose de
Beaumont (whose surname was that of Aurore's grand-uncle) is the
first of the thinly disguised Sandian heroines. She too has a substitute
mother, Soeur Adèle, whose likeness to Madame Alicia extended even
to her beautiful eyes and large nose; and the strapping, outspoken old
Sister of Charity, Soeur Olympe, owes much to the jolliest of the lay
sisters, Theresa. The convent parlor, Rose's cell, the silent assembly
of nuns lining the corridor, are based on faithful recollections. [11] Actual names are put to good use: the most surprising is that of Throck-

morton, remembered from a tomb, but the surnames of former friends and teachers are sported by members of the audience at a school concert—Lady Cadogan, Lady Holland, Lady Gillibrand and l'honorable Monsieur Canning. When Rose sings, "Even Lady Gillibrand said several times 'C'était très jolé' "[12]—a first, mild example of Sand's satire of the English accent and drawl, which she was to make more of later.

Rose's arrival at the convent coincides with visiting day. She sits in the parlour, awaiting admission and listening to an inane conversation between a snobbish French pupil, Béatrix de Vermandois, and her brother. She has begun to feel glad that she has no relations when an English family enters—the rich middle-class Plumkets who have crossed the Channel to visit their seven daughters.

The father was a big man with chubby cheeks, bright eyes and red hair. He looked common-place but happy and good. His wife was six feet tall. Four boys aged from six to ten, as red-haired as their father and as sturdy as their mother, fresh-complexioned as true sons of Albion, looked with curiosity at the grille and showed as much lively impatience as their phlegmatic temperament would allow.[13]

As Rose watches, the seven daughters burst into the parlor:

The dazzling colour of their red hair, so opposed to our notions of beauty, provided unequivocal proof for their father of the fidelity of his spouse. Nothing was more pleasing to his overflowing heart than those eleven red heads ranged around him, without counting the little ones left behind in Monmouthshire.[14]

When the porter opens the grating, all the young English girls throw themselves into their parents' arms.

It was a moment of confusion. In their excitement every one was jostling each other. Exclamations in all keys could be heard. [And here George Sand uses English:] *Ah! Dear Ann! dearest papa! my love! my brother! where's George! and Dick! Sarah! Mary! Mamma!* And all in the piercing tone of voice which the provincials of England possess to a higher degree than we do.[15]

While the aristocratic French pupil sneers, Rose's eyes fill with tears. She watches the mother embracing the oldest red-head while the little boys clutch at their sisters' aprons to get a hug or kiss. For the first time she understands the "bliss of filial love and the treasure of family affections, saying to herself bitterly, 'I shall never know this happiness! A tender and virtuous mother will never press me to her heart like this.' "[16]

It is a revealing little episode and worth quoting at some length because it is not very well known. It is obvious that she enjoyed writing it and that she had witnessed comparable, if less exaggerated, reunions at the *Anglaises* in her time. The families of her friends could not emulate the size of the Plumkets in the pupil-lists, but the three Kellys, the three O'Mullans, the three Carys, the three Gordons, the three Gillibrands, as well as the six Rochejaqueleins are in marked contrast with Aurore's solitariness and lack of a normal family life. Despite its comic aspects, this middle-class English family is given the qualities of frankness, honesty and generosity that Sand was to retain in all her fictional English aristocrats.

She had had much more actual experience of English women than men when she started writing. Her first hero, Fitzgerald, in a juvenile convent tale, had not been much of a success with her friends, and few readers would claim much life for Sir Ralph of *Indiana* (1832). With him we run into the question of literary precedent. In her "days of Corinne" Aurore had no doubt pondered the qualities of Madame de Staël's man of feeling, Lord Nelvil, but Sir Ralph has not much in common with him, for the important feature of all Sand's Englishmen is that they never let the heroine down. Ralph is given a certain steadying, common touch by his surname Brown, and with his bright hair and red cheeks he is at Indiana's side, phlegmatic and indispensable from start to finish—unlike the fickle Frenchman, Raymon. For a general influence on her English heroes I think we need look no further than Rousseau, the idol of her youth, whose Lord Bomston was an English nobleman of sterling qualities and quixotic generosity.

Sand's basic stereotype of English aristocracy is never abandoned, but by the time she wrote *Jeanne*, in 1844, she had managed to breathe enough life into Sir Arthur Harley for Clough, then a Cambridge fellow, to hail him delightedly as an "Englishman—a very veritable hero."[17] What makes him attractive is the blend of the slightly ridiculous and the admirable in him. Sir Arthur understands French well, but he has a pronounced British accent, he gets his tenses and genders muddled, he pronounces *impossible* "immepossible" and *huit jours* "houit jours" and in emergencies always falls back on "Ho!"—uttered "with the indefinable accent of phlegmatic surprise that Englishmen put into that exclamation"[18]—and therefore is fair game for mockery by the villain Marsillat.

On the other hand, he is not only tall and handsome, fresh complexioned and well-dressed but—George Sand gives her Englishman everything—has magnificent teeth and a smooth, unruffled brow. He is eccentric enough to be a democrat, even a practicing socialist, and practically the first succinct observation he utters is "No masters nor slaves; only men."[19] He goes on to prove his belief in the equality of men by proposing to the milkmaid Jeanne, and when she refuses him he follows the noble example of Rousseau's Lord Bomston by offering to set her up with the man of her choice.

Sand's wholehearted admiration of Sir Arthur contrasts strangely with her view of English society, in contemporary letters, as still feudal and, moreover, "unjust, iniquitous, demoralizing, perfidious and brutal."[20] As always, she says that she hates the country and not the people, but it does seem very strange that she should have chosen a rich, English aristocrat as her practicing democrat, a man admired by his French friends as being "exempt from our miserable prejudices."[21] Heart and head, as not infrequently with George Sand, seem to be pulling against each other.

By 1857, when she wrote *La Daniella*, she no longer felt the need to grind a social or political axe, and Lord B. is an affectionate, if somewhat tame, study of an intelligent Englishman, who is treated by his vain and frivolous wife as if he were "the mere mangy dog of the family."[22] Although he is henpecked he is also intelligent, loyal, sensitive, and has a good knowledge of French—excellences that are bound in the long (very long) run to win Lady Harriet's appreciation. Sand's tendency to pontificate about the English is very marked in this novel; she is, for instance, very firm (from the depths of her inexperience of English people at home) about how much nicer and more open-minded they are abroad—though, even then, she adds, to French eyes they always have something comic about them.[23]

This aspect she brings out most strongly in a play, *Flaminio*, which was put on at the Gymnase-Dramatique in 1854. It is a much-altered version of an earlier fantasy, *Teverino*, and is often near to farce. The new character of Miss Barbara Melvil is the source of practically all the comedy. It is valuable to have, in a letter, George Sand's own

comments on which actress should play the part, for it shows her protective attitude toward the Englishwoman. She first gives directions
about the heroine, Lady Sarah Melvil, who, although she is English,
has been brought up in France and has no accent—"or an impercep-
tible and gracious one"—and then goes on to discuss her stepsister
and chaperone, Barbara:

She is aged fifty, an arch-English type well known to me—an eccentric old
maid, good, generous, virile, romantic, virtuous—a type both comic and sympathetic, which I believe to be new to the theatre. It is a good role but not for
Melanie who would make her too funny, too masculine, too like a colonel's
sister. She should be able to make herself loved—supernaturally honest, with
a solid English accent.[24]

Sand's authority here comes from having known in her youth many
strong, hearty Englishwomen in that age group—some ready to laugh
and joke like Sister Theresa, who, when the girls played tricks on her,
would whack them with her broom; others whose Lancashire, Scots
and Irish accents struck the girls as extremely funny. No doubt she
was also bringing to the character of Barbara Melvil her memories of
Englishwomen she had met on her travels, but she probably never
again heard French quite as badly spoken as at the convent. Miss Melvil comes on stage brandishing a rifle, with which she has been shoot-
ing fish, and the boast "Doux carpes d'une coup de fiousil!"[25] She
befriends the bohemian, Flaminio, and yearns to punch the villain,
whose mockery of her she challenges in a defiant speech, typical of
the orthography throughout.

Barbara: Il moque moi, mais je moque lui. (Haut) Je souis une je habiller
moi pas bien en français. Je chassé avec le fiousil, je étudie le philosophy! il
est bien ridiquiolue! Je aimer le poetrie, le miousic, le bonté, le sincerité; je
aimer il signor Flaminio! . . . oh! comme une fils![26]

The blend of amusement and admiration with which George Sand
has always treated her English characters is, however, absent from
Malgrétout (1869), a roman à clé in which she treats her heroine—
another Sarah—with great seriousness. At the age of sixty-five Sand
was looking back twenty years for copy, to her tribulations with So-
lange, Clesinger and Chopin, and seems intent on setting the record

straight about the ingratitude and treachery of her daughter (here, her sister), the gullibility of her lover and her own exemplary conduct. Of the self-sacrificing heroine, whose sanctimonious revelations fill letter after letter, André Maurois wrote: "Sarah Owen comes very close to the author (or to what she thought herself to be).[27]

It is indeed extraordinary to find Sand camouflaged as this twenty-three-year-old Englishwoman, the daughter of Henry Owen, an English lawyer. But it becomes a little less surprising when we learn that she is not in the Ardennes as a tourist; she is half-French. Sarah has been brought up in France by a French mother and therefore has the virtues of both nations. She has the English qualities of reasonableness, reliability, modesty and composure, and she is also beautiful, musical, passionate and generous. In her dual nationality Sarah Owen, in fact, has the same right to perfection as Aurore Dupin's beloved "mère" ("mother"), Alicia (or as she thought her to have been). It is both interesting and touching that George Sand should have fallen back on this girlish ideal in order to present an alternative version of the sorry and ugly tale of her own family strife, which had had no such happy ending. But perhaps it was not too surprising, for her memories of the convent were of a "grande famille féminine" in which there was no discord, only tolerance and tenderness, and of her years there as the happiest and most peaceful of her life.

NOTES

1. George Sand, *Correspondance*, ed. Georges Lubin, 20 vols. (Paris: Garnier, 1964–85). VIII: 127.

2. Thelma Jurgrau, "George Sand's Attitude toward the English," in *George Sand Papers, Conference Proceedings* (New York: Hofstra University, 1980).

3. George Sand, *Histoire de ma Vie* in *Oeuvres Autobiographiques*, ed. Georges Lubin, 2 vols. (Paris: Gallimard 1970–71), I: 862.

4. Ibid., p. 863.

5. Sand, *Correspondance*, I: 19.

6. For details of life at the convent see Sand, *Histoire de ma Vie*, I: 862–1015; and Notes, pp. 1414–33. I am indebted to Lubin's excellent notes throughout.

7. André Maurois, *Lelia, The Life of George Sand*, trans. Gerard Hopkins (London: 1953), p. 41.

8. "C'était mon idéal, mon saint amour, c'était la mère de mon choix."

9. Sand, *Histoire de ma Vie*, I: 925.

10. *Correspondance*, I: 31–82, in particular.

11. George Sand, *Rose et Blanche*, 2 vols. (Bruxelles: 1837), II: chaps. 1–3.

12. Ibid., II: 59.

13. Ibid., II: 9–11.

14. Ibid.

15. Ibid.

16. Ibid.

17. *Correspondance of Arthur Hugh Clough*, ed. F. L. Mulhauser, 2 vols. (Oxford: Oxford University Press, 1957), II: 503.

18. George Sand, *Jeanne* (Paris: 1892), chap. 14, p. 196.

19. Ibid., Prologue, 8. "Pas de maîtres et pas d'esclaves; des hommes et des hommes."

20. Sand, *Correspondance* XII: 229. " . . . injuste, inique, démoralisatrice, perfide et brutal."

21. Sand, *Jeanne*, chap. 13, p. 175.

22. George Sand, *La Daniella* (Paris: 1862), chap. 11, p. 114.

23. Ibid., p. 247.

24. Sand, *Correspondance*, XII: 299.

25. Sand, *Flaminio*, in *Théâtre complet*, 4 vols. (Paris: Michel Lévy, 1866–67), I: 23, "Two carps with one rifle-shot!"

26. Ibid., p. 299. The comedy depends upon the ungrammatical French, which a translation cannot convey: "He mocks me but I mock him. (Loudly) I am a ridiculous person, I don't speak French well, I don't dress myself well in French. I hunt with the rifle, I study philosophy, it is very ridiculous! I love poetry, music, goodness, sincerity; I love signor Flaminio! . . . oh, like a son!"

27. André Maurois, Preface to *Malgrétout* (Les Cahiers ardennais, n.d.), p. 5.

6

Trollope's Choice: Frances Trollope Reads George Sand

Marie-Jacques Hoog

Paris, April, 1835: Frances Trollope, the English traveller now well established by the instant success of her *Domestic Manners of the Americans*, arrives and promptly sets out to write her letters, soon to be published as *Paris and the Parisians*.[1] She is older for this, her third visit, but the Paris of young France has grown younger since the rights of passage of July, 1830.

With the boldness of an English clergyman's daughter, she decides not to mourn too much over the white banners or the renowned lilies, symbols of the fading honors of her country's rival, now torn down, tramped upon. She resolutely turns her eyes away from the new tricolored flag—"those three stripes, terrible heraldry"—and concentrates on amusing herself," a business never performed anywhere with so much ease as in Paris, this gay, bright, noisy, restless city—this city of the living."[2] And one of the most irresistible of those living Parisians will soon be George Sand.

The overall conditions are most favorable for the British visitor, even in the absence of the "center round which all that is gay and English revolves":[3] the English Embassy. In fact, the present moment could not be more pregnant with expectations. Everything seems new: the Madeleine is completed—"why might not our National Gallery have risen as noble, as simple, as beautiful as this?"[4]

A new effigy of Napoleon crowns the Colonne Vendôme. The gardens and the streets of Paris bristle with *farouches jeunes gens* ("wild youths"), with their new, dark looks, their new idiom. At the Luxembourg a new chamber is erected, handsome though built of wood, to house the "monstrous trial." It will open on May 5, when The Chamber of Peers will try the Lyons political prisoners and their Paris accomplices, one hundred and twenty-one in all.[5] This test of the new July Monarchy is stirring up all the passions of the "Great Nation." In her secluded village of Nohant, George Sand is packing to attend the session: her new friend Michel de Bourges is a central figure in it. Women, she will discover, are not admitted. But dressed as a schoolboy, Sand is present on May 20.[6] So she appears—at least part of her—in Trollope's text:

It is said, indeed, that in one of the tribunes set apart for the public, a small white hand has been seen to caress some jet-black curls upon the head of a boy; and it was said, too, that the boy called himself George S—–d; but I have heard of no other instance of anyone not furnished with that important symbol of prerogative, *une barbe au menton*, who has ventured within the prescribed limits.[7]

Hand and head: good similes for Trollope's choice when she discusses Sand's works, later in her book. French is still French she says, but a new slang is insinuating itself among "The Young Men of Paris," whose idiom and manners prevail in young France. They classify the French population under two great divisions: the *rococo* and the *décousu*. *Rococo* contains "all varieties of old-fashionism," including the author and her taste for the French classics, from Corneille and Boileau to Staël and Chateaubriand. *Décousu* is the fashionable epithet "given by the sober-minded to all that smacks of the rambling nonsense of the new-school of authors," be they novelists, dramatists or poets; to all shades of republicans, from the avowed eulogist of the "spirited Robespierre" to the gentler disciples of Lamennais, to most of the schoolboys, including George Sand, and all of the fishwives of Paris.[8]

The first thing to do, if you are as *rococo* as Frances Trollope, when you land in Paris is to go see Mlle Mars and her *Beau Idéal* in *Tartuffe*. Next, you go to the Louvre and admire "Le Déluge" of that *rococo* Nicolas Poussin. Then you dash to a salon, where you discuss again, the topic of the day, the Monstrous Trial, in a fashionable potpourri, divided between the opinions of the "Although" and the "Because." Then to church, to inspect the younger, *décousu* clergy. Only then can you sit and reflect about the "Literature of the Revolutionary School," that is, the Romantics of the day. The reader is warned of the coming rout of the *décousu*-type novel, with Sand as a possible exception.[9]

Trollope, with her keen journalistic eye, shows us, dramatically, the sudden rise to prominence of two groups in the new French society: the young men, with their "lean and hungry looks," and literary women: "nowhere higher efforts of the female mind are more honored than in France," she says.[10] She helps us understand how young Sand managed to make it so quickly to the top of that moveable feast which is Paris. But the dynamics of Trollope's book are such that it will take the reader ten more "literary letters"—out of the seventy-two that compose the two volumes—to get to the full-length chapter devoted exclusively to Sand, the only author to receive such treatment.

Meanwhile, along the way, we hear of *La Marquise*[11] which provides the libretto of a *petite comédie*, preceeding that brilliant trifle, *spectacle par excellence*, *Le Cheval de Bronze*, at the Comic Opera: "This fable must, I think, be taken, though greatly changed, from a story of George Sand. It has perhaps little in it worth talking about, but it is a fair specimen of one of that most agreeable of French nationalities, a natural, easy, playful little piece."[12]

This strategy of putting in foil the presentation of Sand is necessitated by two predicaments. The major one is that, in France as well as in Victorian England, Sand is present, the center of controversial debates. In 1835 *Indiana*, *Valentine*, *Lélia*, are hot pieces. Since then, Sand has published more sober works: *Le Secrétaire intime*, light short stories—*Leone Leoni* and *André*—and the first six of the serialized *Lettres d'un Voyageur*. But the renegade of Venice has blurred her Parisian image. And Trollope will quietly choose to ignore the "novels of rebellion" as well as the scandalous aspects of Sand's *vita*.

The other obstacle to Sand's early recognition is that she evidently is glorified most by precisely that nonsensical group of "The Young Men," who have attracted Trollope's immediate attention but none of her sympathies. Yet they are the same "bons enfants" to whom Sand dedicates the best pages of her *Lettre d'un Oncle*, so admired by Liszt, where she claims she owes her life to friendship.[13] For Trollope, they partake of that "outrageous school of literary extravagance" that fills the French stage with absurdities, from *Le Monomane* to *Angelo tyran de Padoue*. Indeed, Victor Hugo, so liked in England for his *Notre-*

Dame de Paris (if only Westminster Abbey were celebrated in such a
way!) is vindicated here three times: Esmeralda! Triboulet! Heroes of
"The Idiot Era!" The *décousu* school is not only the mirror but the
cause behind the deconstruction of the French social material as Trollope sees it: the Morgue and its Horrible Murders are the reflection of
a literature of "depravity," an amplification of *La Tour de Nesle*.
Sand will, much later in the book, be shown in a contrast with all that
"trash."

Strong sympathies drive Trollope toward Sand. Both women are
professional writers; both are famed travellers. It is obvious through
the whole book that Trollope is biased in favor of women authors,
especially when they are daughters of ministers. When in Letter
LXXXVII she examines the new French publications, she puts Lamartine, Tocqueville and Mme Tastu on the same level. She is always
talking about actresses—the French Mlle Mars or Marie Dorval, the
English Mrs. Bartley, Mrs. Butler or the famous Madame Siddons,
who appears in Staël's *Corinne*. Corinne is everywhere, she finds:
"the memory of Madame de Staël seems enshrined in every woman's
heart. And the glory she has brought to her country appears to shed
its beams upon every female in it." Then Trollope bows to Mrs.
Somerville and ventures into a funny little piece about the "fishwives"
their harangues to the king, their very special vintage of poetry, and
the respectful treatment bestowed upon them by the French press, which
names them "ces dames des Halles", a title as incongruous in French
as saying "the ladies of Billingsgate."[14]

At the extreme opposite of the social scale, Trollope takes us now
to the Faubourg Saint-Germain and her most exclusive circle: as early
as mid-May, she had been privileged to sit among Mme Récamier's
intimates. We are introduced into the "beautiful little *salon*" with its
rich draperies of white silk, and the delicate blue accents mixed with
the mirrors, the flowers, the harp, and, above it all, the magnificent
picture by Gérard of *Corinne at Cap Misène*. The "perfect loveliness"
of Madame, forever pledged to wear white, is soon enhanced by the
"fine forehead and eyes, delightful voice, graceful turn of expression"
of the guest of honor, le Vicomte de Chateaubriand. The conversation
falls on Staël: Récamier's "intimacy and ever enduring affection for
Madame de Staël has given her a still higher interest in my eyes."
Then they talk about Lamartine, Delavigne, Dumas, Hugo, and "some
others." "Our Byron, Scott, etc., followed."[15]

There will be subsequent visits by Trollope to l'Abbaye-aux-bois: we shall sit listening to *l'Enchanteur* read a portion of his *Mémoires*.[16] The diminutive salon will symbolize so well the spirit of Paris for Trollope that she will close her book on the very last soirée spent there. My hypothesis, though, is that the "some others" discussed by l'Abbaye guests must have included mention of George Sand. She was very much on the minds of her friends through her "fresh break" with Musset in March. Mme Récamier, with Sainte-Beuve and Sosthènes de la Rochefoucauld, has been trying for a long time to meet Sand and to have her meet Chateaubriand. The month of May must have brought the young and dark mistress of *La Vallée Noire* within these silky, white, Parisian walls.[17]

"Sand's talent is irresistible" wrote Trollope, who can read her in the text; for like most English women of her class, she has been reading French since childhood.[18] She makes no attempt to meet Sand, feeling perhaps that, as a mother of "young and tender hearts," she should not be seen in the "mansarde bleue," where Sand holds open house.[19]

Sand's name resounds on both sides of the Channel. In February 1833, the *Atheneum* speaks of her works with praise, then the *Foreign Quarterly Review* devotes a twenty-page article to all her novels to date.[20] "More than Hugo or Balzac," wrote Patricia Thomson in her *George Sand and the Victorians*, "she stood for the English reader as a symbol of the post-revolutionary writing in France."[21] She made the strongest impression of all French writers in the 1830s and 1840s. If in the spring of 1835 *La Revue Brittannique* becomes critical of Sand, Sainte-Beuve, in *La Revue des Deux Mondes* of May 15, in his "Portraits de Femmes," promptly compares her to Staël and celebrates her "glory." In January 1836, *Blackwood's Magazines* still speaks of Sand's "several and very pleasing successful romances." It is not until March and April 1836—about the time of Trollope's publication of *Paris and the Parisians*, that the same magazine, along with the *Quarterly Review*, reverses its views and launches into a series of vicious attacks, using words like "poison."[22]

In Paris, in the spring of 1835, Sand is in print everywhere—in bookstores, in periodicals, in lending libraries. In December 1834, Bonnaire began to publish a series of *Romans et Nouvelles*, which, along with chapters of the *Secrétaire intime*, includes short stories such as *La Marquise*, *Metella*, *Lavinia "an old tale."* Meanwhile, *La Re-*

vue des Deux Mondes had been publishing Sand's prose regularly since January 15, 1833, concurrently with *La Revue de Paris*. *La Cinquième Lettre d'un Voyageur* appears in the issue of January 15; along with *Myrza*. The novel *André*, so highly praised by Liszt, appears in March and April;[23] side by side with *La Nuit de Mai* by Musset, *La Sixième Lettre d'un Voyageur*, addressed to Everard-Michel de Bourges, appears June 15 and *Mattea* appears July 1. These titles are the very ones Trollope later discusses in her *Letter LXIII*, in a chapter coming more than half-way through her second and last volume of *Paris and the Parisians* in 1835.[24]

She entitles her nine pages "George Sand" and proceeds with much caution to deal with "the lady who writes under the signature of George Sand." She is prompted, she says, by her deeply felt "love of truth and justice," to separate the French writer from "the pack," from the terrible "school which derives its power from displaying all that is worst and vilest in the human heart."[25] (We shall hear Sand, many years later in her *Histoire de ma Vie*, admit that every young disciple of Hugo was wearing "des oripeaux bizarres" (strange finery) in those eccentric days.[26]) That pen, says Trollope, is unequalled in her powers of writing. There is "the divine spirit of real genius in her," but it is "strained, bruised" (the very epithets with which she will qualify Liberty as it is practiced in France at the time). If only Sand would boldly free herself from that "slough," that "whirlpool," and take off in soaring flight, she could become a French Walter Scott. The whole world lays claims on her genius, for genius has no nation, but speaks a universal language.[27]

Out of "propriety," Trollope ignores those books "which ought never to have been written," even if they contain such passages as will make the reader's heart glow "with admiration of the thoughts that one so proudly quotes and boasts of as coming from the pen of a woman."[28] In fact, Sand's magical "grace of expression is never so animated and inspired" as when she lets her genius "carry her far above and quite out of sight of the whole *décousu* school." Trollope finds proof of her statement in a rapid analysis of *André*, a short novel not quite *faultless*, because an innocent creature "falls into indiscretion with her lover—and this to no avail, fictionally speaking—*before* she marries him.[29] However, the "little story" is conceived in "a spirit of purity and delicacy really angelic."[30] The "before she marries him" is certainly dictated to Sand by the "clique." A novelist herself, Trollope cannot refrain from admiring Sand's subtle treatment of Geneviève, the *grisette*, and the cameo scene in which the young flower girl appears minutely studying the flowers in the fields, so as to be able to duplicate them in silk—a refined simile for the mimetic problems of fiction writing that both women, Sand and Trollope, know only too well.[31]

She proceeds to quote, in French, some carefully chosen, fanciful Sandisms, mostly having to do with poetry. She seems to be aware that Sand, in her early days, never refers to herself as a novelist, but only as an artist or a poet. "Instead of wondering where poetry is, shouldn't we ask ourselves where it is not?" Trollope delights in these poetic paradoxes. She finds also a new moral code for the future, when disgust and sorrow will be "stamped as vices", while "love, hope and admiration" will be rewarded as virtues. With a new code of this kind, life would become an act of constant Thanksgiving. In Sand, she finds a teacher of meliorism.

In another series of excerpts from *Les Lettres d'un Voyageur*—"an absolute masterpiece"—Trollope brings to light Sand's poetic secrets, which she seems "to share with prophets and gypsies" in occasional "shootings of bold new thoughts, philosophical and metaphysical". However it is done "so lightly, so playfully that it should seem she was only jesting when she appears to aim wildly at objects so much beyond a woman's ken." Her conservative heart rejoices to the light-hearted tone with which Sand addresses herself to the social problem:[32] "*You* govern all those nasty fools," she writes Everard. "Meanwhile, *I* shall sing perched on a branch in the sun." Trollope could not suspect from her reading that Sand was arriving at her political turning point. Regarding that spring, Sand writes much later: "I'm reaching the time when my eyes are opening on a new perspective: politics."[33] In the turmoil of the "Monstrous Trial" she will become a committed socialist, a figure familiar to the twentieth century reader.

Trollope now concerns herself with the descriptive powers of the novelist, with a short, delicately chosen excerpt from *Mattea*, a "little story that is beautiful, one hardly knows why":[34]

The guitar is an instrument whose existence takes reality only in Venice, that silent and sonorous city. When a gondola glides over this river of phosphorescent ink, where each stroke of the oar dives with a flash of lightning, while a hail of small, light notes, neatly and playfully, gambols on the strings on which an invisible hand travels nimbly, one would like to linger on this soft but distinctive melody, which flirts with the ears of the passers-by and flees along the great shadows of the palaces, as if to call the Belles to their windows and to pass by, telling them: "this serenade is not for you, and you won't even know where it comes from and where it is going."[35]

"Could Rousseau himself," asks Trollope, "have chosen apter words? Do the words not seem an echo to the sounds she describes?"[36] Such a judgment, so early in her day, when musicality of prose was still virtually ignored, should suffice to qualify Trollope as a perceptive critic, who also recognizes descriptive powers, loftiness of thought and ethical dynamism when she sees them.

An even more remarkable statement by Trollope reveals her modernity: "The private history of an author ought never to mix itself with a judgment of his works."[37] She admits later: "Of that Sand, I know but little." But she senses an affinity between her own, vagrant life, and what she feels Sand's fate must be: "in some way or another, unfortunate." Going back to Letter V in which she records, page after page, Sand's struggle against the temptation of suicide, Trollope is deeply moved by the cry: "Let him die, damn little George!"[38] and by the famous, lyrical call: "O eternal silence!" which was to inspire Vigny's *Destinées*.[39]

Trollope closes her pages by quoting the well-known: "I lived all wrong," an admission so pathetically close to the Augustinian *Confessions*. And says that "she could go on for ever with this beautiful prose." She cuts short by exhorting her author to "break from whatever cloud" and "devote the rest of her life to the tranquil development of her extraordinary talents."[40]

In these voluble pages, mixed with British cant and Victorian progressism, we also find much more than what Patricia Thomson called "formal praises."[41] They are vibrant, genuine, elaborate praises. Trollope's categories will remain with the English reader for the rest of the century and beyond: the musical, delicate descriptive power, the poetic, soaring elevation of the mind, the generous and therapeutic faith in humanity. If Sand, in one of Henry James' many comments on her works, is jokingly called "fictionist too . . . *rococo* at the present time," on the other hand, C. S. Lewis writes: "She is infinitely more than a novelist. She is a poet."[42] Charlotte Brontë writing to Lewis, agreed with Trollope: "Most of her faults spring from the excess of her good qualities. I believe . . . the longer she lives, the better she will grow."[43]

Not only the categories but the choice of text remain as basic references long after the French reader has dismissed them. Miss Mitford praised *André* ("that gentle and inocuous pastorale"); Robert Browning, in Florence, "is in an enthusiasm about *André*." And James, in 1897, asks: "Has *André* the exquisite dropped out of knowledge?" He liked to pronounce titles like *André*, *Mauprat* or *Teverino*, "for the mere sweet sound of them, without the least expectation of an answer." Hardy, who "got many hints from his readings of George Sand" reproduced a scene of *André* in *Tess of the d'Urbervilles* and ended his speech of 1912 by quoting *André*, chapter 3: "*Poesie* cannot die." Trollope's choice.[44]

As for *Lettres d'un Voyageur*, Thomson concurs with Trollope that they "contain some of the finest, freshest and most lyrical evocative passages, and strike a note of intimacy with the reader," which Sand, never, from that time, lost. The *Lettres* are constantly referred to in England: Matthew Arnold, for instance, put them on his list of essential works of Sand. Mrs. Browning praises the "noble elevation of *Lettres d'un Voyageur*." As for Mazzini, who has read them at the time of personal despair, he sees in them the guide to recovery, the road from individual right to a new sense of social duty: he never travelled without the book.[45]

The second point I want to make is that the Trollopian treatment of George Sand, in its approach and dynamics, is germaine to the two texts that Chateaubriand will devote to Sand, at the end of 1837. In *La Vie de Rancé*, we find a splendid digression devoted to Sand, using Mlle de Scudéry's prose as a springboard;[46] apparently, it was inspired by the literary conversation with Trollope about "some other authors." Two passages in *Les Mémoires d'Outre-Tombe* have the laudatory and protective tone familiar to Trollope:[47] Chateaubriand speaks of "the author of *Valentine*" as giving birth to "perilous wonders" and discusses her case for five pages. Are these texts born from the gentle intervention of Madame de Récamier, who in the spring of 1835 so generously opened her door to Mrs. Trollope and her daughters and who, during the same period, was plotting with Sosthènes de la Rochefoucauld to "arrange" a meeting? Georges Lubin discusses briefly that "religious ambush," where we see Sand, cropped hair, hands crossed, like a Mary Magdalen, listening humbly to her "bien-pensants'' Parisian friends who want to save her soul and try to sever her ties with her Berrichon and *décousu* friends.[48]

Not least noteworthy is Trollope's clairvoyance, although with regard to politics, she is too reactionary for that.[49] When Trollope exhorts Sand to a poetic transformation, she does it at the very moment when Sand, not only in her political life, or sentimental life, but in all aspects of her spiritual life, has reached the last turning point—the final step of a long painful initiation process, the shamanistic rebirth that started in the Caves of Oliero.[50] The modern reader of *Histoire de ma Vie* and of *Correspondance II*—especially the March letters to Sainte-Beuve and to Liszt—can see her suffering her last and most perilous identity crisis. But on April 8, 1835, in a fundamental Rite of Spring, "the miracle took place."[51] (See the "Prière d'une matinée de printemps" written and dated April 8 Nohant, published a year later in "*La Revue des Duex Mondes* and then omitted from the tradebook edition of *Les Lettres*, suppressed even in the clipping that Sand kept in her scrapbook *Sketches and Hints*.[52]) At the age of thirty-one, she has finally completed her own "individuation." She has shed all exterior influence. She is free to soar up and away from the *décousu* school. She feels obliged to rewrite *Lélia*. She will soon write *Mauprat*, the story of a masked beast transformed by beauty. From then on, her topic will be the metamorphosis of the subject by the hand of woman. She has forty years to go, eighty books to write. She will indeed, "bloom in the tranquil development of her extraordinary talent."[53] She has chosen for herself the path forseen by the English writer: in effect, she has made Trollope's choice.

NOTES

1. Frances (Fanny) Milton Trollope, 1780-1865, writer traveller. Biographies by Ternan Anthony Trollope and Eileen Bigland. *Domestic Manners of the Americans* is her first work, published by Whittaker simultaneously in London and New York, 1832; by Baudry's Foreign Library in Paris, 1832; and by Gosselin (publisher of Tocqueville, Cooper and Sand) in 1833. After her adventurous trip and stay in America, first with Frances White at New Harmony on the Wabash and then by herself with her children and A. Hervieu at Cincinnati, she wrote about the American ways in such a critical manner that a verb was promptly fashioned in the States after her name: "Careful, fellow Americans, she is out to trollopize us all!" See also Frances Trollope, *Paris and the Parisians*, 2 vols. (London: Bentley, 1836); 1 vol. (Paris: Gal-

iagni, 1836). All quotations come from this text, which is itself divided into Books I and II. The book was published in French by Weissbrugh Père, 3 vols. (Brussels and Leipzig: Allgemeine Niederlandishe Buchlandung, 1836). Apart from her fiction (*Tremordyn Cliff* . . .) she wrote travelogues: *Belgium and Western Germany*, *Vienna and the Austrians*, *Western France*, *Visit to Italy*. At this time Sand published her *Lettres d'un Voyageur*, and Stendhal, who had read both travellers, engaged in writing his *Mémoires d'un Touriste*. The travel book, as a genre, was in full bloom.

2. Trollope, *Paris*, Book I, Letter I, p. 4.

3. Ibid.

4. Ibid.

5. See George Sand's *Correspondance*, ed. Georges Lubin (Paris: Garnier, 1965), II: 865, n. 1; "C'est le procès dit d'Avril parce qu'il rassemblait les responsables des divers mouvements insurrectionnels d'avril 1834, la Cour des Pairs ayant déclaré connexes tous les faits qui s'étaient passés dans diverses villes de France que ce fut Lyon, Paris (la rue Transnonain), Epinal ou Marseille." See also Sand's *Histoire de ma Vie* in *Oeuvres Autobiographiques*, II: passim; and Lubin (Paris: La Pléïade, 1971), p. 1372, note.

6. See Sand's *Histoire de ma Vie* II: 331: "in order not to be spotted as a woman alone among all these young men, I went back to my little boy's outfit, which permitted me to sit without being seen at the famous Séance of May 20th at the Luxembourg."

7. Trollope, *Paris,* Book I, Letter XXIV ("Expedition to the Luxembourg.—No admittance for Females.—Portraits of Henri.—Republican Costume.—Quai Voltaire.—Moral Inscriptions.—Anecdote of Marshal Lobeau.—Arrest."), vol. 1, p. 146; also Letter II, p. 140.

8. Ibid., Letter III ("Slang.—*Les Jeunes Gens de Paris*.—*La Jeune France*.—*Rococo*.—*Décousu*."), p. 12.

9. Ibid., Letter IX (Literature of the Revolutionary School.—Its low estimation in France.) "With the exception of history . . . no single work has appeared since the revolution of 1830 that has obtained a substantial . . . reputation for any author unknown before that period; not even among all the unbridled ebullition of imagination, though restrained neither by decorum, principle, nor taste,—not even here (excepting from one female [in footnote, G. Sand] pen, which might become, were it the pleasure of the hand that wields it, the first now extant in the world of fiction) has anything appeared likely to survive its author" (p. 42).

10. Ibid., Book II, Letter LI ("Parisian women—Rousseau's failure to describe them.—Their great influence in Society.—Their grace in Conversation.—Difficulty of growing old.—Do the ladies of France or those of England manage it best?") "Women, that powerful portion of the human race" (p. 64).

11. Ibid., Book I, Letter XXXVIII, p. 262.

12. Ibid.

13. Sand, *Correspondance*, II: 835. Sand dedicated Letter VI to Liszt. Here we deal with Letter V.

14. Trollope, *Paris*, Book II, p. 70. Trollope referred to them in French as *"les poissardes."*

15. L'Abbaye-aux-bois, ibid., Letter XXX. ("Madame Récamier.—Her morning parties.—Gérard's picture of Corinne.—Miniature of Mme de Staël.—M. de Chateaubriand.—Conversation on the degree in which the French Language is understood by Foreigners.—The necessity of speaking French.")

16. These readings, which *l'Enchanteur* started in February, 1834 on Mme Récamier's invitation at L'Abbaye-aux-bois, interested publishers in the new *Mémoires d'Outre-Tombe*: A contract was signed in March 1836. See *Mémoires d'Outre-Tombe* (Paris: Pléïade, 1971).

17. The "guet-apens religieux" hypothesis is based on Chateaubriand's *Mémoires* (part 4, XI: 7) and Sosthènes de la Rochefoucauld's *Mémoires*, Archives Doudeauville, château de Bonnétable, carton 245, 699, and 700, quoted by Levaillant-Moulinier; Lubin, in Sand's *Correspondance*, vol. II, places the incident in 1833; May, 1835 seems more plausible because of Sand's letter to Sosthènes that very month, begging for money for the families of the *Procès Monstre*, and the date of May 16 indicated by Sosthènes for the meeting between Sand, *l'Enchanteur* and himself.

18. Trollope quotes freely from Corneille, Boileau, Racine, and goes from English to French and vice versa without warning.

19. Trollope, *Paris*, Book II, p. 182, Letter LXIII ("George Sand").

20. Patricia Thomson, *George Sand and the Victorians* (New York: Columbia University Press, 1970), p. 11. Some attacks in *La Revue Britannique* in early 1835 and amplified in 1836 prompted one of Sainte-Beuve's "Portraits de femmes" quoted by Lubin in Sand's *Oeuvres Autobiographiques*, II: 1453: "Oh you whom opinion already proclaims the first in literature since Madame de Staël, you have in you, I know, in your admiration towards her, something like a feeling of thanksgiving, deep and tender for all the good things that she would have brought to you. . . . In your glory there will always be a first bond which attaches you to her." Trollope follows the same line when she writes that Madame de Staël "is followed, sought, looked at, listened to, and moreover, beloved and esteemed, by a very large circle of the first society in Paris, among whom are numbered some of the most illustrious literary names in France." Trollope, *Paris*, Book I, p. 191.

21. Ibid., pp. 12-27.

22. Crocker, author of the "famous-infamous" article in the *Quarterly Review*, April, 1836, hopes that his intervention will have the same effect as "labelling vials or packets POISON." Thomson, *George Sand*, pp. 14-15.

23. Sand *Correspondance* II: 20 April 1835: "On vient de m'apporter *André* que je n'ai pas encore lu. Tout le monde m'en fait l'éloge" (p. 814).

24. Trollope, *Paris*, Book II, pp. 180-89.

25. Ibid., p. 181.

26. Sand, *Histoire de ma Vie*, II: 159. Trollope called this same period "the Idiot Era." *Paris*, Book II, p. 34.

27. Trollope, *Paris*, Book II, p. 183.

28. Ibid., p. 182.

29. Ibid., p. 183.

30. Ibid.

31. Ibid., p. 184.

32. Ibid., p. 185. See George Sand, "Lettre à Everard," in Sand, *Ouevres Autobiographiques*, II: 786; and idem, *Histoire de ma Vie*, II: 355.

33. Sand, *Histoire de ma Vie*, II: 195: "Le moment où j'ouvrais les yeux était solennel dans l'histoire." And p. 33: "L'année 1835 où, pour la première fois de ma vie, je me sentis gagnée par un vif intérêt aux événements d'actualité."

34. Trollope, *Paris*, Book II, p. 186. Later (p. 205) she will read Sand's *Lavinia* under the trees of the Tuileries and call it "that beautiful story about nothing at all," translating felicitously at the same time Sand's wish to have written "une histoire sur rien" (expressed in her preface to *Les Lettres à Marcie*), and the still current French expression "un je ne sais quoi."

35. Ibid.

36. Ibid.

37. Ibid., p. 187.

38. Ibid.; and Sand *Lettres d'un Voyageur*, vols. IV and V ("Qui vivra de ma pensée?"), in Sand, *Oeuvres Autobiographiques*, II: 746.

39. Vigny's famous poem in *Les Destinées*, "Le Mont des Oliviers," borrows its conclusion from some Sandian themes. Three elements come from Sand's *Lettres*: the Garden of Olives, the Just, the cosmic silence.

40. F. Trollope, *Paris*, passim.

41. Thomson, *George Sand and the Victorians*, p. 19: "There were many references to George Sand in journals and Bulwer-Lytton. Mrs. Trollope and G. W. Reynolds more formally added their praises and Thackeray his censure."

42. Ibid., passim.

43. Ibid.

44. Ibid., pp. 46, 51, 185 and 226.

45. Ibid., pp. 34, 58 and 93.

46. *Vie de Rancé*, in *Oeuvres Romanesques & Voyages*, I: 1000.

47. Ibid., I: 1143; II: 91-96, 374. The chapter "De quelques femmes" as well as the *Vie de Rancé* seems to have been written at the end of 1837.

48. See note 20 and Lubin who, in Sand's *Correspondance*, II: 291, quoted Rochefoucauld, *Mémoires*, liasse 1057, dated May 14, 1835.

49. Anthony Trollope, in his *An Autobiography* (London: Oxford University Press, 1980), said that Trollope was "so pleased with her luck in making personal contacts with the ruling class, with historians like Thiers and Guizot, notables like Chateaubriand or Récamier." "With her," he writes later, "politics were always an affair of the heart" (p. 22).

50. *George Sand*, Acts of the Sand Colloquium at Cérisy-la-Salle, ed. Simone Vierne (Paris: Cédès, 1983), "*Les Lettres d'un Voyageur*, texte initiatique."

51. In Sand, *Ouevres Autobiographiques*, II: 1455. See also idem, *Correspondance*, II: 871. (To Liszt): "Je me sens renaître." "Le feu de l'enthousiasme . . . a rallumé sa flamme." "Je me fais un bonheur que personne ne peut plus me prendre." "Le Dieu n'est pas encore descendu en moi, mais je suis en train de lui bâtir un temple."

52. Sand, *Ouevres Autobiographiques*, II: 173: "Pastiche, que me veux-tu?"

53. Ibid., pp. 623-24, "Sketches and Hints," with the same date and place, "April 8, Nohant."

7

George Sand and the Seamless Theater

Julia Frey

THE PUPPET THEATRE AT NOHANT

One evening in 1847, Maurice Sand had prepared a surprise for his mother. After dinner in the big dining room at Nohant, he and Eugène Lambert, who both had been studying art with Eugène Delacroix, ushered George Sand and the rest of the Nohant household, residents and guests alike, into the billiard room under the stairs. There the impromptu audience was treated to a new and, as it would happen, most important family entertainment: the first production of the Nohant Puppet Theatre. The theatre would be continuously active for the next twenty-five years, growing from its original status of four finger puppets, whose puppeteers hid behind a blanket, to a vast permanent theatre containing both a four-by-eight-foot puppet stage set high above a *faux marbre* wall to hide the puppeteers and a small stage for live actors. It seats sixty spectators and can still be visited today.

Thirty-five plays were produced during the next seven years and by 1876, the year of George Sand's death, more than one hundred fifty-nine plays had been presented in a repertory that varied from spur-of-the-moment skits to carefully written theatrical works. Fourteen of the plays were preserved in *Théâtre des Marionnettes*, published posthumously under Maurice Sand's name in 1890.[1] This puppet theatre has been undeservedly neglected by scholars of George Sand, for it was a significant influence in her life and work.

THE "ARTIST'S COLONY" AT NOHANT

Unlike many writers of her time, George Sand disliked Paris despite her easy access to literary circles there. She preferred to live at Nohant, near Chateauroux, on the property she had inherited from her grandmother. After 1834 she resided there most of the time and travelled infrequently to Paris. She saw Nohant as a haven from the scandal that haunted her personal life and from the political and social conservatism she had tried unsuccessfully to combat. The relative calm of her private world nurtured her active creative and social life.

When her friends wanted to see her, they generally went to Nohant, where she had created around her a sort of microcosm of French art and letters in the mid-nineteenth century. Nohant was a close-knit community of family and visitors, some of whom stayed for years. Most of its members were actors, writers, artists and musicians. At different times, Delacroix painted flowers in the garden, Flaubert discoursed on society in the dining room and Alexandre Manceau and Maurice Sand ran an engraving studio in one of the outbuildings. Over the years, a wide spectrum of works was created at Nohant, ranging from George Sand's many novels, to Chopin's sonatas, to the puppet plays, which were the product of many hands and minds.

Although Sand writes of "the Nohant theatre, painted, sculpted, lighted, composed and spoken by Maurice all by himself,"[2] she also gives a list of at least ten individuals, some, like the actor Sully-Lévy, very well-known, who were her son's associates in writing, directing and presenting the plays.[3] It is even possible that the plays published under Maurice's name were not written by him alone, as the title page would indicate, but that he served as the collector of works that were really collaborations. The very nature of the kind of relaxed group activity that created the puppet plays at Nohant would tend to support this conclusion.

Although Maurice created most of the puppets and George Sand considered herself to be their wardrobe mistress, there was abundant opportunity for the guests to lend their talents to the creation of characters, sets, scripts and musical accompaniments.[4] Maurice quickly e⸒ ⸲blished a reputation as a puppeteer, which gave the production a guaranty of quality and a sheen of professionalism. This undoubtedly provided a measure of real artistic gratification to his team of assistants and gave to the entire process an air of meaningful creative collabora-

This puppet, Aurore, was made by Maurice Sand, George Sand's son and was named after Maurice's daughter. It was used for one of the puppet plays produced at Nohant and is now in the collection of Christiane Smeets-Sand, Gargilesse, France. *(Photograph by Julia Frey.)*

tion. Although the theatre, as well as some of the sets and about sixty
puppets, have been preserved, many of the creations incidental to the
plays—music, lighting effects, props, presentation poems and *canevas*—are lost.[5]

WRITERS AND PUPPETS

Surprisingly, it was common for intellectuals at that time to be interested in puppet theatre, and many wrote about it or used it as a
theatrical tool.[6] Although marionette theatre in French is an ancient
tradition, it reached a pinnacle of development during the eighteenth
and nineteenth centuries. Polichinelle, the traditional puppet and *commedia dell'arte* libertine, was supplemented by the working-man
Guignol, and the repertory of plays for these heroes and their entourage of stock characters grew to encompass not only legend and fairy
tale but also satire, parody and political commentary. Both traditional
and abstract puppets were used as representations of ideals and stere-
otypes, as imitators of life and initiators of fantasy in puppet theatres
not only for children, or for sideshow, fairground and boulevard publics, but also in salon and cabaret puppet theatres, presenting plays for
an invited audience of adults, an activity that became increasingly
fashionable in Parisian artistic circles.

The heightened interest in puppet theatre during the second half of
the nineteenth century arose in part from the taste for fantasy and
dépaysement (an attempt to disorient one's habitual thought patterns
through travel or unsettling experiences) that were endemic to European Romanticism and Symbolism. The nineteenth-century rejection
of the rules of classical theatre, devotion to the "reign of imagination"
and respect for nonconformity brought new recognition and popularity
to puppet theatre and to its versatility as a theatrical form.[7]

The French literary movements of the entire century, including Realism, were marked by a renascent interest in folk art of all kinds. The
adoption of puppet theatre by café and salon sophisticates was in part
glamorized by its continuing vitality as street entertainment for the
working class. The names of the writers and artists who worked with
puppet theatre at the time are still familiar. They include George Sand;
the poet and playwright Paul Claudel; the Belgian Symbolist Maurice
Maeterlinck; the Impressionist art critic Edmond Duranty; Maurice
Bouchor, best known as a gifted translator of Shakespeare; Henri Ri-

vière, whose *tableaux* from the celebrated Chat Noir nightclub are on permanent exhibition at the Montmartre Museum in Paris and others. Given the fashion of puppet theatre in the world of Paris intellectuals, it is not astonishing that a great deal of energy was devoted to it in George Sand's household. The Nohant guests flocked to participate in an art form that allowed them a broad range of expression from child-like playfulness to political badinage to ethereal fantasy.

BEYOND DILETTANTISM

Maurice, the undisputed director of the theatre, applied his passionate interest in art and theatre to the puppets, creating more than one hundred twenty-five characters and finding ingenious methods of giving the scenes detail and realism. He excelled in creating illusions, going to such lengths as making identical puppets of several sizes to represent characters moving toward or away from the footlights. He also evinced a scholarly interest in theatre by writing and illustrating with Alexandre Manceau a definitive work on *commedia dell'arte* entitled *Masques et Bouffons* (1860). After George Sand's death in 1876, Maurice moved to his house at Passy and continued to produce puppet shows until his own death in 1890.

His level of commitment to this exercise far exceeds the bounds of dilettantism. A handsome—perhaps dashing—and intelligent creative artist, Maurice was the apple of his mother's eye. He lived most of his adult life at Nohant and, in spite of his mother's hardworking example, never devoted himself seriously to any remunerative occupation. He tried and failed in a number of fields: literary, political and artistic. Puppet theatre was, in the long run, his most sustained profession.

Contemporary accounts reveal the standard of excellence achieved by the Nohant stage. The memoirs of Juliette Lamber-Adam, an early feminist and a frequent visitor to Nohant, record her introduction to the puppet theatre in 1868. She wrote that the puppet personalities were so much a part of daily life and conversation at Nohant that she and her daughter knew the characters' names before they had even seen them on stage and recognized them at once when they finally did see them. George Sand presided over the evening performances and assigned seats to her guests, who wore full evening dress. As the "astonishing curtain," hand painted by Maurice, rose on the set of *Alonzi*

Alonzo le Bâtard, ou le brigand de las Sierras, Balandard, the puppet stage manager appeared on stage and encouraged the audience to speak to his puppet actors and thereby to influence the action and even the play's outcome. He granted "universal suffrage" to the spectators—including the ladies—so they could vote on what they wanted to happen next. Shortly after, the gestures and motions of the puppets, their skillfully carved and painted figures and the exquisitely decorated and illuminated stage created a "stupefying realism" in which Juliette Lamber-Adam reports finding herself in dialogue with puppets that seemed little short of human.[8]

A later account by Louis Lemercier de Neuville, one of the leading puppeteers of the Paris intellectual set, described Maurice's puppet theatre at Passy, where most of the puppets and sets from the Nohant theatre had been moved. According to Lemercier de Neuville's *Histoire anecdotique des marionnettes*, Maurice had installed a street organ to serve as a backstage orchestra, had invented ingenious devices to produce sound effects such as thunder, rain, trains and raging seas and used a sophisticated lighting system (electricity was not yet available) to simulate nightfall and a variety of mood-evoking light effects on stage. "The number of stage sets would make the Paris Opera seem inadequate," Lemercier de Neuville noted, and he found the workshops where the puppets were built and stored most impressive. Altogether, Lemercier de Neuville called Maurice's theatre "undeniably the most perfect that has ever existed."[9] Yet despite their quality, the productions were never open to the public. Lemercier de Neuville, for example, lamented that he was not one of the Nohant "intimates" and had never seen a performance.

THEATRE IN AN ARMCHAIR

What was it, then, that preoccupied the Nohant circle, and particularly George and Maurice Sand, with puppet theatre for thirty years? George Sand's essay "Le Théâtre des marionnettes de Nohant" gives both simple and complex reasons. This careful study (ninety-one manuscript pages) of the techniques and creative invention used by Maurice in the Nohant theatre was originally written as a preface to the first publication of Maurice's puppet play *Jouets et mystères*.[10] It describes in detail the philosophical principles behind puppet theatre and tries to pinpoint the reasons for the pleasure it gave her. She proposes similar theories in her two novels about puppets, *Le Diable aux champs* (1855) and *L'Homme de neige* (1859).

Plain entertainment is the most basic. In *Le Diable aux champs*, one of her characters comments, "We go to the theatre to have fun and be distracted from the cares of reality. And when I'm there, I don't want anyone to force me to think about real problems."[11] The theatre entertained the performers, during the days or weeks of preparation, just as much as it did the spectators. In the long evenings at Nohant when the day's work was done, everyone gathered in the salon, and until George Sand retired to her nightly writing, the assembled members of her extended family devoted themselves to a variety of amusements, ranging from conversation to embroidery to word games and theatrical skits. People took turns suggesting activities, and although many different enterprises occupied the candlelit group over the years, it was not until the inauguration of the puppet theatre that there was a major theme to the Nohant activity. This is not to say that everyone participated in the productions. There was too much individuality in the household for that. People continued to amuse themselves singly or in small groups with whatever particularly attracted them—a tendency that had foiled earlier attempts to put on plays, since it was hard to get enough people to act in them on a regular basis.

The spontaneity and improvisation characteristic of puppet theatre made it easy to adapt to Nohant's needs. Whoever wanted to work on a play did so, and then everyone gathered for the gala presentation. George Sand refers to such flexibility frequently in discussing the Nohant theatre, and it corresponds to a tendency of her own fiction writing. She excelled in constructing plots on the spot, often drawing upon life situations she had at hand. The result in many of her novels was a flavor of autobiography, fictionalized reportage, and improvisation, in which events were often included for their own interest rather than for their contribution to plot or character development. George Sand's taste for improvisation was reflected in nearly all her choices for evening activities at Nohant: charades, skits, situation comedies, and impromptu operettas. She attempted to create a *commedia dell'arte* but abandoned the idea for lack of a full cast of characters. Once again, she discovered that:

One theatre which is always possible is puppet theatre. It requires little space, costs next to nothing, and takes only one or at most two people to move the puppets and keep the dialogue going. Thus it is within the grasp of anyone who has wit, a quick tongue, talent or a sense of humor; and if you add inventiveness and taste, a puppet theatre can take on singularly interesting dimensions.[12]

Puppet theatre also matched George Sand's own sense of the absurd. Giving free reign to unrelated or incoherent actions, verbal nonsense, exaggerated coincidences, anti-establishment behavior, bawdy humor and fisticuffs disputes, it gave a sense of elemental involvement in life's realities precisely because it short-circuited "realism." Although many of the Nohant plays had a political thrust, influence of any sort beyond the limits of Nohant was not a consideration since the plays were never open to the public. What they apparently accomplished instead was to provide an opportunity for unbridled political self-expression and—for George Sand herself—relief from what she saw as the futility of her own political involvement and from her feelings of powerlessness to change anything in society.

Let us find something else for our children to do . . . marionettes, stories, tales, anything you wish, but something which will take us away from our passions, our materialistic preoccupations, our bitterness; from those sad family hatreds we call political, religious and philosophical differences.[13]

Examination of the plays shows that neither the most prominent national issues nor profound treatment of smaller ones was needed to provoke the desired cathartic effect. Most of the plays deal with local or minor political situations whose interest and importance is lost in the obscurity of the past. Yet the fourteen extant plays may be too small or too unrepresentative a sample to show how far the Nohant theatre could and did involve itself politically. Whatever the exact ingredients of those evenings of puppet entertainment were, they must have created within the confines of Nohant a world in which the wicked and corrupt were given their comeuppance with quick, sharp blows— physical and verbal—and a social outcast could be honorable if he were pure of heart and stood for just causes. It was a world that George Sand could not have elsewhere—a world in which "universal suffrage" gave every member of society a hand in the outcome of the events on the stage.

A last possible reason for George Sand's love for puppet theatre is that it was conducive to her creative labors when she returned to her room later in the evening. She may well have chosen it and other similar entertainments as stimuli to her imagination. She offers what might seem substantiating testimony to this possibility in a touching portrait of herself seated in the orchestra while Maurice practiced scene changes; no puppets were present but her fantasy took wing in the mere ambiance of the puppet stage:

It was intensely pleasurable for me. The metamorphosis created by the foot-lights is surprising: tones seem to change, relief stands out, depths are hollow, things become magically transparent. I was so fascinated by watching the beautiful backdrops reveal their secrets and become forests, water and moun-tains, floating in an artificial atmosphere which gave the impression of being really hot or cold, that I used to beg Maurice to put on a show of stage sets alone. . . . Watching, I felt as if I were really traveling as the scenes changed, supplemented by my revery; and I could happily have spent the rest of my life there, for at the age I have currently attained, the most agreeable voyage is the one that can be taken in an armchair.[14]

THE CHARACTERISTICS OF THE NOHANT PUPPET PLAYS

The Nohant elite found creative stimulation in its own company and indulged in all the sins of the literary *chapelles* of the time. Occasion-ally, its members resorted to jealousies, infighting and outright feuds, but generally they presented a united front against the outside world, hitting the "enemy" with a verbal barrage of ridicule, sacrilege and gossip. The puppet plays, as shall be seen, also contain these ele-ments, and their subject matter reflects the concerns of the authors, both humorous and serious.

The titles of thirty-four of the Nohant plays are still known, al-though twenty of them are now lost. From these titles—such as "L'Auberge du haricot vert" ("Green Bean Hotel"); "Le Moine" ("The Monk"); "Sang, sérénades et bandits" ("Blood, Bandits and Serenades"); "Une Femme et un sac de nuit" ("A Woman and an Overnight Bag")—the plays appear to have been mostly comedies or parodies. The plots of the fourteen extant plays can be grouped as follows: six farces, four political comedies, two fairy tales and two parodies. They all have in common broad humor, slapstick comedy, physical violence, puns, and in many cases, stock characters who appear in play after play. Unfortunately, most of the subject matter is too ephemeral to be durable, and only one or two of them are used as repertory pieces in puppet theatres today.[15]

Humor in the plays depends chiefly on caricature and satire. Part of the fun for Nohant elite was, in George Sand's words,

momentary impressions, a ridiculous event in the world of politics or art, local gossip, an amusing or singular anecdote, the visit of some absurd intruding personage whom we caricatured unbeknownst to him. Anything could be the theme of the plays which were written as scripts in several hours and sometimes played the same evening.[16]

They are full of "in-jokes" and references to current events. An example is *Nous dînons chez le Colonel*, subtitled a "salty slice of military life" ("une pièce militaire salée"), presented in January, 1867. The play pokes fun at the billeting of French army officers in the homes of two respectable ladies, a common occurrence in France at that time and no doubt a source of irritation, particularly in peacetime. The play may well have referred to a situation and individuals the audience knew personally. The core of the plot is a case of mistaken identity in which two army captains, who have become their hostesses' lovers, come home drunk from dinner at the Colonel's and accidentally enter the wrong houses. Indigestion prevents any indiscretions and when daylight puts the correct lovers back into the right houses, marriage ensues.

The play's humor is found almost exclusively in the situation, scatology and puns. Both the latter are exemplified in the names of the characters whose English equivalents are: Miss Euphemism, Colonel Stiffneck, Captain Dumbox, Captain Brightshit, and Madam Greenfart. There is also a mention of Madam Greenfart's confessor, Father Soften'emup. Other puns abound. Some are accessible, but many refer to people who presumably were in the audience. Some are merely random. Almost without exception the puns are intentionally far-fetched and silly. Few are translatable.

The use of ridicule, caricature and parody tended to unite the members of the Nohant household in a common attitude toward the outside world, both as a kind of elitism that spared no one in its indictments, and as a fantasy-level retaliation against anything that was hurtful or objectionable. Their indulgence in these forms of criticism yielded a hybrid vocabulary, humor, morality and tone that would have been incomprehensible to outsiders. Other examples of this phenomenon abound in all "salon" literature and all satire aimed at a limited public.

Indeed, according to Ernst Kris, the ultimate psychological benefit of comic gestures such as caricature and parody is the imagined annihilation of the person caricatured.[17] They are parallel to the kind of retaliation of the weak against the strong that we see when a crowd resorts to the parading, disfiguring, insulting and finally burning of a public figure in effigy.

Caricature and parody work as humor because of their highly specific imitation. Part of the pleasure for the audience is in deciphering the hieroglyphic or riddle of the caricature. This also leads to the ephemerality of such humor, for once identification of the original subject is no longer possible, the caricature itself is no longer interesting. For example, in *La Rosière de Viremollet*, the confusion of the words *imperative* ("impératif") and *empress* ("impératrice") by a local farmer is belabored to the point of dullness. In the same play, ironic dialog concerning states' rights, military services and so on is of little interest to the contemporary reader.

Altogether, the quality of the Nohant plays rarely rises above that of "salon" art, created on the spur of the moment for a specific audience at a specific time. For George Sand herself, however, that is their charm:

It is always a mistake to think the plays would have the same value if they were transcribed and conserved. Their existence was not planned and we remember them with delight precisely because we really have retained only a confused idea of them, and our imagination has embellished them after the fact.[18]

She appears to have changed her mind later in life, for in her essay on puppets she admits that she encouraged Maurice to write the plays down and defends the quality of the *canevas* as literature. Wondering about the effect of reading a *canevas* as opposed to that of seeing the play on stage, she read several and decided that in fact they created a very original impression.[19] She said that since the *canevas* capsulize and abbreviate the action, the rapid-fire, unembroidered dialogs were agreeable to read, and that having seen the original plays with all their improvisation and visual effects, she was doubly impressed with her son's talent at the end of each production.

Her opinion notwithstanding, like all theatre, Maurice's *canevas* must have been better presented on the stage. In any case, today they do not maintain the interest of someone who merely reads them. From what is known of the role of audience participation, improvisation, wisecracks and so on in these productions, what made them attractive was largely the theatricality of the shows, the burlesque quality of the theatre itself and the impressive artistic quality of the sets, puppets and stage effects.

GEORGE SAND AND PUPPETS

Although George Sand was both audience and wardrobe mistress for these plays, there is no concrete evidence that she ever actively produced any of her own work on the tiny stage. Sand critic Maurice Toesca suggested that her interest in writing plays for live actors sprang from the development of the puppet theatre at Nohant and that perhaps the puppets presented early stages of some of her plays, testing them at home, so to speak, before she wrote the final version, but none of George Sand's published theatre is specifically intended for marionettes, nor are any of the extant puppet plays reflected in her work.[20] She did however produce a few early versions of her plays on the small stage for live actors that shared the billiard room with the puppet theatre at Nohant. At least one of them, ''Nello ou le joueur de violon,'' was ultimately produced at the Odeon Theatre on September 15, 1855, under the title *Maître Favilla*.[21]

Although puppet theatre is a plot element and stylistic device in two of her novels, it is not critical to her work as a novelist *per se*. However, her writing about puppets gives us insight into her philosophical and psychological attitudes, into some of her feelings of powerlessness as a woman, and into her relationship to her son, the chief puppeteer of Nohant. Above all it illuminates her struggles as a creator, an iconoclast, an intellectual and member of an elite. Most of these elements are revealed in her vision of the puppeteer as a metaphor for the outsider to society and its values who nonetheless finds himself in the role of commentator on and participant in that society. The puppeteer who can, from his hidden position in the puppet theatre, anonymously portray, criticize and idealize the world around him, reenters that world as a full-fledged member the minute he ducks out from behind the stage. No one knows, as he blends into the crowd, that what the puppets said is his responsibility. He is a mysterious wanderer/artist or a whimsical dilettante, often in disguise or invisible backstage, living as he chooses, able to enter and leave society when he pleases.

The puppeteer—hero of *L'Homme de neige*—is an almost perfect match to the stereotype of the nineteenth-century Romantic hero or "bohemian" as described by Cesar Graña.[22] He leads a double life in which he is faithful to his own ideals but is not an outcast—it is he who chooses whether he will be an artist or a homogeneous member of the crowd. He is a sort of Gypsy or street-fair showman, but at the same time he is well-bred, well-educated and an intellectual. Although he has left the domain of art patronage to submit his work to the judgment of public taste, and is thus free in his puppet plays to reject the preconceived canons of taste and imagination required by a patron, his occupation is enslaved to the whim of public approval. Like many artists of the time, he responds to this job insecurity by glorifying risk and the need to live on a shoestring. His integrity and refusal to sell out to bourgeois materialistic ideals, his rejection of these ideals as having created "the inherent valuelessness of [bourgeois'] lives and the internal anonymity of their souls" are in some ways rationalizations for his uncertain financial situation.[23] Also, his decision to be an artist rather than an artisan "useful to everyone" is not so much a moral decision as a psychological need.[24] His work creates intense, if ambivalent, feelings in him: "enormous excitement, followed by great depression, a lot of procrastination and nonchalance about getting to work, feverish animation and overwhelming gaiety or emotion while I am at it, exhaustion and self-hate when I take off my mask and become once more a man as stale as any other."[25]

This image of the impassioned, hypersensitive artist, the alienated Romantic hero who criticizes, rejects and rises above the confines of bourgeois society, was of more than passing interest to George Sand. It is a reflection of many of her personal preoccupations. The hero's personality and behavior in many ways are also thinly disguised versions of her son's. The relationship between mother and son was unusually intense and rich. One profound advantage to George Sand of her son's "profession" was that this activity, unlike many others he might have chosen, permitted him to remain at Nohant, close to her.

However, she must have felt ambivalent about his choice of career. His work with puppets, like his dabbling in other artistic fields, was not publicly recognized, so he achieved no wide reputation to compensate for having chosen a trade that "after all could hardly make him rich."[26].

Not only does George Sand's puppeteer embody the elements of the Romantic hero who represented the anxieties of an entire generation of French intellectual youth and enable her to write out her ambivalence about her "failed" son's style of life, but ultimately her hero permits her to resolve in fiction conflicts she could not resolve in her own life. As a woman who both lived within and openly rejected the restrictions of nineteenth-century bourgeois society, she was made to suffer from her attempts to achieve personal freedom and integrity. She had no anonymity and struggled daily to live as she chose. Unlike her, the puppeteer could criticize with impunity. Unlike her, he could have a private life that was distant from his professional and political life. The freedom of his theatre to express unbridled, illogical human responses may well have appeased some of the rage and hopelessness she felt at repeatedly seeing her own demands for passion and genius blocked by her society. However, in her ambiguous portrayal of the value of the puppeteer in society, she may also be showing not only her ambivalence about Maurice but also her ambivalence about the comparative values of her own social, creative and psychological stances. Her description of the addictive quality of the passions engendered by creative work speaks eloquently of her own addiction, and reveals perhaps the guilt she felt at putting her role as a creative artist before her other roles as woman, mother, breadwinner and intellectual in a world that simultaneously rejected and idolized her for her choices.

NOTES

1. The plays included for publication were: *Le Flageolet* (*The Penny-Whistle*), 1863; *Nous dînons chez le Colonel* (*We Dine with the Colonel*), 1867; *La Clémence de Titus* (*The Forgiveness of Titus*), 1867; *Funeste oubli, fatale baignoire* (*Fateful Slip, Fatal Bathtub*), 1868; *Jouets et mystères* (*Toys and Mysteries*), 1871; *Les Esprits frappeurs* (*The Spirit Rappers*), 1871; *Le Candidat de Trépigny* (*The Trepigny Candidate*), 1874; *Le Lundi de la Comtesse* (*The Countess' Monday*), 1874; *Une Nuit à Chateauroux* (*One Night at Chateauroux*), 1875; *La Chambre bleue* (*The Blue Bedroom*), 1875; *J'ai oublié mon panier* (*I Forgot My Basket*), 1875; *La Rosière de Viremollet* (*The*

Viremollet Rose-Arbor), 1879; *Zut! ou la petite chaussette bleue* (*Darn! Or the Little Blue Sock*), 1884; *Balandard aux enfers* (*Balandard in Hell*), 1886. All translations from the French are by the author unless otherwise noted.

2. George Sand, "Le Théâtre des marionnettes de Nohant" *Oeuvres Autobiographiques*, 2 vols. (Paris: Gallimard, 1970–71), II: 1276. This work is hereafter cited as *Oeuvres*.

3. *Oeuvres*, p. 1273.

4. Sand wrote fondly, for example, of her role in inventing one of the characters: "I am the one who made up the monster. Its vast maw, designed to swallow up Pierrot, was made out of a pair of pink-lined bedroom slippers, and its body, of a bluish satin sleeve. Thus this monster, which still exists today and is still called the "green monster," has always been blue! The numerous spectators who have watched it over the years have never noticed." Ibid., p. 1251.

5. *Canevas* is a theatrical term referring to a list of scenes and a summary of dialog written on a piece of cloth or paper, which was then tacked up inside the puppet theatre, to remind the puppeteers of the plot as they improvised the dialog during the performance.

6. See J. B. Frey, "Writers and Puppets in Nineteenth-Century France: The Study of a Phenomenon" (Ph.D. thesis, Yale University, 1977). Available from University Microfilms, Ann Arbor, Mich.

7. See Gaston Baty and René Chavance, *Histoire des marionnettes* (Paris: Presses Universitaires de France, 1959), p. 96: "But the dawn of Romanticism cast new light on puppet theatre. When existence is no longer limited to so-called real life, when the barriers between the world of exterior appearances and the world of dreams are cast down, the puppet comes into its own. Psychological traits can be clearly drawn without losing their relationship to humanity. Novalis proclaimed that puppet theatre is the essence of all theatre."

8. Juliette Lamber-Adam, *Mes Sentiments et nos idées avant 1870* (Paris, 1905), pp. 269–72.

9. Lemercier de Neuville, *Histoire anecdotique des marionnettes* (Paris, 1892). André Maurois, in *Lélia*, his biography of George Sand, also described the puppet theatre. He indicated an equivalent degree of backstage ingenuity, writing: "By means of a rotating drum, moon and sun could be made to move in their nightly and diurnal round. Rain could fall and lightning zig-zag across the backdrop," trans. Gerard Hopkins (New York: Harper & Brothers, 1954), p. 365.

10. In *Le Temps*, May 13, 1876. His mother's essay was published in two parts on May 11–12. Intended for inclusion in *Histoire de ma Vie*, this was the last piece of writing she published before her death. Charles Magnin, a major critic and theorist of theatre in nineteenth-century France, considered it

the most important contribution to puppet theatre in his time. Preface to *Histoire des marionnettes en Europe* (Paris, 1882), n.p.

11. *Le Diable aux champs* (Paris, 1855), p. 227.

12. *Oeuvres*, p. 1250.

13. Ibid., p. 1276.

14. Ibid., p. 1273.

15. English audiences may wish to consult the long out-of-print *Maurice Sand's Plays for Marionettes*, trans. Babette and Glenn Hughes (New York: Samuel French, 1931), which presents five of the plays in skillful English versions: *The Rose-Queen of Viremollet, The Clemency of Titus, The Flageolet, He Dines at the Colonel's* and *The Spirit Rappers*.

16. *Oeuvres*, p. 1251.

17. Ernst Kris, *Psychoanalytic Explorations in Art* (New York: International Universities Press, 1952).

18. George Sand, *L'Homme de neige*, 3 vols. (Paris: Michel Lévy, 1869), II: 197.

19. A number of the original, unpublished *canevas* are still in the collection of Christiane Smeets-Sand in Gargilesse, France.

20. Maurice Toesca, *Le Plus grand amour de George Sand* (Paris: Albin Michel, 1962), p. 162.

21. Maurois, *Lélia*, p. 365, n.1.

22. Cesar Graña, *Modernity and its Discontents: French Society and the French Man of Letters in the Nineteenth Century* (New York: Basic Books, 1964).

23. Ibid., p. 47.

24. Sand, *L'Homme de neige*, III: 13.

25. Ibid., II: 289.

26. Ibid., III: 120.

8

Musset's *Lorenzaccio*: George Sand's Ultimate Gift

Alex Szogyi

Lorenzaccio is a play in search of an identity. Even now, one hundred and fifty years after its genesis, Musset's great play, perhaps the most ambitious and ecstatically beautiful of the entire nineteenth century in France, is still not sufficiently well known all over the world or even among the French. The problem perhaps lies in Musset's immense scaffolding (the work must be adapted and shortened to be performed in one convenient stage evening); despite many adaptations, no individual interpretation has ever achieved the status of the official acting text to be performed everywhere. This is standard procedure for the Shakespeare plays, and although we never hear much about the actual shortening and adaptation, we rarely see a Shakespeare play in its entirety. It is Musset who was the first major playwright to style his theatre to the Shakespearian esthetic, and it is perhaps because his play is so eminently influenced by Shakespeare that it presents similar problems in staging.

It was not until 1896 that Sarah Bernhardt took it upon herself to be the first famous interpreter of the quasi-effeminate hero, thereby launching a tradition in which the role was the property of virile actresses rather than young, sensitive leading men. *Lorenzaccio* is often called the "Hamlet" of the French stage, and that is perhaps why Sarah Bernhardt was drawn to it, knowing she could interpret the role more amply than any actor. This is standard Kabuki style, *à rebours*; the actress can better incarnate the essence of the man. It was Gérard Philipe who gave the role its first and perhaps definitive interpretation for our time. His rare mastery of sensitive lyricism in a male chrysalis gave the part a deep subtlety.

Few have forgotten his incandescent performance as Lorenzo, in Jean Vilar's adaptation for the Théâtre National Populaire.[1] I had the privilege of seeing the production with Uta Hagen, and I can still recall the excitement nearly thirty years ago of the nearly bare stage and provocative lighting as well as the haunting sonorous catch-in-the-throat richness of Gérard Philipe's voice.

George Sand scholars know that Musset might perhaps never have written the play without benefit of her version, *Une Conspiration en 1537*, which she gave to Musset as a personal gesture.[2] It was her first play, and scholars have been able to situate it as having been written in 1831 or 1832, at the latest, thereby pre-dating Musset's creation by about a year. After a reading of Sand's play, we may readily see that all the essentials of Musset's play are given. Sand and Musset both had as primary source the Florentine historian, Varchi, who provided them both with an ample helping of the magnificent dialogue.

Sand took the trouble to fathom Lorenzo's mind more than Musset ever did. Anyone adapting the play (I was commissioned to do so by the Virginia Museum Theatre, in 1978) can readily understand that Musset often confused the issue, creating a Hamlet figure who was a pawn in a political power struggle among the families and factions of renaissance Florence, a young man in search of a cause, hanging on to it for dear death so that he might purge himself of his murderous feelings. Musset's anti-hero is distinctly Hamletian, a young man in search of a definitive identity. In his quintessentially romantic play, the Hamlet figure falls idealistically in love with murder and death. Sand's view was much more pragmatic and even Freudian *avant la lettre*.

There is only one major element of Sand's play, her original assessment of the celebrated story of Duke Alexander's death at the hands of Lorenzo of Medici, which Musset categorically rejected. *Chez* Sand, the motivation for the killing of Duke Alexander is an inherent hatred bubbling within Lorenzo, who would wish to kill the man who coveted his sister. George Sand combined instinctive feminism with an understanding of the Italian psyche to produce a decided emphasis on the innocence and appealing youth of Lorenzo's sister. We see the girl appear after the murder, violently reacting to it, turning from the horror provoked by the act to intense love and trust in the murderer.

George Sand thus opted for *Sturm and Drang* melodrama and, in a sense, *grand guignol*, as we are told the lurid details of the actual murder. Musset preferred the Romantic touch, a poetic litote, an almost classical refusal to make the murder shocking or in any way obtrusive. Catterina becomes an accomplice of Lorenzo in George Sand's long one-act tableau (almost a pre-figuration of Oreste and Electre in Jean-Paul Sartre's *Les Mouches*).

Musset changed all of that. His mighty scaffolding is tripartite. Lorenzo is caught in the web of a power struggle between the forces for and against freedom in Florence. Musset makes the city of Florence the true protagonist, rendered lyric through a rare use of mellifluous prose. Lorenzo seeks a Father figure and chooses the white-haired patriarch, Filippo Strozzi, who also seeks revenge for the victimization of his sons by the other families of Florence. Lorenzo is *persona non grata* in Florence because he has given vent to a natural wildness of character, decapitating statues in Rome, fatally fascinated by crime even though he cannot bear the sight of a naked sword. His final act of murder becomes *chez* Musset a form of existential self-immolation which might have appealed to Jean-Paul Sartre in the conception of his early plays. Lorenzo slowly defines himself in terms of a crime which will free him from the murderous feelings lurking within him. His is *un pur*, a pure young fellow who wears the cloak of sin and crime for reasons he can barely fathom. He takes pleasure in destructive, adolescent acts. Slowly, over the five tableaux of George Sand's play, he comprehends that the Duke, in whose service he lives, is a worthless sinner and heartless seducer. Lorenzo adopts Filippo Strozzi's crusade and takes it upon himself to assuage Strozzi's suffering by killing the Duke. Lorenzo's final destructive act is a complicated revenge, a liberation from sin, a purging of his nature and a compassionate act, as well. The precipitating factor, the final straw, is similar in Sand and Musset but significantly different. In Sand's work, Catterina is the sister who takes hold of Lorenzo and pushes him even further than he would wish to go. She is the Sandian woman, par excellence. In Musset's vision, she is Lorenzo's aunt, and his outrage at the Duke Alexander's desire to seduce a member of his family is not directly complicated with flaming incestuous desire.

Lorenzaccio is way ahead of its time in that Lorenzo's complicated sexuality needs a violent outburst and an expiation. In purely psychosexual terms, violence is often a direct by-product of an inability to perform sexually. Lorenzo is so bottled up that he virtually bursts forth verbally and murderously. In neither play does Lorenzaccio have a love object. Yet we see and hear his overweening desire to stimulate himself to orgasmic glory. His behavior in Musset's play is that of a pimp-prostitute subordinating himself to the role of minion, spiritual lover of the Duke. Lorenzo is also pre-Baudelairian in that the double postulate of virtue and sin exist side by side inside of his psyche. He is spiritually if not physically bisexual, and his only strong feelings are for the elderly Strozzi. His self-loathing leads to a counterfeited effeminacy, theatrically rooted to his fear of bloodshed. Lorenzo nearly faints at the sight of a sword because he knows instinctively that he will one day be called on to use one. Sand's Lorenzo is much bloodier. When he has finally disposed of the Duke, he describes the act to his young sister, and they revel in the acceptance of the crime. The death scene *chez* Sand is hyperbolic, mingling blood and dripping sensuality. *Chez* Musset it is rather a classic pantomime. We are caught up in Lorenzo's ecstatic realization that he has purged himself of the crime, once and for all, by committing it: "Dieu de bonté, quel moment!" The murder in Musset's terms is sheer poetry. *Chez* Sand it is graphic and horrible. How ultimately ironic that Sand's fairly short one-act play should use hyperbolic methods only in the murder scene, otherwise sticking fairly close to the historical facts recounted by the historian Varchi. Musset's talky play opts for classical restraint precisely at the moment when the classical theatre would have banished the scene altogether.

George Sand's play is a historical scene of the kind that was popular in the first decade of the nineteenth century. She used a blueprint formula with genuine dialogue taken from the chronicles of the time. Musset made his play a romantic tract with long tirades at the center of the play devoted to discussions of tyranny and freedom. These tirades are not without interest. They remind us of Beaumarchais' monologues to the audience in *The Marriage of Figaro*, sections automatically omitted in popular performances.

Musset's *Lorenzaccio* is still basically Sand's play, however. It would be instructive to perform both of them together.[3] Musset's is totally decipherable when we see Sand's alongside it. George Sand as a playwright bears a similarity to Balzac and Henry James. The dialogues in their novels were highly dramatic, and their works are supremely theatrical in concept. What they all three lack is the ability to create stage shorthand which is liberated from narrative description. True play-wrights do not need novelistic exposition to make the drama live. Sand is a writer of deeply logical prose; Musset is a poet with a flair for drama.

A Conspiracy in 1537 is, nevertheless, one of Sand's best plays. She understands Lorenzo viscerally. This is perhaps because the bi-sexual basis of the play is part and parcel of Sand's own psychological makeup. Musset had no such problems, as far as we know, and he therefore needed to feed his psyche with politics, vendetta, revenge, sin and ultimate purity of intention. Sand understood instinctually what an incestuous longing could be and the feelings of a man who had not defined his masculinity. In that sense, Sand's play is more modern than Musset's in its visceral comprehension of the psychological mo-tivations of Lorenzo. Her Lorenzo could never be a Musset hero. Her sense of logic and proportion are void of the soul of poetry. Yet she gave the play to Musset, *en connaissance de cause*, perhaps suggest-ing in her fashion that Musset was Lorenzo in spirit. She was capable of this kind of subtle reverse suggestiveness in her other work. *Lucre-zia Floriani*, in which she metamorphosed Chopin into a Polish tyrant and turned herself into a retired Italian actress and mother submitting to the tyrannical behavior of the Chopin figure, a young and domi-neering Polish prince. George Sand knew how to role-play in the realm of fiction.

In *La Genèse de Lorenzaccio* (Paris: Marcel Didier, 1964), Paul Dimoff gives us the clearest delineation of the genesis of the Musset play.[4] Although he did not comprehend the basic difference between Sand's and Musset's conceptions in modern psychosexual terms, Di-moff does trace the Varchi-Sand-Musset itinerary most effectively. The manuscript of *A Conspiracy in 1537* (E848 of the collection Spoel-berch of Louvenjoul) is made up of twenty-one sheets of one small notebook. The writing and the spelling of the document clearly place it among the earliest manuscripts of George Sand, probably dating back to 1831 or 1832. The notebook originated from the papers of Jules Sandeau himself. It then became the property of Marie Dorval, who received it from Sandeau: she had been *his* mistress at a certain moment, before Sand. This preamble simply serves to tell us that Musset had a copy of the play (in his possession) for only a short time before he conceived his own. He wrote *Lorenzaccio* before he and George Sand journeyed to Italy together in 1834. Among the relics of George

Sand that Mme Lauth-Sand, her granddaughter, kept was a large note-book, commonly known in the family as the *Red Book*, after the color of its binding. The label pasted on the inside read: "1829–1830: lit-erary fragments." The first twenty-eight pages of the red book contain another work, *Jehan Cauvin*, which is followed by a title page of *A Conspiracy in 1537: Historical Scene* and a list of the characters of the play. This list is the same contained in the Louvenjoul manuscript. Then one can see twenty irregularly torn-out pages, removed close to the binding, followed by works of George Sand's youth.

The torn pages, the number of which correspond exactly to the number of pages in the Louvenjoul manuscript, evidently contained the text of *A Conspiracy in 1537*. Possession of the red book probably led George Sand to forget about the destiny of the older manuscript, and so she never claimed it from Sandeau. When Alfred de Musset wished to have it at his disposal during the composition of his play, she must have detached the pages of the red book. The list of characters would not have been of paramount interest since Musset changed the char-acters, adding, subtracting and revising identities.

George Sand took care to call her play a historic scene. At this early date, she did not as yet have much pretension to literary ambition, perhaps only desirous of earning a living as a writer. The existence of a historical scene with the signature of Sand was only recently discov-ered. It was in 1899 that Mme Wladimir Karenin made an allusion to a manuscript in which she believed she saw the prototype of *Loren-zaccio*. Two years later, in a thesis devoted to Musset's theatre, M. Lafoscade indicated that he had read the document and gave a sum-mary description of it. Other scholars (Messrs Pierre Gauthier and Léon Sèche) followed suit, but it remained for M. Dimoff to publish the complete historical scene in the *Revue de Paris* of 1921.[5]

The historical scene was a modest genre. The public enjoyed the genre, especially those written by Ludovic Vitet. *La Revue de Paris*, in which George Sand dreamed of being published, had printed two historical scenes in 1830, one of them by Prosper Mérimée (*Les Mé-contents*). We will probably never know why *A Conspiracy in 1537* did not see the light of day at that time. Sand's modesty was probably at the root of it. Vitet pontificated that a historical scene should present historical facts in dramatic form but without the pretension of compos-ing a full-fledged drama. The unity of action and drama was a felici-tous result of the arrangement of historical facts. For Vitet, the dramatic details at the heart of a tale were purely accidental gold, a good fortune for all concerned with the facts. The difficulty of the genre was the specific choice of subject. The facts would arrange themselves into scenes, concrete and picturesque tableaux, rather than abstract dry notions of historical truth. The living dialogues illustrated the psychological truths inherent in the history. The writer filled in historical silences with scenes interpreting the rapport of facts. The writer fashioned art inherent in history.

George Sand's timing was inexorable. She chose Italy and specifically Florence, suddenly in vogue because of its renaissance historical panorama. We cannot be sure how she found her subject. Jean Pommier tells us that she had asked a friend to conduct historical research for her in 1831. M. Jean Giraud thinks she discovered the subject of her play in a literary history of Italy published by Guinguiné, in which the plays and the crime of Lorenzo of Medici were reported in several brief sentences, alluding to the work of Varchi. Pommier adds that Sismondi, in his work *The Italian Republics of the Middle Ages*, could just as well have informed Sand of Lorenzo's crime. Although Varchi names Catterina as Lorenzo's aunt, sister of his mother, George Sand chose to make her Lorenzo's sister. Guinguiné had spoken of a young and beautiful Florentine damsel whom some had pointed out to be his aunt or his sister. M. Lafoscade conjectured that it was perhaps Henri de Latouche who directed Sand to Graevius' *Theasurus Antiquatum et Historiam Italiae*, which may have led her directly to Varchi, the *only* work in Italian among a host of Latin lucubrations.

Once in possession of her subject, George Sand obeyed Vitet by refusing to construct a drama, although she noticed that Varchi contained within his pages the stuff of a most ample and complex play. She limited herself to setting the scene for the direct preparation for the execution of Duke Alexander by Lorenzo. She deliberately neglected all the episodes in Varchi which gave local color and background evidence. She precipitated events, clustering them together in so short a time that she didn't even need the twenty-four hours granted to a classical tragedy. Docile, with very few exceptions, she kept only the situation and effects that illuminate the heart of the story.

Sand did make a few errors and take historic license, nevertheless. She called Alexander Grand-Duke instead of Duke of Florence. She spoke of Clement VII as reigning pope in 1537, even though Paul III had replaced him in 1534; she presented Valori as the apostolic commissioner of Florence, whereas in 1534 he no longer fulfilled any mission whatsoever for the pope. Sand may have taken insufficient notes while skimming through the history of Florence. If she confused Giomo with the Hungarian and made one person of the two, the fault lies with the Leyden edition, which omitted a comma where one was needed. If she dated the death of Alexander of Medici as 1537, instead of 1536, the fault lies with erroneous dates which appear in other works. If she made Catterina the sister and not the aunt of Lorenzo, she had ample authority from Guinguiné. It may simply be that Sand instinctively comprehended the dramatic advantage of making the girl his sister, thereby creating high incestuous drama. She hinted at the implicit rivalry between Lorenzo and Alexander for the affections of the sister. Musset gave Lorenzo a more complex motivation: his Lorenzo killed the Duke because he had become part of his psyche. Lorenzaccio of Musset killed to prevent his own shame at procuring a votive sexual gift for his oppressor. Despite these small betrayals of history, nowhere can one truly seize George Sand in flagrante delicto of impertinence to historical fact. Musset followed Sand in most of her dramatic choices.

Whenever Sand allowed her imagination to take over, unbridled, she produced the memorable moments of her historical scene. When Varchi did not furnish the basis of a character, Sand created it freely. M. Lafoscade referred to the strong virgin who is Sand's spiritual daughter. More curious and original is her Lorenzo, troubled in the last tableau, after the Duke's murder, justifying his act to his sister and making her his accomplice. This was most probably the origin for Musset of the *idée fixe* of the crime itself, the conviction that he was finally fulfilled by the committing of it, thus becoming the avenger of justice for which he was destined, disguised by humankind's perfidy and disabused of his generous illusions, skeptical of the political consequences of his act. Sand gave Varchi's Lorenzo *envergure*, a historical status, and Musset provided him with poetic schizophrenia.

A Conspiracy in 1537 was the work of a novice, but it turns out to be a work of intense depth and promise. Musset was undoubtedly a good judge of such matters. He used Sand's gift to give his own work the complex dimension it needed. What Paul Dimoff and the other critics did not envisage was that Musset had not written only a romantic historical drama but rather a Sartrian essay in existential self-definition, much ahead of its time. Musset's theatre was not often performed during his lifetime. It came into its own in an era when its concerns were philosophically and psychologically more viable.

Sand instinctively singled out Lorenzo's sister, his alter ego, as the true protagonist. It is Catterina's choice which gives Sand's play a final coherence. Musset muddled the waters with a penchant for Shakespeare, thereby elevating the Cardinal Cibo and his sister-in-law, the Marquise de Cibo, to the dramatic forefront, creating a sinful dramatic couple as counterpoint for the other flawed Florentines. George Sand's feminist-incestuous approach is more elemental than Musset's. Musset intellectualized the drama, allowing Lorenzo five long, convoluted acts to become a full-fledged murderer who purges himself by an ironic act of murder which is an ultimate suicide. In Musset's version, Catterina is long since out of the dramatic picture. Sand, finally, is logically Sartrian while Musset's version was more than aromatic Shakespeare. Had Musset and Sand known one another when Sand's career was further along, George Sand might very well have written a full-length play and kept it for herself. As it is, she made of it a unique gift and revealed yet another of her most winning lifelong characteristics, as an inspiration to her artist friends. Balzac, Mérimée and Flaubert all came under her personal and literary spell. With Balzac there was literary symbiosis and mutual inspiration in minor works. The Flaubert-Sand correspondence defined them both in each other's eyes and for the world. Most significantly, her generous gift to Musset made possible what is now acknowledged to be the greatest dramatic work of the nineteenth century. Although we can never be privy to the conversations they had together concerning the life and times of Lorenzo of Medici, it is highly likely that the intertextual twists and turns, from Varchi of the Renaissance to the final masterwork of Alfred de Musset, were indelibly influenced by the coherent literary logic of George Sand.

NOTES

1. The Théâtre National Populaire, under the direction of Jean Vilar, first performed *Lorenzaccio* in the Cour d'Honneur of the Palais des Papes in Avignon, July 15, 1952. They later toured in the United States. The use of sound and light and pageantry was so remarkable that the production is often recalled even thirty years later with the most singular esthetic pleasure. Gérard Philipe's sonorous voice was perhaps never used to better advantage.

2. The text of George Sand's play is available only in Paul Dimoff's *La Genèse de Lorenzaccio* (Paris: Librairie Marcel Didier, 1964), in the editions of the Société des Textes français modernes (pp. 81–146.) All references to the development of the plays are taken from this volume.

3. *Lorenzaccio* has had a difficult time becoming known. Although the Stratford Ontario Shakespeare Festival has performed it, no professional production has yet been forthcoming in New York. I do believe the Sand play would help clarify Musset's epic. Perhaps one day it will be possible to do this in a university setting.

4. This volume is a gold mine. It contains fragments from the *Storia Fiorentina of Varchi* (pp. 1–80), *Une Conspiration en 1537* (pp. 81–146), various strategies in the writing of *Lorenzaccio* (pp. 147–66), scenes which were not used in *Lorenzaccio* (pp. 167–84) and *Lorenzaccio*, the play itself (pp. 185–471). As is the case for some of the great long plays of the world, such as *Hamlet* (and *Lorenzaccio* has often been called the French *Hamlet*), each production or version is an adaptation. At least five of them have been performed in London and Paris in the last few years. Each adaptor is collaborating with Sand and Musset. Will the definitive version of the play be in English or French?

5. *Lorenzaccio* is one of the few important plays of the past to need the reconstruction of scholars and theatre professionals. Musset's theatre, like Stendhal's work, was minimally performed during his lifetime and only came into its own a century later. Certain of the mid-nineteenth-century writers were not truly of their time. Stendhal realized this and spoke of the year 1935 as "his" time, long after his lifetime. Musset, now a classic, created works which were profoundly inspired by Shakespeare and not truly comprehended in the Romantic era. His is the purest of all Romantic styles and is only now being amply interpreted.

9

Fredrika Bremer: Sweden's First Feminist

Doris R. Asmundsson

Fredrika Bremer, a novelist and social reformer who lived from 1801 to 1865, was Sweden's earliest feminist writer. She achieved international fame and stated frequently that much of her success in social reform could be traced to her literary and personal contacts in England and America.

The daughter of a wealthy Swedish landowner, Bremer was educated at home by private tutors in French, German and English. When she and her sister Charlotte studied geography, their governess, to encourage their interest, presented each child with her own kingdom. Charlotte was given France and Fredrika England.[1] The gift foreshadowed a lifelong preference for, and association with, England. At fifteen Bremer was allowed to read novels and found those of Richardson, Fielding, Burney and Scott particularly enjoyable. She had great admiration for Sir Charles Grandison and his peerless Harriet, but Richardson's *Clarissa* had a different effect upon her. She stated with indignation that for all decent women the name Lovelace was "synonymous with Satan."[2] Unable to endure reading about Lovelace's brutality, Bremer could not finish *Clarissa*. Nevertheless, this novel was to have profound influence on her life. Because of the hatred she felt toward Lovelace as an exploiter of women, Bremer decided to become a defender of women's rights.

Bremer and her sisters travelled on the continent with their parents and spent a winter in Paris where they had the best music, singing and painting teachers. At twenty Bremer was presented to society and was expected eventually to marry well. But meanwhile she was intolerably bored with the idle routine of embroidery and piano practice and considered her home life "painful." Having been impressed by the work of the Sisters of Charity in Paris, she longed to do similar work in Stockholm, but there was no such institution. She then began to write *Sketches of Everyday Life*. It was published anonymously in 1830, but the name of the author soon came out. Although Bremer immediately became popular and received a gold medal from the Swedish Academy, she preferred to stay out of the limelight and devote herself to her writing and her private work for the poor. She rejected the many marriage proposals she received, stating that she never intended to marry. At thirty Bremer's physical and mental state was better than it had been in her twenties when she had chafed against the boredom of her idle existence.

In 1831 Bremer met a young English girl, Frances Lewin, who had married a Swede. Under the influence of this intellectual girl, Bremer's mind was opened to new philosophical ideas, notably those of Bentham, Locke and Mill. She wrote to Frances: "You put Locke and Bentham in my hands and with the principle of Utilitarianism kindled a new light in me. I cannot describe how everything . . . was changed within me—from depression, despair—to courage, hope and joy. . . . What a beautiful life lies before me now!"[3] Bremer was indeed carried away by the writings of Bentham and Locke. Although Bentham's utilitarianism as the sole basis of morality did not satisfy her and she later strayed from a rigid application of its principles, its influences can be seen in her efforts to make women's lives useful and significant.

At her English friend's suggestion, Bremer spent part of the winter of 1834 studying Harriet Martineau's *Illustrations of Political Economy*. The theories of the English socialist Robert Owen for the improvement of humanity also excited her—almost as much as the works of her "beloved Miss Martineau"—and she daily made resolutions to do something useful in a similar way.[4] She began to correspond with Harriet Martineau and Maria Edgeworth.

As the years passed, Bremer continued to turn out her novels of Swedish domestic life, many of which were translated into other languages. In February, 1843 she received the first copies of her novel *The Neighbours*, translated into English by Mary Howitt, and she confided to a friend that as a child she had wept tears of longing that she might some day "become someone" for Sweden. Now she was amazed that her modest pictures of Swedish life should be successful in Germany and Holland and, more important, in a country "as rich in romantic literature" and with such "fastidious taste" as England.[5] It is probable that Fredrika Bremer's fame in England, in the beginning at least, owed something to the fact that English curiosity about Sweden had been aroused by a book published in 1837 by a Scottish clergyman, Samuel Laing, *A Tour of Sweden*, which was highly critical of Swedish life and morality. Whatever the reasons, English reviewers as well as readers welcomed Bremer's works, which were favorably compared with the meager English literary output of that decade. The *Athenaeum* hailed her novels as an innovation, and *Fraser's Magazine* credited them with reviving the dying art of novel reading.[6]

The Brontës were also reading her; in February of 1849, Charlotte noted in her diary that Anne was "engaged with one of Fredrika Bremer's tales."[7] Although Bremer's first and ultimately most popular novel, *The Neighbours*, was published in England in 1842, Charlotte Brontë seems not to have read it until after the publication of her own *Jane Eyre* in 1847. In her *Life of Charlotte Brontë*, Elizabeth Gaskell revealed that on reading *The Neighbours*, Charlotte was sure that everyone would see a resemblance between Francesca, its Swedish heroine, and Jane Eyre.[8]

Bremer was always restless and eager to travel. As early as 1830 she had expressed a desire to visit England to learn more about the important problems that England "works out for the benefit of mankind."[9] But such a trip was far in the future. During the 1830's and early 1840's, she spent much of her time at the estate of a Norwegian countess, and after the death of the countess announced to the amazed Bremer family that she intended to make a trip to America. Overcoming all opposition, she finally sailed for the United States via London in 1849. A cholera epidemic limited her stay in London to three days, but she was able at last to meet her English translators, William and Mary Howitt, who gave her a warm welcome.

At the age of forty-eight, Fredrika Bremer arrived in New York in October, 1849 for what would turn out to be a two-year stay, longer than she had originally anticipated. Because her books were as popular in America—mostly in pirated editions—as those of Dickens, she was lionized at literary soirées in New York where she met William Cullen Bryant and Washington Irving, among many others, and was photographed by Matthew Brady. Physically frail, Bremer found the exuberant American welcome exhausting and escaped to New England for three months. There she was a guest of Emerson, of whom she drew a sketch; Longfellow; Lowell and Hawthorne. John Greenleaf Whittier dedicated a poem to her which read in part:

> Seeress of the misty Norland,
> Daughter of the Vikings bold.[10]

She met many abolitionists, among them William Lloyd Garrison and Julia Ward Howe. Bremer disapproved of slavery but thought she ought to investigate slave plantations personally. Later, after a stay at a South Carolina plantation, she condemned slavery "as a great lie in the life of human freedom, and especially in the New World." Of Harriet Beecher Stowe Bremer said: "Honor and blessing be hers! What will not that people become who can produce such daughters!" She also remarked that the slavery problem would be solved "if women would but awake."[11] Later, in Sweden, she arranged for the Swedish translation of *Uncle Tom's Cabin*.

Bremer visited Scandinavian settlements in the Midwest, and the enthusiastic picture of that life presented in her book *Homes of the New World: Impressions of America* was largely responsible for the great wave of Scandinavian emigration following the Civil War. Published in New York in 1853, the book went through five printings within a month and was also translated into Danish, Dutch, French and German.[12] While in America, Bremer attended Millard Fillmore's inauguration in Washington and met with exponents of women's rights such as Dorothea Dix, Lucretia Mott, Lucy Stone and, of course, Harriet Beecher Stowe.

After two exciting years in America, Bremer returned to England in 1851 on her way home. Her visit had several purposes: to renew her acquaintance with the Howitts; to meet the author of *Alton Locke*, Charles Kingsley; to see the Crystal Palace Exhibition and to investigate social problems in England as she had done in America. The last aim was characteristic of her utilitarian approach to travel. She hoped on her return to arouse the slumbering life in Sweden "with the example of [England], more than ever at this moment an example worth admiration and—imitation."[13]

On landing in Liverpool, Bremer went to stay for a week at the home of James Martineau, Harriet's clergyman brother. On her departure, Martineau gave her a letter of introduction to his friend Francis N. Newman, an Oxford professor and brother of Cardinal Newman. Martineau hoped that Newman would find the ''interest and pleasure in her society and conversation'' that he had felt. But more important, the introduction was to prevent Bremer from ''carrying home without correction the impressions in favour of socialistic doctrine which she . . . received from the writings of Mr. Kingsley.''[14] Martineau believed that Kingsley's *Alton Locke*, a novel advocating social reform, had strengthened the dangerous sympathies aroused by Bremer's visits to socialist communities in America. Martineau feared that her pen might be used to serve ''the delusive schemes of these people'' and hoped that Newman's knowledge of these subjects would ''afford her true guidance.''[15]; In this instance, however, his hopes were doomed; Bremer made no mention of her meeting with Newman, but her friendship and subsequent correspondence with Kingsley flourished. She wrote to him that she was eager ''to see, to thank, to converse with the *Author of Alton Locke*.''[16] She had read the book on her voyage back to England and was moved by his depiction of the suffering of the poor and the need for reform. The anticipated meeting was successful on both sides. Kingsley found Bremer to be ''one of the most highly cultivated women'' he had ever conversed with, and her sweetness and womanliness ''even more attractive than her intellect.'' She thought of him as a younger brother.[17]

In London Bremer had a room at John Chapman's where her fellow boarder was George Eliot, then Chapman's assistant editor of the *Westminster Review*. Upon Bremer's arrival at the end of September, George Eliot wrote of her to a friend in less than glowing terms. She found the Swedish author ''equally unprepossessing to eye and ear'' and found it necessary to remind herself constantly that this was really the famous Fredrika Bremer. Shortly after, she softened to the extent of saying that all the world was ''doing its *devoir* to the great little authoress Miss Bremer.'' Later she commented favorably on Bremer's sketches of flowers, landscapes and people. Those of Emerson and Jenny Lind, George Eliot found ''marvelously like.''[18]

Bremer later travelled to Manchester to meet Mrs. Gaskell who, like Kingsley, had written novels of social significance. Her concern for the exploited factory workers of her native city is expressed in the novel *Mary Barton*. Gaskell saw Bremer as ''a quaint, droll little lady

. . . very plain and rather untidy,'' but, like George Eliot, she soon fell under the spell of her quiet charm.[19] Because of their mutual concern for oppressed people, they became fast friends and faithful correspondents in the following years.

Ever since Bremer had read *The Old Governess*, a plea for better treatment of these aged women, she had been eager to meet its author Anna Maria Hall. (Bremer was later to found a home in Stockholm for indigent women.) The Halls invited her to their Surrey estate and never had ''a more interesting or more amusing visitor.'' Mrs. Hall described her as ''small and delicate, not unlike Maria Edgeworth in form, and somewhat like her in manner.'' Eager to fulfill Bremer's desire to see and learn everything about England that might be useful in Sweden, the Halls brought her to large farms as well as cottages, to ancient churches and to Windsor Castle. She was disappointed at not seeing Queen Victoria, but as they were driving out, the royal carriage arrived. In her excitement, Bremer dropped a much-beloved umbrella out the window. Prince Albert sent a footman to return it, and, said Mrs. Hall, ''little did the Royal Lady and her illustrious husband know whom they had thus befriended.''[20] When Victoria bowed and smiled, Bremer understood the magic secret of her popularity; yet her social conscience troubled her and she complained: ''Why should this Queen fortify her throne with stables and dog kennels? Why not rather build it upon warm and loving hearts?''[21] Although herself a wealthy woman, Bremer never lost her sympathy for ordinary people.

Anna Maria Hall was sympathetic to Bremer's desire for social justice and for improvement in the position of women. She saw her not as a ''rights-of-women'' woman—to Hall a vulgar idea—but one who was ''anxious for the emancipation of her sex . . . from the heavy thralldom'' under which they labored.[22]

While in England, Bremer had an opportunity to investigate socialism of the English variety, which drew its support from an educated class and from some earnest members of the clergy such as Kingsley. The most important aspect of her visit was the chance to ''see and greet this dawn of a new and better day in the world.''[23] She had little sympathy for the Chartists, however, whose socialism had no religious connection. She condemned any movement, however benevolent, that overlooked religion. Christian socialism was the only answer, she believed, and she was confident that England would lead the way. But the Swedes seem to have taken Fredrika Bremer more seriously than she had expected since Sweden has ultimately led the world in social reform, without religious overtones, however.

In 1854 a cholera epidemic left thousands of orphans in Stockholm, but this melancholy event was turned to good account by Bremer's establishment of the Women's Union for the Care of Children. Believing that a universal organization of women might accomplish much in the fields of social welfare and international peace, Bremer wrote an "Invitation to a Peace Alliance" and sent it to the editor of the London *Times*. She told him it would be published simultaneously in Sweden, Russia, France, Germany and America and that she was particularly anxious to have it published in England because she knew that "no hearts and minds in the world will be more ready to respond . . . than those of the benevolent and high-minded English people." [24] The opening of the "Invitation to a Peace Alliance" has a somewhat familiar ring to modern ears:

At a time like this, when the Powers of the West arm themselves against those of the East, and enter into a struggle threatening to spread over several of the countries of Europe, . . . we have ventured a thought, a hope, that through women a peaceful alliance might be concluded, opposing the direful effects of war, and contributing . . . to the development of a state of peace, love and well-being. [25]

The "Invitation" suggested that national associations of women unite for the purpose of caring for the destitute of all types. The editor of the London *Times* published the "Invitation" with a disparaging disclaimer, and since the international organization failed to materialize, the women of England and the rest of the world were evidently not as interested in unity and peace as the Stockholm women, who strongly supported all of Bremer's ideas. It is a tribute to Bremer, however, that after almost one hundred thirty years the women's organization of Sweden is still known as the Fredrika Bremer Forbündet.

Bremer believed, then, in 1855 that the emancipation of women was the factor "on which depends the true liberation of mankind," and she sent an American friend "a little book that I have written for the same cause." [26] Bremer, possibly influenced by Gaskell, realized that literature was her best vehicle for protest. The book was *Hertha*, and into it she poured all of her indignation, her theories and her aspirations on the subject of women. Like almost all her other works, it is now too dated and too melodramatic to interest the modern reader: Hertha is a sanctimonious and long-suffering heroine in a class with Elsie Dinsmore. Nevertheless, the publication of the book in 1856 created a sensation, and it was blamed for the breakup of families. Bremer, who had risked a loss of popularity in publishing *Hertha*, was attacked by the sensational press and called "a blue stocking."[27] But the book, coming to the attention of King Oscar I, who had recently come the throne, influenced his decision to take up the question of women's independence. *Hertha* was mentioned in parliamentary debates, and when the law was finally passed, Bremer's friends described it as "Hertha's triumph in the Riksdag."[28] On June 15, 1858, it was established by royal decree that unmarried women of twenty-five, after applying to court, were entitled to the same rights as men of legal age. In 1863 the necessity of petitioning court was abolished, and by 1884 the age of majority for women was declared the same as for men—twenty-one. *Hertha*, it would appear, played a large part in winning civil rights for Swedish women. In 1886 women of twenty-five with an annual income of twenty-two pounds were granted the right to vote, while the militant suffragettes in England and America had to fight for the vote until 1918.

But Fredrika Bremer now realized that legal freedom alone did not solve all of women's problems; the happiness and welfare of the individual must still be provided for. Influenced by Anna Maria Hall's book on the fate of aged governesses, Bremer in 1855 established the Relief and Pension Fund for Swedish Governesses and later a home for aged gentlewomen, most of whom were former governesses. As a preventive measure in the late 1850's, she founded a Women's College of Teacher Training to insure that women in this profession would be well trained and thus successful and happy. In 1863 Mary Howitt's daughter Margaret came to Stockholm to live with Bremer while taking courses at the Women's College.

It is difficult to compare the success of the efforts of Fredrika Bremer with that of her contemporaries in the women's movement in England and America. Perhaps because she was a famous woman when Sweden had no others and because her fame was international, what she advocated was adopted with little resistance. In the last ten years of her life, she was able almost alone to organize a woman's society and a home for aged women, to establish schools for teacher training

and for the deaf, and through her novel *Hertha* to influence legislation
to emancipate women. Her success might also be laid to the fact that
circumstances in Sweden were undoubtedly more favorable for reform
than in England and America where political and economic strife were
more prevalent. Sweden, with a relatively small population of homogeneous people, experienced little of the social upheavals of nineteenth-century Europe and America. It is also worth noting that Fredrika Bremer, in contrast to some of her foreign contemporaries, devoted
herself to the cause of women with complete dedication. In America
Dorothea Dix, Lucy Stone and Harriet Beecher Stowe worked respec-
tively for prison reform, women's suffrage and the abolition of slavery. In England Harriet Martineau's interest in women's affairs was
diluted by an interest in political economy and foreign affairs. Barbara
Leigh Smith and Bessie Rayner Parkes made valuable contributions to
the women's movement, but their activity was in the nature of an
interlude and necessarily declined after marriage. Bremer, in contrast,
devoted her entire life to the cause of women. Her interest began with
her awakening through utilitarianism to the fact that her life might
become useful and happy. Having been saved herself, she became
convinced as time went on that she must devote herself entirely to the
salvation of women.

Fredrika Bremer died on December 31, 1865, and was mourned in
Sweden and throughout the world. Margaret Howitt then decided it
was time to publish as a memorial *Twelve Months with Fredrika Bremer*. The book was widely reviewed in the British press, favorably for
the most part. Bremer's reputation had evidently not suffered any serious decline in the twenty years since she rose to fame in England
and America. As late as 1929, another Englishwoman paid tribute to
Fredrika Bremer. The novelist Angela Thirkell, in an article entitled
"Mamsell Fredrika" in the *Fortnightly Review*, said she had been
reading Miss Bremer for nearly thirty years and still found her "as
charming as ever."[29]

Now, one hundred fifteen years after her death, Fredrika Bremer's
memory lives on in only a few places outside Sweden: in Philadelphia,
a room is dedicated to her in the American Swedish Historical Museum, and in Minneapolis a public school has been named for her. But
in Sweden the Fredrika Bremer Society lives on, publishing a magazine entitled *Hertha*.

NOTES

1. *Life, Letters and Posthumous Works of Fredrika Bremer*, ed. Charlotte Bremer, trans. Fredrick Milow (New York: Worthington, 1880), p. 42.

2. Klara Johanson and Ellen Kleman, eds., *Fredrika Bremers Brev*, 4 vols. (Stockholm: P. J. Norstedt, 1915–20), I: 136. This and all succeeding passages from these volumes are translated from the Swedish by the author.

3. Ibid., I: 155.

4. Ibid., I: 279.

5. Ibid., II: 316.

6. *Athenaeum*, no. 784 (November 5, 1842), 949; *Fraser's Magazine* 28 (November, 1843), 505.

7. Clement K. Shorter, *The Brontës* (London: Dent, 1914), II: 23.

8. Elizabeth Gaskell, *The Life of Charlotte Brontë* (London: Smith, Elder & Co., 1900), p. 233.

9. Bremer, *Life, Letters*, p. 193.

10. "To Fredrika Bremer," John G. Whittier, *The Complete Poetical Works of Whittier* (Boston: Houghton Mifflin & Co., 1894), p. 183.

11. Fredrika Bremer, *Homes of the World* (London: Arthur Hill, Virtue & Co., 1853), II: 12.

12. Signe Alice Rooth, "Fredrika Bremer, 1801–1865" in *Abroad in America: Visitors to the New Nation, 1776–1914* (Reading, Mass.: Addison-Wesley, 1976), pp. 116–21. Signe Rooth is also the author of *Seeress of the North* (Philadelphia: American-Swedish Historical Society, 1955), the definitive treatment of Fredrika Bremer's visit to America.

13. Johanson and Kleman, *Fredrika Bremers Brev*, IV: 551.

14. Charles Kingsley, a clergyman, novelist and exponent of Christian socialism, is remembered today chiefly for *Westward, Ho!* and a children's book, *The Water Babies*.

15. James Drummond and C. B. Upton, eds., *The Life and Letters of James Martineau* (New York: Dodd, Mead & Co., 1902), II: 294.

16. ALS dated October 14, 1851, in the Yale University Library.

17. Charles Kingsley, *His Letters and Memories of His Life*, ed. by his wife [Frances Eliza (Grenfell) Kingsley] (London: Scribner, Armstrong & Co., 1877), p. 170.

18. Gordon S. Haight, ed., *The George Eliot Letters*, 9 vols. (New Haven: Yale University Press, 1955–78), I: 365–67.

19. ALS dated October 29, 1851, in the Berg Collection, New York Public Library.

20. S. C. Hall, *A Book of Memories of Great Men and Women of the Age* (London: Virtue & Co., 1871), pp. 411–18.

21. Fredrika Bremer, *England in 1851* (Boulogne: Merridew, 1853), pp. 131–34.

22. Hall, *Book of Memories*, p. 411.

23. Johanson and Kleman, *Fredrika Bremers Brev*, III: 225.

24. Ibid., III: 349.

25. Ibid., III: 562–64.

26. Ibid., IV: 572.

27. *Stockholm Dagens Nyheter*, August 19, 1862.

28. Ibid.

29. *Fortnightly Review*, n.s., 126 (August, 1929), 217–29.

10

An Introduction to the Life and Times of Louise Otto

Ruth-Ellen Boetcher Joeres

The subject of women writers in nineteenth-century Germany is by no means a popular one: when it is raised, the embarrassed silence is generally broken only by a comment here or there on the wives of Romantic writers who were active behind the scenes, in salons or as often anonymous contributors to their husbands' efforts or by a comment about the one widely known writer, Annette von Droste-Hülshoff, whose reclusive life-style bore similarity to that of Emily Dickinson. Yet according to Louise Otto, a writer whose life spanned most of the last century, more women were writing then than at any other time in the history of that country.[1] An investigation thus seems both appropriate and long overdue, an examination not only of the actual group of women writers and what they wrote but most certainly of the possible reasons why such enforced anonymity ever came about in the first place. For the limits imposed by a chapter, even a superficial survey seems too extensive; what will therefore be pursued here is a discussion of just one of the many, of a representative of a particular faction among myriad factions: given the many-sided nature of her life and her writings, a look at her can serve as an introduction to the world of nineteenth-century German women writers and can give some contextual substance to an age that accommodated her along with Emily Dickinson and George Eliot.

Louise Otto (1819–95) was a poet, the author of a number of lengthy novels and an activist in the causes of political liberalism and feminism.[2] In the often heavily tendentious prose that her novels exhibit, it is made clear that the overriding passion of her life was her social involvement, the fervent republicanism that she espoused in the 1840's and a lasting concern with the formation of a German women's movement. Her abiding and intense preoccupation with Germany and its social problems indeed left her little time for purely literary pursuits.

The consistency that marked her lifelong philosophy of liberalism is evident in the polemic writings of her later years, after her founding in 1865 of the National German Women's Organization, the first association of its size and scope to deal exclusively with the social and political problems of German women rather than with the philanthropic good deeds that marked all other groups of women at that time. It is felt as well in her fictional works, her novels, novellas, her poetry, even in the two opera libretti that she published in 1852 and 1872. Consistency can, of course, indicate stagnation—a belief that was radical in the 1840's might well be outlived and stale by the 1870's—but the maintenance of a firm, progressive stance throughout a lifetime is especially notable when one reflects on the rapid and often devastating changes that marked German politics during the years of Otto's life. In her particular case, the secure and happy middle-class upbringing that she enjoyed helped in creating a certain degree of self-confidence and optimism. Meissen, the city in which she was born on March 26, 1819, was at that time an idyllic town in a reasonably progressive province, far removed from the hectic pace of the nearest big cities Dresden and Leipzig. Her father, a public official, was a firm believer in a good education for his four daughters, and his demand that they also develop a knowledge of current political and social concepts helped create an open-mindedness in them, a mental curiosity not common in the young women of the day. Her mother, a member of one of Meissen's artistic families, exposed Otto and her sisters to aesthetic ideas and no doubt reinforced the bourgeois idealistic belief in the importance of an aesthetic education.

But Otto's life did not continue its serene pattern. The death of her eldest sister in 1831 and of both parents and the young poet whom she was to marry in 1835–36; the death of her husband, August Peters, in 1864 after only six years of marriage; frequent illness and considerable harassment during the years of reaction after the 1848 revolution were the sorts of catastrophes that might well have led her into a compliant and submissive middle age. Yet one need only compare Otto's radical

statements of the 1840's, when revolution was rife and liberal sentiments widespread, with the more mature, yet equally liberal, emotions
expressed in much of her semi-autobiographical work *The Life of Women
in the German Empire* (1876) to sense the consistency.[3] After the empire was established, a satisfied inactivity took hold not only of the
populace at large but also of many of Otto's sister writers whose work,
like hers, had initially been marked by social criticism. Her continued
progressivism is thus all the more unique and remarkable.

Louise Otto's multi-volumed novels appeared from 1843 on. She
was also a frequent contributor to a number of progressive journals in
the 1840's and the founder and editor of *The Women's Newspaper*,
the first significant journal for German women, from 1849–52, and of
New Paths, the organ of her national women's organization, from 1866
until her death in 1895, as well as the author of several compilations
of verse and many polemic works. Her poetry and her prose fiction
tend toward wordiness and overstatement, and one frequently has the
feeling that there was not the necessary time for a judicious editing of
such a mass of words. She was clearly a socially critical writer, for
she primarily and deliberately dealt with social and political issues or
(in the historical novels of the reactionary 1850's, when political concerns were better expressed in private) with larger moral issues that
nevertheless were scarcely masked treatments of the problems of her
times. Not all of her female characters are exclusively involved with
what were considered traditional female spheres of activity; especially
in the early novels there are strong and competent women, writers and
social activists, whose occasional avoidance of love and marriage is
not made to seem tragic or pitiful. Except in the historical novels, the
interest is solely in the present; there are no utopias, no dream-like
sequences involving a golden age that was yet to appear. The idealism
and optimism that characterize her polemic writings are present in the
novels as well, but it is a realistic idealism that never leaves the realm
of the possible.

Despite the abundance of novels with their multifaceted themes, their
condemnation of rigid thinking, and the positive conception of liberal
ideas, it is the aforementioned *Life of Women in the German Empire*
that must be considered the most eloquent representation of Louise
Otto's philosophy. This semi-documentary work is as close as Otto
ever got to an autobiography, for it is teeming with information not
only about the general topic of women in the nineteenth century but

more specifically about her own upbringing and experiences, including samples of her poetry as well as sections on her philosophy of life, particularly as it relates to her thoughts on women. As a portrait of middle-class German female life in the last century, it is a veritable goldmine of facts, unique in its concerns and detail; as a personal account, it is revealing and welcome in its subjectivity; and, as seen in the context of Otto's *oeuvre*, it is the best written and most perceptive.

The Life of Women is divided pedantically into three sections, labeled "past," "present," and "future," with the greatest attention paid to the first of them, an extensive picture of life earlier in the century. What a fascinating picture it is, with discussions of everything from sewing in the days before sewing machines to comments on the lack of formal education and decent schooling for girls. Personal observations abound; there is no doubt about Otto's own perspective even in the midst of an apparently objective statement like the following:

By means of selected illustrations that we shall borrow from the past, the younger generation will also be able to imagine how things were in the German nation at a time when looms were just beginning to supplant the spinning wheel, but no sewing machines were around to compete with handiwork; when crafts and industry were not yet at the stage where they would surpass every sort of female labor at home; when there were no matches and no gas, no trains and no telegraphs; when most of what in our economy is now called necessity and not luxury was either not available or only at considerable discomfort,—or it was only for those grand people who live in castles; when there were still many women among the populace who could not write and could only read printed materials or nothing at all; when there were women who were considered cute because they couldn't spell right; when the schooling of girls ended with their confirmation at 14; when even the oldest women were treated like children and needed a guardian when they went to court; and when it was considered daring for a woman to write under her own name. (Pp. v–vi)

The section on the past is extremely diverse in its array of topics, but the message that is delivered is less nostalgic than it is revealing in its account of the usefulness of a woman at a time when the running of a house was indeed her ultimate task and responsibility. Since growing technical benefits have removed a great deal of that responsibility—a development that Louise Otto welcomes and stresses throughout the volume—it is, she claims, time to give women some other equally important mission. Within this first section, there is not only an abundance of information centering primarily on the impact of technical change in the lives of women, but there are lyricism and fascination as well, an optimistic mood and barely contained excitement.

One of the most vivid chapters, for example, is entitled "Light and Fire"; it concerns the difficulties of producing light when one was confined to sulphur and lighter and flint in the days before the phosphorous match had been invented. When that invention came about ("and all distress came to an end," she comments), the deed was "as world-shaking, as liberating, as symbolic as the laying of railroad track" (p. 26). The idea of new tasks and realms of activities for women is consistently present: "Since gas not only gives us light, but also serves for cooking, since heating by means of air, water, and steam will eventually eliminate heating with ovens—how much female working power will be freed in every house and can—indeed must!—be applied to other areas of labor!" (P. 29)

A similar theme is developed in the long description of sewing where, once she has acknowledged that sewing itself is useful since it allows women time to think, and provides, in fact, an opportunity for young girls to be read to, she nevertheless welcomes the invention of the sewing machine:

The more menial and mechanical jobs are taken away from the human *hand* as industry progresses, the more the human *spirit* can triumph, can work its way to a loftier realm of mental achievement and joyful creativity—indeed, it is not only permitted to rise higher, it must do so, it must reach for a higher plane. What I say is not just for men—women are also affected. The more handiwork is taken from them by means of new inventions and the progress of industry, the more strength they will have for loftier goals, the more rapidly they will move toward the solution of women's problems. (pp. 47–48)

Particularly interesting touches are provided in the witty section on fashion and the tyranny of the dictators of fashion and in the autobiographical section on travel and the special difficulties women have had to face in undertaking any journey alone. In the case of fashion, the comments are cleverly bound up with a history of the century that stresses both the helplessness of the individual in the face of often

arbitrary variations and the occasionally liberating effect of even mind-
less or exploitative change. Striking examples of the latter include the
decision to have corset stays fasten in the front (which Louise Otto
terms a "major move toward feminine independence" (p. 77) and the
invention of the crinoline (useful particularly in cases of pregnancy,
as Napoleon's Eugenie, the pregnant inventor, determined).

As to the picture of travel in the nineteenth century, there is a sense
of the revealing of another world, a new freedom that Otto experienced during her first journey alone. On the other hand, there are also
the indignities she suffered at the hands of many skeptics who saw in
her travelling alone an insult or a disgrace. A child of the new age, as
she calls herself, she welcomes the trains, sees in them a means to
facilitate travel particularly for women alone, praises the English trains
with their separate compartments for women and claims that trains and
the steam engine have opened up a new era for all.

The leitmotifs introduced in this first section, namely the stamina
and vitality of women in the past but also the limitations that were
imposed upon their sphere of activity, are pursued in somewhat different form in the less passionate section entitled "present." Most interesting here are the many observations on writing, especially as they
reveal Otto's own philosophy on the skill with which she earned her
living. Never absent is her insistence on the importance of a social
conscience: in a discussion of the usurpation of seamstress work by
male tailors, for example, she speaks of her own strong involvement
in the cause of the seamstresses, then adds:

I shall no doubt describe one day in my autobiography how hard I worked for
the cause of the seamstresses! At that time, I had no organization to back me
up, no comrades to help me, I was not the experienced, older woman that I
am now, I was just a young thing, a fledgling poet! And the issue was after
all so prosaic that most of my sister writers in the service of the Muse would
never have involved themselves with such a topic. (P. 160)

The concern with the world around her is complemented by her motivation for writing: the idealism that marks her philosophy of life sur-
faces here again. "Ah, let us repeat it," she remarks:

. . . our efforts are not for money alone. On the contrary! With our memories
of the past in which there was dedication to art or science out of an inner

drive, where one plunged in without having to ask first whether it was a proper career, where one wrote in order to write, in order to please oneself, and because one had something to say—not for money—where at the beginning of a literary career one was happy not only to see oneself in print, but to have a mouthpiece to express one's views, and where it was still considered daring, a courageous emergence from the circle of femininity, if one risked introducing her name to a public in the press—we above all have been hurt countless times when in today's world a woman chooses to write to earn money and when even poems and articles expressing one's opinion on either political or feminist topics are only written and submitted because of the honorarium. It seems like an endless insult, a hideous degradation, and nothing could be farther from my mind than to favor material interests in my discussion of improvements for women. (Pp. 183–84)

What follows, however, marks a clear break between the nonmaterialistic, almost abstract vision of what life should be, the vision of loftier aims that Otto expounds so often in her polemic writings and the no-nonsense approach that she evidences in the section on how women should write. The generalization that women are not only the guardians of morality but also of poetry (understood in the larger context of all writing) is abruptly followed by several startling ideas that are different from what we, who view women's literature from another perspective, have been led to expect. Despite the fact that women, living in an inner world and often barred from participation in the public world, tended to favor the forms of diary and letter to express their thoughts and ideas, for her part Louise Otto condemns both. She finds the former marked by ''massive subjectivity'' and ''nervous sensitivity'' (p. 239), thinks of the latter as increasingly unnecessary in a world where trains reduce the space between potential correspondents and telegrams and postcards provide the necessary means to communicate whatever has to be said. She observes that literature is cheap and available everywhere, thanks to less expensive editions and an abundance of journals, and she concludes that the odds of a favorable reaction to an outpouring of private thoughts are slim. She is highly critical of the burning need to publish every personal confession and to see one's own name in print. In light of her own harried existence, it is not surprising to hear her claim that ''the world certainly has better things to do than to read time and again the effusions of an individual heart and the same tired old phrases of some beautiful soul'' (p. 241). She encourages reading rather than writing, sees a need for

rigorous mental training and stresses the importance of eliminating dil-
ettantish and wasteful hours that should be better spent in the pursuit
of positive goals. Indeed, if there is a group of whom she is most
critical here, it is middle-class women, relieved of all the responsibilities that they bore in their more rigorous past and as yet unable to
find new and meaningful activities. Whether it is dabbling in art or
music or writing, whether it is the dallying away of time at balls or in
the learning of a genteel skill for the sake of public appearance, Louise
Otto thunders her disapproval and overtly or implicitly provides evidence of her own useful life to suggest an alternative path of action.

The final section of the text is the briefest, but it is equally important and interesting. "Hopes for the Future" contains a compendium
of her own beliefs and aspirations, but it is, as she emphasizes, no
utopian vision, for she has no time for dreams and merely wishes to
elucidate her philosophy of what she hopes the next years will bring.
Even here, she cannot neglect what she sees as the progress that has
already been made:

People claim that aging makes one conservative and reactionary, that the old
are against progress and innovation, that they will not move ahead with humanity, but will instead lose faith in the world. In my opinion, the older one
gets, the more firmly one believes that the world is advancing despite all the
barriers set up, that what was impossible is now possible, that what was once
miraculous is now commonplace. (P. 250)

Her fascination with technical developments is illustrated once again
in a lyrical account of those innovations.[4] She supplements this account by listing less material changes, all of which had already occurred: the improvements in girls' schooling, the addition of subjects
like gymnastics, the entrance of women into the work force in greater
numbers than ever before, the training of women to be white-collar
workers, and the most welcome of all changes, the growing sentiment
to train women as lawyers and doctors. Otto views the prospect of
women doctors in no less dramatic terms than as the chance to save
countless lives that would otherwise be lost because of false modesty:
women have been taught to feel shame and in most cases, she claims,
would literally prefer to die rather than share their intimate problems
with a male doctor. But there is a nagging and general dissatisfaction
as well with the slowness of progress for women, particularly in the

political sphere, and it is here that she moves from listing the accomplishments of the past to the hopes for the future. Pages are devoted to a rousing plea for involving women in political life, for imitating the British and Americans in their progressive ways. A hesitant but definite statement on the need for female suffrage emerges, a rare thought in 1876, when the subject was broached in Germany only by the occasional iconoclast in an otherwise stagnant political world. The moderation that marked the German feminist movement under Louise Otto is tempered by this touch of radicalism, which seems reminiscent of her early strong support for working women in the 1840's and her vocal role in the 1848 revolution.

As at many other points in the course of this rich work, Louise Otto turns to poetry at its conclusion when she finds that prose does not have the impact she needs. The poems she has chosen are highly tendentious, limited in scope to the immediate situation, but their fervency is notable. The most interesting of them is an allegorical meeting of three years, 1865, 1875, and 1965, on the occasion in 1875 of the tenth anniversary of the Leipzig Organization for Educating Women (which was founded shortly before the National German Women's Organization with the purpose of expanding educational and work opportunities for women). The optimistic and confident words of 1965 seem ironic from our twentieth-century vantage point: Louise Otto's firm belief that all problems concerning women's rights would be settled by that year has hardly been fulfilled in Germany or elsewhere. What is most significant, however, is not so much the unfulfilled prophecy, as it is Otto's own impatience with dwelling on the future and her vigorous demand that the present remain centrally important and that we learn from the lessons of the past. When 1875 interrupts the look into the future by warning against revelation and stating that the goals are yet to be won, when we as readers are thus abruptly brought back to the tenth-anniversary celebration, we see the optimistic message of Louise Otto's entire life brought home: it is the process, the change, the action, that are important to her, and she is not even scintillated by a look into a future that she will never experience.

Louise Otto's active life seems to have allowed her little time for perfection of a literary style, and she, like a number of her compatriots, was too swept along by the happenings of the day to retreat and deliberate, to shape her words, to dwell for too long on the importance of how to write. Nevertheless, anyone who can make the past come alive as she does in *The Life of Women in the German Empire* should not be consigned to dusty oblivion. The cultural and historical portrait that she provides gives depth and meaning to our understanding of the life of bourgeois German women in the last century, allows us a unique look not only at the rarely revealed personal aspects of Otto's life but also at the scope of a middle-class German woman's world at a time when she was beginning to question in earnest the need for the confinement that had been traditionally imposed upon her.

When Elaine Showalter says that she wants to make ''an attempt to fill in the terrain between those literary landmarks [Austen, the Brontës, Eliot, and Woolf],'' she is embarking upon a course that historians of literature should follow.[5] Her effort to fill in some of the gaps in our knowledge of lesser-known American and British women writers is almost certainly an approach that is valid and appropriate. In that regard, if Louise Otto had written nothing but *The Life of Women*, she would be worth noting, for as a German feminist who spent her life working for the betterment of her sisters, she attempted to unite women in a common experience of their past, their present, and their hoped-for future, an effort given its strongest impulse in this treatise. Here she best mirrors a woman's life in the nineteenth century: in her depiction of rapid technical change not necessarily accompanied by an equally important social change, she gives a rationale, a sense of why progress in women's issues was slower in that country; in the process she provides an astoundingly readable and lively characterization of her own productive life and philosophy.

NOTES

1. Louise Otto, *Das Recht der Frauen auf Erwerb: Blick auf das Frauenleben der Gegenwart* (*Women's Right to Work: Views of Women's Life Today*) (Hamburg: Hoffmann & Campe, 1866), p. 95.

2. For those readers who understand German, I refer them to the most complete modern compilation of Louise Otto's thought and work yet to emerge: namely, my *Die Anfänge der deutschen Frauenbewegung: Louise Otto-Peters* (Frankfurt/Main: Fischer, 1983).

3. Louise Otto, *Frauenleben im deutschen Reich: Erinnerungen aus der Vergangenheit mit Hinweis auf Gegenwart und Zukunft* (*The Life of Women in the German Empire: Reminiscences of the Past with a Look at the Present and the Future*) (Leipzig: Moritz Schäfer, 1876). Page numbers for quotations

from this text are listed in parentheses following each citation. The translations are my own.

4. Otto, *The Life of Women*, p. 250. The passage referred to is the following:

> All we need to do is to ponder all the changes we have experienced, and what can help here are the examples I have provided from a past I actually witnessed: If anybody had said 50 or 60 years ago that any child could make fire with the use of a small stick of wood, he would have been laughed out of the room.
>
> If anybody had claimed 30 or 40 years ago, upon seeing the first locomotive and the first propeller steamer, that one might soon encircle the earth in 80 or 90 days, he would have been considered a jokester. Pleasure trips undertaken by ladies without male protection were at that time very much the exception to the rule.
>
> If anyone had said 20 or 30 years ago that water would be delivered to our homes and would come up more or less on its own to every floor and that no maid would have to carry it any more, that we could cook with gas and petroleum and without wood and coal etc.—he would have been accused of telling fairy tales.
>
> If anyone would have imagined some 10 or 20 years ago that in place of the pretty little sewing table there would be a sewing machine, or that a washing machine would be in the washroom, he would have been greeted with derision.
>
> These are reforms and revolutions in the economic sphere that are supplemented by countless greater ones—and it goes on and on and continues to go on! (Pp. 250–51)

5. Elaine Showalter, *A Literature of Their Own: British Women Novelists from Brontë to Lessing* (Princeton, N.J.: Princeton University Press, 1977), p. vii.

11

Annette von Droste-Hülshoff and Critics of "Die Judenbuche"

Maruta Lietina-Ray

Annette von Droste-Hülshoff is acknowledged to be the most important German woman writer of the nineteenth century, and her novella "Die Judenbuche" ("The Jews' Beech Tree") is recognized as a masterpiece. The novella has been translated into eight languages and is required reading in much of West Germany. Yet, though generally praised, it is frequently faulted for "errors" and "mistakes"; it is not accorded the autonomy of a work of art with its own artistic integrity or approached with the same respect shown works by German male authors. Most critics also refer to Droste in a patronizing way as "Annette," although none refer to male authors in this fashion. The critical opinions expressed are so unusual that they raise the question of whether there is a difference in the way important women writers' work is critically received and whether the writers' sex does not influence both male and female critics. Drawing upon criticism published on Droste's "Judenbuche" over the past hundred forty years in Germany and the United States, this chapter will study the image of the woman writer and will concentrate on the consistency or change in critical views of a woman's work.

The novella begins with a poetic epigraph that introduces social prejudice as the theme of the story. The story is about everyday life in an isolated rural community, about the customs, mores, and relationships of the villagers and about the relationships between the villagers and the ruling aristocracy. The content is reflected in Droste's own title for the story, "A Portrayal of the Customs of the Hill Country of Westphalia." This title was changed to "The Jews' Beech Tree" by the editor of the newspaper in which the novella was first published in 1842. Droste's own title was relegated to the position of subtitle and has remained such ever since. Unfortunately, most critics ignore the subtitle, which more appropriately indicates the content of the story. Thus, Clemens Heselhaus, for example, says that Droste's title has become "superfluous," although "it very aptly states the intention of the author to simultaneously render a portrayal of the customs, practices, and mores."[1]

The story focuses on Friedrich Mergel whose parents' notoriety rubs off upon him. When the Jew Aaron is murdered, the villagers suspect Mergel to be the killer. Droste's narrative provides no grounds for their suspicions, and it is only endemic social prejudice that makes Mergel into the murderer. By the same token, Johannes, an illegitimate look-alike for Mergel and probably his cousin, is regarded with equal but different prejudice as naive, innocent, simpleminded and incapable of doing evil. After the murder both Mergel and Johannes disappear, and the murderer is never brought to justice. The Jewish community purchases the beech tree under which Aaron's body was found and inscribes on the bark in Hebrew the sentence "When you approach this place, the same thing will happen to you that you did to me," to stand as a living memorial of the murder.

The story resumes twenty-eight years later when a broken old man returns to the village. He is recognized as Johannes. Yet, when he subsequently commits suicide by hanging himself on the beech tree, the Baron, who acts as the local judge and jury, orders that people be told that the suicide is Friedrich and not Johannes, as everyone had thought. Even in death prejudice against Friedrich prevails.

Despite the fact that the true murderer is never positively identified, most critics of the story perceive it to be a murder mystery. Friedrich is taken to be the murderer, and the Baron's "identification" of the corpse is assumed to be infallible. The critics then proceed to analyze how and why Friedrich became a murderer. Having made these a priori assumptions, critics then complain that the remainder of the story dealing with the mores, practices and life of the Westphalians is extrinsic and irrelevant to the "murder" story.

Droste was inspired to write her story after reading an allegedly true account, written down by her uncle, of similar events, which occurred in Westphalia in the eighteenth century.[2] It is the tale of a villager who murders a Jew, flees and is captured by slave traders, spends years as a slave in Algeria, returns to his native village and is pardoned but eventually hangs himself in the woods. This eighteenth-century story must be mentioned because it has become a major focus for the analysis of the novella. Heselhaus believes that precisely in its deviation from the source, the novella becomes a work of art.[3] That this is indeed the case is confirmed by Droste herself in a letter written to a friend three years before the work was published. She emphasizes that the character of the murderer in the source is very different from the character of *her* (Droste's italics) Mergel.[4] Thus, though acknowledging that her inspiration was drawn from the source, Droste differentiates between her work and the source and confirms that her work is the product of a conscious creative process.

Among the critics who were interested in comparing Droste's novella with its historical "model," Walter Silz notes that Droste departed "radically from her 'source,' " and Julius Schwering feels that "Annette is taking liberties" with the "model."[5] Heinz Rölleke also accuses Droste of "deviating" from the model, because she "cruelly" lets Mergel end up in the carrion pit, while in the model the suicide is buried in a cemetery.[6] Reading such criticism one wonders why Shakespeare's or Brecht's plays are not similarly judged on their historical accuracy or faithfulness to their sources. In Droste's case, perhaps the critics are preoccupied with the "model" because of their inclination not to take the creativity of a woman writer seriously and to show how she has muddled the "truth." Whatever the motive, these critics have denied the novella its artistic autonomy.

While much attention has been devoted to the source, which is essentially peripheral to the novella, little attention has been given to the story's poetic epigraph. The epigraph states that it is impossible for one human being to judge another fairly, and expressly forbids anyone to judge his inferiors. Most critics simply ignore the poem, probably because, as their interpretations suggest, the poem does not fit their inductive murder-mystery explication. If the poem is mentioned, it is dissociated from the rest of the novella. Thus Heselhaus wants to make the author of the poem different from the rest of the novella, because "if the two are *not* differentiated, one would have consequently to assume that Droste indeed has left open the question whether Friedrich Mergel is or is not involved in the murder."[7] The poem has nothing to do with a murder mystery, which is what Heselhaus wanted the novella to be. Therefore, the epigraph must be removed to make the story fit the critic's scheme.

In dealing with the content, critics also ignore the author's portrayal of the customs and mores of the Westphalians. Theodore Fontane in 1890 complains that the novella consists of two stories and too much material for its scope.

I feel that the story of the uncle [Friedrich's uncle, suspected father of Johannes], deserves to be made into the focus and the story about the Jews would then be omitted, but if Annette wanted rather to tell the latter tale, which also has much to recommend it, then the former with the uncle should have been only a minor incident, not a rival plot.[8]

Again, what Droste has written is not thought to be of central importance. Instead, the critic's personal wishes, how he would have written the story, are the basis for the criticism. Emil Staiger similarly asserted that the village wedding scene is superfluous and does not contribute to the murder story.[9] If Staiger had studied the content of the work, he would have seen it as one of many village weddings in the novella and one that portrays the Baron's blindness to the true relationships among his villagers whom he does not really know. Since Droste has given the reader ample proof of the absence of intimacy between the Baron and his people, the Baron's identification of the body at the end of the novella should seem all the more questionable.

It is also noteworthy that many German critics never question the Baron's identification of the corpse. It would appear that they respect too greatly the social authority vested in the Baron. Robert Koenig states: "The Baron, together with his family, is an appealing personality. Unprejudiced, fair, and brimming with love for his neighbor, he is not only a circumspect guardian of order, but also a helpful friend and counselor to the villagers."[10] Erik Wolf states: "Authority as an 'office' is always right and must be maintained against insubordination."[11] In contrast to this, an English-speaking critic, Betty N. Weber, believes that Droste exposed the limitations of feudalistic protection. Though seemingly solicitous of its subjects, "rather than institute measures for preventing destitution, the aristocracy provides niggardly refuge for the casualties of the existing order."[12] That the novella ends in 1789, the year of the French Revolution, is a further indication to Weber of the underlying social injustice depicted in the novella.

That the Baron's word is to be trusted, while the narrator's, Droste's, is not, appears most clearly in discussions of the final scene, when the Baron looks intently at a scar on the body of the suicide before announcing that the suicide is to be called "Friedrich." Nowhere before in the story has such a scar been mentioned, therefore, objectively seen, it cannot serve as a positive means of identification. Yet some critics persist in referring to it as the decisive factor in solving the mystery, while chastizing Droste for "forgetting" to include it earlier in the story. They overlook the fact that in an earlier fragment of the novella Droste did endow Friedrich with a scar but removed it in all later versions.[13] This must have been done to conceal the identity of the murderer. The only critic who perceived the scar differently, as a topos of recognition going back to Ulysses, is Gerard Oppermann. He summarizes the attacks on Droste for "forgetting" to include the scar earlier and then says, "Is this objection justified or can ways and arguments be found to vindicate the writer in the eyes of her exegetes?"[14] He is not simply offering a new interpretation of the novella but trying to find ways to show that Droste is acting deliberately and that the absence of the scar is not the result of sloppy writing. The appropriateness of Oppermann's argument is seen from the fact that Droste criticism is all too often ad hominem.

Exception is also taken to Droste because she is "merciless." Ernest Feist finds that Droste's ending is devoid of the "mercy" that otherwise governs the "maternal heart" of the author.[15] Thus it appears that for a woman writer certain attitudes and subjects are deemed suitable, others not; her literary work should reflect maternal instincts, justice, goodness and kindness. One marvels that the reverse demands are not made of male authors: reflection of paternal instincts, injustice, evil, and cruelty.

In addition to criticism directed at specific aspects of the novella, sweeping evaluations abound. Levin Schücking in 1862 calls it one of the "most excellent '*Dorfgeschichten*' in German literature."[16] Julian Schmidt said that the atmosphere of the story bespeaks great talent, while the plot is maddeningly confused.[17] Adele Schopenhauer feels it successfully captures reality.[18] The contradictory nature of Droste criticism is exemplified by Fontane (1890) and Paul Ernst (1904). Fontane wrote that "pretty and noteworthy as it is," he "would not rank it among the best works; although it exudes atmosphere and is very effective, still it lacks artistry and technique."[19] Ernst wrote that "Die

Judenbuche'' belongs among the most outstanding novellas ever written in Germany. Yet, he claimed that Droste did not write it; *it wrote itself*: "Now Annette belongs to those writers who only minimally consciously guide the creative process. . . . We have in Annette's work the result of an unintentional activity of artistic imagination." Furthermore, Ernst says that Droste's "conscious artistic will" was very limited and therefore she should be called a dilettante. "Thus we have here a truly remarkable example of the independent existence of artistic form."[20] Rudolf A. Schroder similarly comments that it appears that "Annette" has attained the pinnacle of art almost in a semiconscious state, while others have to struggle step by step to reach such perfection.[21]

A brief look at the criticism of Droste's poetry—and Droste was primarily a poet—yields a very different picture. Commentators are generally more appreciative of its uniqueness and originality, and they make a genuine effort to understand what Droste is saying. Ironically, the very qualities—uniqueness, originality, individuality—for which her poetry is lauded call forth negative opinions when they appear in her novella, which is nevertheless considered among the best ever written in the German language. Since 1962 most critics of her poetry refer to the author as "Droste," and of fourteen critics surveyed, only two men and two women still refer to her as "Annette." They do so in the extreme, however, speaking even of "Annette-poems" and "Annette-research" (imagine: "Tom-novels, Tom-research" when speaking of Thomas Mann).

In summary, what then is the image of Droste the writer as reflected in criticism of her "Judenbuche"? Referring to her persistently as "Annette," critics demonstrate a familiar, patronizing and disrespectful attitude. Criticism is frequently ad hominem. Droste is seen as an inept dilettante who cannot even retell the facts found in her source correctly. She has poor control of the novella form and poor technique. She is not feminine or maternal because she is cruel to her hero. She does not know her own plot and in fact does not even write the novella. It writes itself. She is seldom given credit for conscious creative artistry; yet the paradox remains that the novella is a masterpiece of German literature.

This general image of Droste as a bungling dilettante who is not responsible for the excellence of her novella remained constant from the 1840's until the mid-1960's, when some critics began to approach the work differently. Unlike their predecessors, who did not attend to the text but forced it into their own preconceptions about what Droste should or would have said, other critics now look at what has actually been written. It happens that for the most part these critics are American women, and their work has not yet had an appreciable impact on critics in Germany.[22] Their approach to Droste's work does not seem a matter of "feminist" literary criticism but rather an outgrowth of their literary-critical training. Their methods are different from those of the German critics. Thus the critic's nationality or country of training seems to influence the type of criticism more than his or her sex. Americans of both sexes appear more open-minded and sex blind, while German critics of both sexes seem to approach Droste's work with less respect than that shown to male writers. It is unfortunate that there are no other nineteenth-century German women writers of Droste's stature, for a comparison of the critical reception of several women writers would prove revealing. One is left to wonder whether some German literary criticism is not governed by the critic's own social and cultural prejudice—against women in general and against aristocratic, neurotic spinster-poets who dabble in prose, that is, Droste, in particular.

NOTES

1. Clemens Heselhaus, *Annette von Droste-Hülshoff: Werk und Leben* (Dusseldorf: A. Bagel, 1971), p. 155. This and all subsequent translations from the German are mine.

2. August von Haxthausen, "Geschichte eines Algierer-Sklaven," *Wünschelruthe. Ein Zeitblatt*, ed. H[einrich] Straube and J[ohann] P[eter] von Hornthal (Gottingen), nos. 11–15, February 5–19, 1818, pp. 41f., 46f., 50f., 55, 59f.

3. Heselhaus, *Annette von Droste-Hülshoff*, p. 158.

4. *Die Briefe der Annette von Droste-Hülshoff*, ed. Karl Schulte Kemminghausen, 2 vols. (Darmstadt: Wissenschaftliche Buchgesellschaft, 1968), I: 367.

5. Heinz Rölleke, *Annette von Droste-Hülshoff: "Die Judenbuche"* (Bad Homburg, Berlin, Zurich: Gehlen, 1970), p. 195, lists the critiques of Huffer, 1880; Redegeld, 1895; Franzos, 1897; Loewenberg, 1920; Keck, 1925; Ocke, 1927; Meisel, 1928; and Flaskamp, 1937. See also Walter Silz, *Realism and Reality* (Chapel Hill: University of North Carolina Press, 1954), p. 46. Robert Koenig, *Annette von Droste-Hülshoff. Ein Lebens- und Literaturbild* (Heidelberg, 1883), p. 22, quotes Julius Schwering.

6. Heinze Rölleke, "Erzähltes Mysterium: Studie zur 'Judenbuche' der Annette von Droste-Hülshoff," *DVjs*, 42 (1968), 417.

7. Heselhaus, *Annette von Droste-Hülshoff*, p. 152. Here Heselhaus is referring to the murder of the forester Brandis.

8. Rölleke, *Annette von Droste-Hülshoff*, p. 189.

9. Emil Staiger, *Annette von Droste-Hülshoff* (Horgen-Zurich and Leipzig: Münster-Presse, 1933), p. 60. This is offset by Edson Chick, "Voices in Discord: Some Observations on 'Die Judenbuche,'" *GO* 42 (March 1969), pp. 147–57.

10. Koenig, *Annette von Droste-Hülshoff*, p. 38.

11. Erik Wolf, *Vom Wesen des Rechts in deutscher Dichtung: Hölderlin. Stifter. Hebel. Droste.* (Frankfurt: Klostermann, 1946), p. 235.

12. Betty Nance Weber, "Droste's 'Judenbuche': Westphalia in International Context," *Germanic Review* 50 (1975), 210, n. 27.

13. For discussion of the scar, see Maruta Lietina-Ray, "Das Recht der öffentlichen Meinung: Über das Vorurteil in der 'Judenbuche,'" *Zeitschrift fur deutsche Philologie, Sonderheft: Annette von Droste-Hülshoff, "Die Judenbuche." Neue Studien und Interpretationen* 99 (1979), 99–109. See also Heselhaus, *Annette von Droste-Hülshoff*, p. 153, and Rölleke, *Annette von Droste-Hülshoff*, p. 231.

14. Gerard Oppermann, "Die Narbe des Friedrich Mergel: Zur Aufklärung eines literarischen Motivs in Annette von Droste-Hülshoff's 'Die Judenbuche,'" *DVjs*, 50 (1976), 449.

15. Ernst Feist, " 'Die Judenbuche' von Annette von Droste-Hülshoff," *Monatshefte*, 35 (December, 1943), 415.

16. Levin Schücking as quoted in Rölleke, *Annette von Droste-Hülshoff*, p. 188.

17. Julian Schmidt as quoted in Clemens Heselhaus, "Statt einer Wirkungsgeschichte: Die Aufnahme der postumen Werke der Droste," *Jahrbuch der Droste-Gesellschaft* 5 (1972), 131.

18. Adele Schopenhauer as quoted in Rölleke, *Annette von Droste-Hülshoff*, 188.

19. Fontane as quoted in Ibid.

20. All Ernst quotations are from Rölleke, *Annette von Droste-Hülshoff*, pp. 189–92.

21. Rudolf A. Schroder as quoted in Rölleke, *Annette von Droste-Hülshoff*, p. 193.

22. For such criticism see: (1) Jane K. Brown, "The Real Mystery in Droste-Hülshoff's 'Die Judenbuche,'" *MLR*, 73 (October, 1978), 835–45; (2) Janet K. King, "Conscience and Conviction in 'Die Judenbuche,'" *Monatshefte* 64 (Winter, 1972), 349–55; (3) Betty Nance Weber, see note 12; and (4) Maruta Lietina-Ray, see note 13. By comparison, at a three-day Colloquium on "Die

Judenbuche'' sponsored by the Droste-Gesellschaft in Münster, West Germany in November 1978, only two of the fourteen lecturers deviated from the murder-mystery interpretation of the novella. The major papers read at the colloquium have been published; see note 13.

12

Toward a New Freedom: Rahel Varnhagen and the German Women Writers before 1848

Doris Starr Guilloton

Given the restricted status of women in Germany until recently, it is all the more noteworthy that the cause of their emancipation was championed nearly two hundred years ago. Its major spokeswomen—first Rahel Varnhagen and then Luise Mühlbach, Countesse Hahn-Hahn and Fanny Lewald—represent the two literary generations between 1790 and 1850 known as German Romanticism and "Young Germany" (*Junqes Deutschland*). During the Romantic period, to be sure, the idea of feminism was barely hinted at. But its roots can be found in Rahel Varnhagen von Ense, famous for her literary salon in Berlin and considered the German Mme de Staël.[1] Not an activist in the strict sense of the word, she nevertheless set forth women's right to self-determination and recommended a reevaluation of their status, both in the family and in society.[2]

Although she was unquestionably the most prominent women's advocate of her time in Germany, there were other writers who shared in her quest for women's identity. For example, Sophie Mereau (later married to Clemens Brentano), espoused—in the guise of fiction—women's emancipation in her belletristic journals and novels.[3] The wives of the Schlegel brothers, Dorothea and Caroline, found a vehicle for their feminist stance in the major Romantic journal *Athenaeum* (1798–1800). Their anonymous contributions express the conviction that women have a natural right to share in intellectual and social life.[4] In 1832, with the translation of Mary Wollstonecraft's *Vindication of the Rights of Woman* (1792), Henriette Herz also helped pave the way to the later women's movement in Germany.[5]

These Romantic feminists furthered the cause also through their personal involvement in public life. They founded literary salons, which became centers for the exchange of the leading intellectual and political views of the time. Rahel Varnhagen and Henriette Herz played an active part in their Berlin salons; Caroline and Dorothea Schlegel left their mark on the Jena circle (*Jenaer Schule*). Bettina von Arnim, however, the most celebrated writer of her day and famous for her soirées in Berlin and Rome, did not take a feminist stand (as had been erroneously assumed by the critics). The most frequented salon was that of Rahel Varnhagen. Despite financial difficulties, health problems and political complications, she managed to conduct her Berlin salon from 1789 until the Napoleonic invasion of 1806, and then again from 1819 until shortly before her death in 1833. Poets and philosophers, princes and diplomats, sympathizers with the *Ancien Régime* and liberals of *Young Germany* valued her opinion and vied for her attention.[6]

Although Rahel Varnhagen did not use her salon explicitly as a feminist platform, she was perceived as a pioneer of women's intellectual emancipation in her own circles as one may gather from her husband's memoirs.[7] The women's issue had been in the air since the Age of Reason, and her class was aware of the fashionable practice of letter writing. This legacy of the eighteenth-century epistolary genre, the so-called *Women's Letters* (*Frauenbriefe*)—or the many moralistic journals of the time—were controlled by women and attested to their involvement in education and human rights issues. Varnhagen surely knew of the Gottsched couple, champions of Enlightenment in the early part of the eighteenth century, who had promoted the women's cause through their insistence on female education.[8] Theodor Gottlieb von Hippel's *On the Improvement of Women's Lot in Society* (*Uber die bürgerliche Verbesserung der Weiber*, 1792), inspired by the human rights proclamation of the French Revolution, continued to stimulate the self-confidence of women. He had stipulated a priori that the idea of woman's ''inferiority'' was merely a fallacy of social convention.[9]

New support for women's sense of identity came from Fichte's perception of the universe as a projection of the self—the philosophy of German Idealism, which made no distinction between the sexes—

extolling the spiritual force as the unifying and equalizing basis of all creation. For Rahel Varnhagen, who was acquainted with Fichte's writings, this was a reinforcement of her own belief in the equality of the sexes. Later, she found Hegel's philosophy similarly supportive of her views.[10] She was, however, most indebted to Schleiermacher, whose *Catechism of Reason for Noble Women* provided the framework for her approach to the problem of women's emancipation. She liked to quote him as for instance in the following passage: "*Creed*: I believe that I do not live to obey . . . but to be and to become . . . and I believe in the power of the will and of education . . . to make me independent of the bonds of sex."[11] Varnhagen assimilated all these ideas in the hope of giving women's lives new purpose and direction.[12]

Her feminism surfaced in three volumes of correspondence and diary records.[13] In reviewing them Carlyle declared her "a singular biographic phenomenon of her century; a woman of genius, of true depth and worth . . . a woman equal to the highest thought of her century. . . . the highest philosopher, or poet, or artist was not above her, but of a like element and rank with her."[14] Although Varnhagen's pioneering ideas on women are scattered throughout her writings in an almost off-handed manner, their message is forceful. She focused on personal freedom, marriage and family, motherhood and its legal implications, education and the political organization of women.

By the early 1790's Varnhagen expressed the need for greater mobility of women and the removal of social restrictions. She was critical of the double standards of personal conduct, which favored men (I: 63). Twenty-five years later she was still fighting the same tabus that she considered an infringement upon women's freedom. "A woman's desire for greater independence," she wrote 1819, "is interpreted by man as lack of femininity" (II: 564). Rahel Varnhagen was already well aware of sexual politics; she implied in this passage that men, eager to discourage emancipatory behavior, interpret women's drive for independence as some form of biological aberration.

She also took issue with the fact that women were relegated to insignificant work without recourse to independent activities of their own. She wrote bitterly:

While men—at least in their own eyes—view their occupation as important, the execution of which flatters their ambition, and wherein they see progress. . . . we women have forever merely degrading bits and pieces before us, the small tasks and chores that have to relate completely to the man's position. (II: 564)

Considering woman's position in family and marriage, Varnhagen concluded that there is more to her happiness and fulfillment than marriage and children. Even though she believed that family obligations must have priority in a woman's life, she resisted society's view, which takes woman's self-sacrifice for granted. In 1819, she wrote:

It is human ignorance if people imagine that our intellect is different and was created for different purposes, and that for example, we could live completely off our husbands' or our sons' existence. . . . But this is not so; of course, one loves, cherishes, cares for the desires of one's own, complies with them, makes them the center of one's greatest care and most urgent occupation; but they cannot fulfill or strengthen and invigorate us throughout our lives. (II: 564)

She found the difference in status between men and women comparable to that of nations in "that men and women are two different nations in Europe" (I: 312) where the lesser one—women—was at a cruel disadvantage. She agreed with Friedrich Schlegel that the selfish behavior of men was a throwback to the earlier stages of evolution, which leaves women no choice but to manipulate them in turn (II: 116).

In a letter, Varnhagen once described what men in her class would consider the most desirable woman—it would be one "who can teach music, English and Italian, who can speak and write German and French, who performs the most beautiful feminine tasks, is a perfect cook who knows also how to bottle food, and who is happy and understanding to boot" (II: 116f.). On the other hand, she wondered whether the man might ever make it his objective in life to please woman, apart from believing that by marrying her he had done enough for her. "A man thinks he's done all there is to do when he's married a woman; and that is only the beginning of the job," reads one of her diary notes written in French, with the conclusion that actually it would be best if he made her forget he married her (III: 182).[15] Indeed, she considered conventional marriage one of the worst social evils. "Slave trade, wars, marriage!—and people are surprised and patch up things" (I: 259). Influenced by Saint Simon, she later lashed out against marriage as an institution. "Let's level this nuisance to the ground!" she cried out with passion, "and all that is to live on the earth will flourish on it. A real vegetation!" (III: 182) A year before her death she tried to describe what she considered to be an ideal marriage: "Let's have a marriage, and with it freedom as well. One should be able to live in and out of marriage. Let there be a model marriage which speaks for itself through deeds . . . consent based on insight and affection . . . joining what we perceive as the Highest" (III: 550).

While emphasizing the ideal side of marital union, Varnhagen believed that sanctions of the church and the law would be detrimental to it. She also recognized (nearly a century before Engels) that they would reinforce the inherent inequity in a marriage which was rooted in the property rights of the husband.[16] For all these reasons Varnhagen advocated legislation that would consider marriage a private agreement between consenting partners. It should be pointed out that in her own marriage to K. A. Varnhagen, she had achieved the ideal form of an "emancipated" marriage, but she knew that her case was an exception to the rule. With these views she was far ahead of her time. Neither her successors of young Germany nor the later women's movements were receptive to them with the exception of a radical organization, the League for the Protection of Mothers (*Bund für Mutterschutz*) in the 1920's.[17]

Another issue in Rahel Varnhagen's reform plans dealt with maternal rights. She pleaded for the legal protection of both mother and child—whether in or out of wedlock. She condemned the injustice done to both because of social prejudice, penalizing the illegitimate children and stigmatizing the mothers as immoral while men got away with impunity (III: 19). Double standards for men and women, "one moral, the other not," she wrote, "is absolutely unacceptable" (I: 312). Not unlike later feminists, she also insisted that all children—whether legitimate or not—bear their mothers' last name and that mothers control "the assets and power of the families." In this way the female sex would be somewhat compensated for natural and social injustice. "Nature is horrible," she explained, "in that a woman can be misused and can bear a human being against her wish and will. Human institutions have to compensate for this profound insult" (III: 19). It was not until the twentieth century that the problem of illegitimacy and protective laws—however inadequately—was addressed again, thanks to the suffragettes.

For Rahel Varnhagen, education and vocational training were essential for a woman, mainly for the purpose of self-realization. She was not yet as concerned with the economic implications as the women writers of Young Germany would be somewhat later. She demanded access for women to the university lecture halls as regular students, not only as auditors. (In 1811, she herself had been auditor in the classes of Fichte and Schleiermacher.) This was another way of rebelling against those who questioned women's ability for intellectual tasks, for the so-called "männliche Geistesarbeitan," such as writing (III: 10). In contra-distinction to Germaine de Staël, Rahel Varnhagen refused to conceive of a person's sex as a yardstick for the measurement of accomplishment. "Would Fichte's works have been worse if his wife had written them?" (III: 10) In keeping with an eighteenth-century tradition among the educated, Varnhagen's reference to women's vocational abilities does not go much beyond the activity of writing, whereas the next generation would call for a broadening of womens' occupations in the middle class.

Yet unlike the other leading women of the Romantic era who carried out their activities within the shelter of their own social milieu, she became interested in the training of lower-class women. After she had worked together with a great many women during the 1813 Wars of Liberation and again during the 1831 epidemic of Berlin, she decided that they were particularly suited for nursing and social tasks (II: 91; III: 465). Though feminists today might argue that she tried to pigeonhole women into "womanly" jobs, Varnhagen should nevertheless be given credit for promoting their professional abilities at a time when women were inconsequential in the labor market.

Varnhagen was the first leading woman in Germany to sense the need for political organization. To further international understanding during the Wars of Liberation, Varnhagen wanted to establish a European group of women with pacifist aims and as a relief agency during the wars (II: 137). She was convinced that it was "in the nature of men to hurt and destroy" and that therefore women had a mission to counteract this with group action (II: 89). She noted: "I have a plan in mind which calls upon all European women never to participate in war again and to stand together in helping all suffering people; then we would have a guarantee for peace at least as far as we women are concerned'' (II: 126).

Almost twenty years later, on the occasion of Berlin's cholera epidemic, she reiterated her admiration for the untapped capacities of the women in her rescue teams. She was convinced that their civic sense and skills would also make them excellent public administrators. Shortly before her death, in 1833, she wrote: "Women should be on the board of directors of poverty programs; there are a thousand widows and other fine women suited for this" (III: 524). It was, indeed, extraordinary in the society of her time to suggest that women from all walks of life participate actively in public affairs.

Rahel Varnhagen's espousal and articulation of feminist interests coupled with her keen sense of social norms set her far above her Romantic counter-parts. It was only a generation later, in the 1830's and 1840's, that the women writers of Young Germany carried on her work. Luise Müller, Ida Hahn-Hahn and Fanny Lewald were probably the most effective ones. Other known writers of the time like Malvida von Meysenbug and Louise Otto-Peters who pleaded the cause of women were more widely identified with the emancipation of women during the Bismarck era in the last decades of the nineteenth century. Some like Mathilde Franziska Anneke emigrated to the United States and continued their work there.[18]

Varnhagen's immediate successors addressed themselves—usually in the form of fiction—to most of the feminist questions she had raised before them less pragmatically. They, too, requested greater freedom for women in public and private life and protested against their subordinate role in the family. They, too, proposed educational equality and the use of women's vocational potential, but their social frame of reference was different. They focused on the improvement of marriage in its existing form and on better divorce laws rather than pushing for common-law marriage like Varnhagen. They limited themselves mostly to their own classes—the aristocracy and the bourgeoisie—in dealing with emancipatory issues while Varnhagen had used a more universal approach. Essentially, the authors of this new generation shared similar perspectives; only the emphasis and the nuances differed.

Luise Müller, with no fewer than two hundred ninety novels to her name—mostly historical, dealt with women's issues only in those written between 1838 and 1849. In what is viewed as her best novel, *Aphra Behn*, she illustrated the differences of women's struggle according to class levels: their orientation was more ideological in the aristocracy and more economic in the middle class.[19]

It was typical for this group of women writers to deal with the issues of equality in the larger context of socio-political concerns. This is evidenced in ten novels (foremost in *Two Women* and *Faustine*) written *before* 1848 by Countess Hahn-Hahn, who is sometimes called the German George Sand.[20] The various principles of women's emancipation are dealt with in an aristocratic milieu. Based on her own marital problems, and observations gathered during her world travels, her feminist pleas entail a criticism of the double standard of the nobility. Another new element in her writing is her insistence that the sexes should not be fixed in their stereotypical roles any longer but must be considered individuals. The following excerpt illustrates her sense of society's perversity in this domain: "send the girls to the universities and the boys to sewing schools and to the kitchen: after three generations you will know, whether it is impossible [to equal men] and what it means to be the suppressed ones."[21]

Another work bearing witness to women's inequality as an endemic problem of the given class structure was written by Fanny Lewald, a wealthy bourgeoise of the merchant class. In her multi-volume autobiography, *The Story of My Life* (*Meine Lebensgeschichte*, 1811–1845), she gave a vivid picture of the fate of young middle-class women under Metternich:[22]

For five hours every day I sat in the living room at a certain spot by the window and learned how to darn stockings and linen and assisted with tailoring and other work. Two hours were spent at the piano, for one hour I bored myself with my old schoolbooks which I knew by heart from beginning to end, for an additional hour I copied poems to practice my handwriting. In between I did errands between the kitchen and the pantry and between the living room and the children's room . . . and in the evening I had the depressing feeling of not having accomplished anything sensible, deeply envious of my brothers who were privileged to attend the Gymnasium.[23]

The middle class had adopted the leisure ideals of the aristocracy and therefore condemned its daughters to a nonprofessional existence and the expectation of an appropriate marriage. Fanny Lewald realized that the suppression of educational advancement and the idleness imposed on the female members of a household were not only disastrous for women themselves but in many cases ruinous to the economic structure of the whole family.[24] Over the years Fanny Lewald tended to take an ever broader view of feminist causes. Whereas Luise Müller and Ida Hahn-Hahn wrote largely of women's woes, Lewald emphasized in her writings that men, too, needed to be emancipated.

To conclude we should perhaps mention the colorful Luise Aston— Lady Aston by marriage—even though her writings are sparse and hardly known. She was probably the most forceful spokeswoman for the equality of *all* people: women, the working class, and the oppressed in general. Her marriage of fourteen years to an English industrialist had given her insight into the life of the working classes. In her novel, *Revolution and Counterrevolution*, she pleaded for a new order. Her participation on the barricades in Berlin in March 1848, her liberal views, and her free life-style in the manner of George Sand— smoking cigars and wearing men's clothes—provoked the authorities and finally led to her expulsion from that city "as a person dangerous to the state."[25] Astutely, she took this not only as an insult to individual freedom but as a covert anti-feminist act by Prussian authorities.

Unfortunately, these writers abandoned their feminist stance in the reactionary climate that followed the failure of the revolution in March 1848. But they represented an important force in the history of feminism. Their courageous statements during the Restoration period of Metternich enlarged the basis—laid by Rahel Varnhagen—for the new canon adopted by the women's organizations in the era of Bismarck during the last decades of the nineteenth century. Their feminist consciousness led also to the larger evolution of socialism and the concept of women's rights in the twentieth century.

NOTES

1. Vaughan Jennings, *Rahel: Her Life and Letters* (London: Henry S. King, 1876), p. 10. Thomas Carlyle: "We say not that she was equal to de Staël, or the contrary; neither that she might have written far better books. She has ideas unequalled in de Staël; a sincerity, a pure tenderness and genuineness which that celebrated person had not, or had lost." *Critical and Miscellaneous Essays* (Boston: J. Munroe & Co., 1838), p. 534.

For further commentary about Varnhagen in contemporary Germany, see Vilma Lober, "Die Frauen der Romantik im Urteil ihrer Zeit" (Diss., Erlangen, 1947).

2. Isolated references to Varnhagen's feminism can be found in the following biographies: Otto Berdrow, *Rahel Varnhagen: ein Leben und Zeitbild* (Stuttgart: Greiner und Pfeiffer, 1902); Lore Feist, "Rahel Varnhagen: Zwischen

Romantik und Jungem Deutschland" (Diss., Munich/Eberfeld, 1927); Emma Graf, *Rahel Varnhagen und die Romantik* (Berlin: E. Felber, 1903); Vaughan Jennings, *Rahel: Her Life and Letters* (London: Henry S. King, 1876); Ellen Key, *Rahel: Eine biographische Skizze* (Leipzig: Haberland, 1908). Herbert Scurla, *Begegnungen mit Rahel: Der Salon der Rahel Levin* (Berlin: Verlag der Nation, 1966, 4th ed.). In Hannah Arendt's much acclaimed book *Rahel Varnhagen* (Munich: R. Piper, 1962), Varnhagen's feminism is completely disregarded. On the other hand, Claire May's brief study, which appeared in the German Democratic Republic, "Rahel: Ein Berliner Frauenleben im 19. Jahrhundert," *Das neue Berlin* (1949), 22–95, emphasizes her feminist commitment, and it deserves special mention.

3. Sophie Mereau, *Das Blutenalter der Empfindung* (Gotha, 1794), *Eduard und Amanda* (Frankfurt, 1800–1803); her best known journal is *Kalathiskos* (Berlin, 1801–2).

4. Bedrow, *Rahel Varnhagen*, p. 102. Alice Apt, *Caroline und die frühromantische Gesellschaft* (Dresden: Germania, 1936), p. 55. Cf. *Athenaeum*, ed. A. W. and F. Schleel, vol. I, no. 2 (Berlin, 1798–1800), pp. 25, 111, 113; vol. II, no. 1, pp. 4, 20.

5. Her own statements do not indicate an emphatic feminist interest. See Henriette Herz, *Ihr Leben und ihre Erinnerungen*, ed. I. Furst (Berlin: W. Hertz, 1850).

6. For further reference on the salons of Varnhagen and others, see the above-mentioned biographies, as well as Ingeborg Drewitz, *Berliner Salons* (Berlin: Haude und Spener, 1965); Mary Hargrave, *Some German Women and their Salons* (London: T. Werner Laruie, Clifford's Inn, n.d.); Bertha Meyer, *Salon Sketches: Biographic Studies of Berlin Salons* (New York: Block, 1938). Jean-Edouard Spenlé, *Rahel: Mme Varnhagen von Ense. Histoire d'un salon romantique en Allemagne* (Paris: Hachette, 1910); Margaret Sussmann, *Frauen der Romantic* (Stuttgart: Metzler, 1960).

7. Karl August Varnhagen von Ense, *Denkwürdigkeiten und vermischte Schriften*, 25 vols. (Mannheim und Leipzig: Brockhaus, 1837–59), describes his wife's social life and the effect she had on others in vol. VIII.

8. See S. Etta Schreiber, *The German Woman in the Age of Enlightenment: A Study in the Drama from Gottsched to Lessing* (New York: Kings Crown Press, 1948), p. 61; see also Christine Touaillon, *Der deutsche Frauenroman des 18. Jahrhunderts* (Vienna: W. Braumüller, 1919), pp. 57–61.

9. See Helene Lange and Gertrude Baumer, *Die Geschichte der Frauenbewegung in den Kulturländern* (Berlin: Moeser, 1901), I: 8ff.

10. Jennings, *Rahel*, p. 17.

11. *Athenaeum*, vol. I, no. 3, pp. 109ff. from "Katechismus der Vernunft fur edle Frauen."

12. The role of the early Romantic theory for the advancement of the woman

is a moot point. In it, the concept of the woman was exalted as an ideal human being in whom nature and spirit, eros and charity are balanced to make her the redeemer of man and the mediator of Good (see Paul Kluckhohn, *Das Ideengut der deutschen Romantik* [Halle: Niemeyer, 1942], pp. 59ff.). Whether or not this view in the end served the purpose of emancipation may be left undecided.

13. Rahel Varnhagen von Ense, *Rahel, ein Buch des Andenkens fur ihre Freunde*, 3 vols. (Berlin: Duncker und Humblot, 1834). They were edited and published by her husband a year after her death. Hereafter the references to volumes and page numbers are listed in the text. Since the quoted texts have not been published in English, translations from the German are my own.

14. Carlyle, *Critical and Miscellaneous Essays*, p. 534.

15. "Un homme croit avoir tout fait quand il a épousé une femme; cela n'est que le commencement de l'oeuvre. . . . il doit lui faire oublier qu'il l'a épousée!"

16. Wanda Bronska-Pampych, "Ergebnis bei den Marxisten," in *Emanzipation und Ehe*, ed. Christa Rozoll (Munich: Dalp, 1968), p. 127.

17. Katherine Anthony, *Feminism in Germany and Scandinavia* (New York: Holt, 1915), pp. 92ff. For a general history see also Helene Lange, *Die Frauenbewegung in ihren modernen Problemen* (Leipzig: Quelle und Meyer, 1914).

18. Renata Mohrmann, ed., *Texte und Dokumente: Frauenemanzipation im Deutschen Vormarz* (Stuttgart: Reclam, 1978). It contains selected German texts by women writers of the 1848 generation from which my quotes are taken. The translations are my own. See also Hannelore Schröder, ed., *Die Frau ist frei geboren: Texte zur Frauenemanzipation, Band I: 1789–1870* (München: C. H. Beck Verlag, 1979).

19. Renata Mohrmann, *Die andere Frau: Emanzipationsansatze deutscher Schriftstellerinnen im Vorfeld der Achtundvierziger Revolution* (Stuttgart: Metzler, 1977), is the most comprehensive study on the subject. For lexical entries, see E. Friedrichs, *Die deutschsprachigen Schriftstellerinnen des 18. und 19. Jahrhunderts* (Metzler: Stuttgart, 1981). For a discussion of L. Mühlbach, see Mohrmann, *Die andere Frau*, pp. 60–84.

20. Mohrmann, *Die andere Frau*, pp. 85–117.

21. Mohrmann, *Texte und Dokumente*, p. 104.

22. Fanny Lewald, *Meine Lebensgeschichte*, ed. Gisela Brinker-Gabler (Frankfurt: Fischer Verlag, 1980).

23. Mohrmann, *Texte und Dokumente*, p. 16.

24. Ibid., pp. 175–85.

25. L. Aston, *Meine Emanzipation, Verweisung und Rechtfertigung* (Brussels, 1846), p. 18. Cf. Mohrmann, *Die andere Frau*, pp. 141–50.

13

A *Nigilistka* and a *Communarde*: Two Voices of the Nineteenth-Century Russian *Intelligentka*

Isabelle Naginski

The nineteenth century in Russia, by comparison with its European counterpart, is remarkable for having compressed several centuries of intellectual and literary development into one. Yet in this extraordinary cultural ferment, no overwhelmingly great women's voices can be heard—nothing, certainly, to compare with George Sand in France or George Eliot in England. Russia would have to wait for the early twentieth century to produce great literary women, and their chosen medium would be poetry—poets such as the Symbolist Gippius and her younger sisters, Akhmatova and Tsvetaeva.

But the absence of women writers in nineteenth-century Russia is only apparent. Their voices may be muffled, their works hard to find, their manuscripts lost from indifference or neglect, but with renewed interest in feminine *écriture*, Slavicists have rediscovered female voices that had fallen into undeserved obscurity. Until recently, few materials were available to the American public. But feminist scholars have been making up for lost time. I need only mention Barbara Held Monter's recent translation of Karolina Pavlova's *Double Life* (Ann Arbor, Mich.: Ardis, 1978) and Beatrice Stillman's translation of Sofia Kovalevskaia's *Memoirs* (New York: Springer-Verlag, 1978).

Two Russian women who flourished in the 1860's, 1870's and 1880's deserve to be heard for their own sake and as representatives of their time: two sisters, Anna Jaclard (1843–87) and Sofia Kovalevskaia (1850–91), born Anna and Sofia Korvin-Krukovskaia. To listen to them is to acquaint oneself with crucial aspects of Russian intellectual life in the second half of the nineteenth century. For the Korvin-Krukov-skaia sisters are multi-voiced. They articulated the intellectual concerns of their epoch, participated brilliantly in its literary life, and struggled with feminist questions that are still burning issues today.

I have labeled these two women a *communarde*, a female participant of the Paris Commune, and a *nigilistka*, a nihilist woman. The term *communarde* applies mostly to Anna, for she was directly involved in the events that shook France in the wake of the Franco-Prussian war. Anna was secretary of the Comité de Vigilance in the eighteenth *arrondissement* in Paris, in charge of hospitals, schools and prisons; she was a member of the central committee of the Union des Femmes and a founder, with the French feminist writer André Léo, of a daily newspaper, *La Sociale*.[1] The term *communarde* also applies to a lesser degree to Anna's sister Sofia, who visited Paris in April and May 1871 and assisted Anna in her revolutionary duties.[2]

The term *nigilistka* applies foremost to Sofia who wrote a novel by that title. But her older sister Anna was also called "the nihilist girl" by her family in the 1850's. At the time, the terms *nigilist/nigilistka* had become household words in Russia and were used to label an entire generation of young people in the way "beatnik" or "hippie" described the rebellious generations of the 1950s and 1960s in this country.[3] The caricatural tone of an 1864 description of a *nigilistka* in the reactionary paper *Vest'* (*The News*) is typical:

. . . nihilist women are usually very plain, exceedingly ungracious. . . . they dress with no taste and in impossibly filthy fashion, rarely wash their hands, never clean their nails, often wear glasses, always cut their hair short, and sometimes even shave it off. . . . they despise art, use the familiar form of the pronoun "you" with young men, light their cigarettes not from a candle but from other men who smoke, are uninhibited in their choice of expressions, live either alone or in phalansteries, and talk most of all about the exploitation of labor, the silliness of marriage and the family, and about anatomy.[4]

This physical description hardly fits the two Korvin-Krukovskaia sisters. Anna, especially, was a first-class beauty, "virtually a raving beauty," as her sister described her in her *Memoirs*: "tall, slender, with a flawless complexion and a mass of fair hair."[5] It is true, however, that she did go through a phase in which, as Sofia recounts: "she began to dress very simply in black dresses with plain collars, to wear her hair pulled back and covered by a net."[6] But the violence of the caricature is symptomatic of the extreme unease with which the establishment responded to the "new ideas," as they were called in the 1860s, especially as they infiltrated women's consciousnesses and lives.

Although Turgenev's *Fathers and Children* (often mistranslated as *Fathers and Sons*) concentrated on the generational discord between a son and his parents, an equally common pattern in those years was discord between daughters and their parents. As Sofia explains in her *Memoirs*:

. . . it might be said that during the decade between the beginning of the 1860s and the beginning of the 1870s, all the intellectual strata of Russian society were concerned with a single question: the family discord between the old and the young . . . these quarrels arose not from weighty material causes, but from questions of a purely theoretical and abstract nature. . . . the young girls particularly were seized at that time by something like an epidemic of running away from the parental home. . . . now one, now another landowner's daughter had run away—this one to Europe to study, that one to Petersburg, to the "Nihilists."[7]

Indeed, Sofia Kovalevskaia and Anna Jaclard are typical of their time, typical in the Lukácsian sense of being representative in the highest degree. Beatrice Stillman, describing the younger sister, could be speaking of both when she says:

. . . in [Kovalevskaia's] aversion to all form of established authority, whether vested in the monarchy, the landed gentry or one's own parents; her zeal for social reform and desire to render practical service in that struggle; her advocacy of individual rights while denying the validity of personal emotions; her passionate concern with "the woman's question," her infatuation with the natural sciences and in particular her sanguine trust in science itself as the truth that would make men free, Sofia was . . . behaving like a conformist, to the degree that these articles of faith were part of the repertoire of responses of the "girl of the sixties."[8]

One major theme of Sofia's *Memoirs* is to trace the impact of these new ideas not so much on herself as on her sister, and to chart Anna's transformation from a young girl steeped in Romantic historical novels into a young *nigilistka*. Sofia's description of Anna traces the steps taken by an entire generation of brilliant young women growing up in the sixties: Nadezhda Suslova, the first woman physician in Russia, Maria Bokova, prototype for the liberated heroine of Chernyshevsky's *What is to be Done?*, and Anna Evreinova, the first woman lawyer in Russia and editor of the journal *Severnyi vestnik* (*Northern Messenger*).[9] The *Memoirs*, therefore, can be read as a representative statement on the sentimental and intellectual education of a female "child of the century."

The two sisters put into practice the philosophies of their age. A fictitious marriage—the notorious *fiktivnyi brak*—allowed Sofia to escape the despised paternal house, and as a married woman, she was allowed to go abroad and to act as chaperone for her older sister. The trio—Sofia, Anna and Kovalevsky—crossed the border and headed for the cultural centers of Europe. With her gift for mathematics, Sofia went to the universities of Heidelberg and Berlin. She was never allowed to enroll formally in either, but on the basis of her brilliant work on partial differential equations, she was finally (and grudgingly) awarded a doctorate at the University of Göttingen. Kovalevskaia's life is a series of exceptional firsts for a woman: permission to attend (if unofficially) the universities of Germany, a teaching post at the University of Stockholm (the first such position to be held by a woman in Europe), winning the prestigious Bordin prize (the first to be awarded to a woman).

The older sister had a life both more dramatic in content and less successful in terms of achievement. While Sofia devoted herself to science, Anna concentrated her efforts on another preoccupation of her era—revolutionary activism. Sofia flourished in her chosen field, but Anna sacrificed a literary career in the name of revolution. Her efforts in that realm were thwarted and her life took on a distinctly tragic cast after the disastrous outcome of the Paris Commune. The reports in this respect are somewhat contradictory. Some say that she was condemned to forced labor for life; others claim that it was her husband who was imprisoned in Versailles and condemned to deportation and forced labor in New Caledonia. In any case, what is certain is that, with the help of Anna's father who was acquainted with Thiers, and the help of Kovalevsky, the young couple escaped first to Geneva and then to Russia. While Sofia became a great mathematician, Anna did not fulfill her promise as a talented young writer. Her four short stories are still available to us, but any other pieces she might have written are irretrievably lost.

Perhaps Anna is best known, under her maiden name, for having been proposed to by Dostoevsky and for having turned him down. The intellectual affair is sensitively recounted in her sister's *Memoirs*. Anna explains to Sofia her reasons for refusing to marry Dostoevsky and, in so doing she demystifies the role of a famous writer's wife:

. . . at first [she explains] I thought that maybe I could love him. But he needs quite a different wife from me. His wife must devote herself to him completely, completely, she must dedicate her entire life to him, think only about him. And that I cannot do, I myself want to live. And also he is so high-strung, so demanding. It's as if he were constantly taking possession of me, sucking me up in him; with him I could never be myself.[10]

It is hard to discern where "the seeds of revolt," to use Joseph Frank's phrase, were sown in the early life of the Korvin-Krukovskaia sisters: a strict upbringing, a deliberately inadequate education reluctantly provided by a despotic father; a patriarchal society that restricted women's roles to those of a dutiful daughter, obedient wife, and devoted mother.[11] Perhaps the best answer lies in the inordinately great talent these two women possessed, talent they did not always use to the fullest (both sisters died prematurely, Sofia at 41, Anna at 44), talent which did not always bring happiness, recognition, or a sense of fulfillment. It is perhaps in their literary works that their *angoisse*, their feeling of alienation, is best expressed, with almost tragic intensity.

PARTICIPATION IN THE LITERARY LIFE

A mathematician by trade, Sofia embarked on a literary career late in life. Her *Memoirs of Childhood* may at first glance seem to be in the tradition of the very popular genre of the childhood memoir (the *detstvo*) in Russia in the second half of the nineteenth century. But while Tolstoy, Aksakov, and Goncharov, the most famous representatives of that tradition in Russia, followed in the footsteps of their Western male predecessors, Kovalevskaia set herself apart from them by her choice of themes, her narrative strategies and her cast of privileged characters.

Mary G. Mason, in a very interesting article on women's autobiographical *écriture*, has suggested that male and female autobiographies articulate different modes of "interior disclosure": "nowhere in women's autobiographies do we find the patterns established by the two prototypical male autobiographers, Augustine and Rousseau." [12] The archetypical search for an idealized double replaces, in the female autobiography, St. Augustine's "dramatic structure of conversion" and Rousseau's "egoistic secular study of evolving consciousness": "the self-discovery of female identity seems to acknowledge the real presence and recognition of another consciousness, and the disclosure of the female self is linked to the identification of some 'other.' " [13]

Mason's theory is confirmed in Sofia's *Memoirs*, where the "other" is Sofia's sister Anna, who becomes the main character of the *Memoirs* halfway through the book, almost eclipsing her younger and less flamboyant sister. The autobiographer is left very much on the sideline, watching—with a mixture of admiration and envy—the older and more beautiful version of self. The last four chapters of the work concentrate on Anna, her nihilism, her first literary experiments and, finally, her acquaintance with Dostoevsky. The last segment of the *Memoirs* provides a fascinating and candid portrait of the great writer, but it also marks the culminating point of the rivalry between the two sisters. In the love triangle which results, the fifteen-year-old Sofia becomes infatuated with the forty-three-year-old writer, and her hopes are brutally shattered when she realizes that Dostoevsky has fallen in love with Anna. The relationship between the two sisters is temporarily strained.

It is highly significant, in terms of the essential nature of female autobiographies as defined by Mary Mason, that the *Memoirs* do not end with this estrangement between Anna and Sofia but rather with an epiphanic moment of reconciliation. The two sisters are on their way back to the country, having just left Petersburg:

The forest stretched out on both sides of the road, dark, mysterious, impenetrable. Suddenly, as we came out into a clearing, the moon seemed to float out from behind the woods and flooded us with silvery light, so brilliantly and unexpectedly that it gave us an eerie feeling. . . . at that moment, as if by unspoken agreement . . . we put our arms around each other. And both of us felt that there was no more estrangement between us, that we were as close as we had been before. A feeling of inexplicable, boundless joy took hold of us both. [14]

With this scene, the *Memoirs* come to a close. But the ending is not arbitrary. It exemplifies to what an extent Sofia's desire to merge with the idealized sister is the very genesis of the work. Indeed, in the words of Mary Mason, the *raison d'être* of the *Memoirs* could be seen as the need to confront "an overwhelming model or ideal . . . in order that the author's identity be realized." [15]

Sofia's novel *Nigilistka* can also be seen in this light. This work, written just after the *Memoirs*, suggests the extraordinary power of transference provided by literature. The novel concerns a young girl, Vera Barantsova, who arrives in St. Petersburg in 1876 to devote herself to the "nihilist cause." A flashback takes the reader to Vera's childhood, where her search for a worthy cause is pre-figured. She looks toward religion, reads about the Chinese missions and decides to become a missionary. At age fifteen she meets a neighbor, in exile from Petersburg, the liberal professor Vasiltsev. He gives her lessons, and three years later they fall in love, although Vasiltsev is thrice her age. Involved in "revolutionary activities," he is exiled to Viatka in Siberia and soon dies of consumption. Vera's young life is crushed. After her two older sisters leave the paternal house, her father dies, and her mother retires to a convent, thus leaving Vera free to fulfill her revolutionary work. The flashback makes clear Vera's pre-disposition for self-sacrifice and helps explain the outcome of the novel.

Vera attends the "trial of the 193," a true event that took place in Petersburg from October 1877 to January 1878; one hundred and ninety-three young nihilists were being tried for having participated in the "mad summer" of 1874. This episode—defined by the Russian historian Venturi as a "collective act of Rousseauism" [16]—saw thousands of young men and women, university students for the most part, spend their summer in the countryside in answer to "the appeal of the revolutionary Populists." Their mission, as defined by their spokesman Flerovsky in his manifesto, was to: "Go to the people and tell them the whole truth to the very last word. . . . men must live according to the law of nature. . . . all men are equal, all men are born naked; all men are born equally small and weak." [17] In the novel, the judges reserve their harshest sentence for a Jewish medical student Pavlenkov. He is sentenced to twenty years of solitary confinement in the Peter and Paul Fortress in St. Petersburg, a fate "worse than being condemned to be shot or hung." [18] No one, we are told, has ever been able to survive such a sentence for more than three years before succumbing to madness or death. Vera learns that if Pavlenkov were married, his sentence would be commuted to hard labor and exile in Siberia. She decides to sacrifice her life by marrying him and to follow him to Siberia. Her final words as she boards the train for Siberia are: "Is it for me that you cry? . . . Ah, if you only knew how sorry I feel for all of you who are staying behind." [19]

We know that *Nigilistka* was based on a true story, that Sofia had befriended a young woman in Paris, Vera Goncharova, who had married a medical student, Pavlovskii, so as to commute his prison sentence into a Siberian exile. [20] The act of marrying someone for ideological reasons was a common occurrence in Russia at the time, as Sofia knew perfectly well since she herself had contracted such a marriage to escape the hated paternal house. [21] The representative quality of this phenomenon, a "marker" of her generation, would have appealed to her. But there are also indications in the *Memoirs* which point to a deeper connection between the novelist and the subject of *Nigilistka*; notably a passage in a rough draft of the *Memoirs* that analyzes with great sensitivity Sofia's infatuation with Dostoevsky. Significantly, the passage is written in the third person, thus creating a fictional distance between author and character:

[She] understood Dostoevsky. Intuitively she comprehended the marvelous transports of tenderness buried in him. She venerated not only his genius, but also the suffering he had endured. . . . There were also times when she abandoned herself to the wildest fantasies in connection with Dostoevsky. But strange to relate, these fantasies always concerned the past and not the future. Thus, for example, she would sit for hours on end and *imagine herself at hard labor together with Dostoevsky.* [22]

The fantasy may strike the reader as odd. In fact, when Sofia met Dostoevsky in 1865, he had recently returned from ten years of hard labor and exile. On his visits to the Korvin-Krukovskaia sisters, Dostoevsky would describe in vivid detail the mock execution he had undergone in 1849 and the circumstances of his first epileptic seizure in Siberian exile. The fifteen-year-old Sofia thus had much concrete material upon which to build her fantasies. I would suggest, therefore, that in writing *Nigilistka* Sofia transmuted her childish desire for sacrifice by accompanying Dostoevsky in his exile into recounting the story of Vera Goncharova and Pavlovskii in the fictional guise of Vera Barantsova and Pavlenkov. Moreover, since both the fictitious Vera and the real Vera were Sofia's exact contemporaries, the writer could identify quite readily with her heroine. Telling Vera's story, then, was a literary solution to an unfulfilled personal desire of adolescence. But the substitution devise is made even more significant by the fact that the heroine of Sofia's novel is called "nigilistka," a nickname never applied to Sofia herself but one given to Anna by her family, and especially by Dostoevsky. As Sofia notes in her *Memoirs*:

A constant and very burning subject of the arguments between [Anna and Dostoevsky] was nihilism. The debates on this question sometimes continued late into the night, and the longer they talked, the more heated they became; in the heat of the argument they expressed their views much more extremely than either of them really meant to. . . . Beside himself with fury, Dostoevsky would sometimes grab his hat and leave, solemnly announcing that there was no point in arguing with a *nigilistka*.[23]

Thus by writing about a *nigilistka*, Sofia was vicariously fulfilling two desires. One, she lived out fictionally and through her heroine her earlier dream of self-sacrifice and devotion to a man by following him into exile. Two, in the fiction *she* became the *nigilistka* instead of her sister, thus taking over the sister's role in her relationship with Dostoevsky as the favorite. By substituting an authorial persona in the sister's place, by recreating a girlhood mythology in which she becomes the chosen one, Sofia's novel is neither as straightforwardly political nor as far removed from the autobiographical mode as it might at first appear.

Limited space does not allow me as detailed a discussion of Anna's literary production as I would like. She published four short stories. The first two, written when she was in her early twenties, appeared in Dostoevsky's journal *Epokha*.[24] The last two, written much later, were published in *Severnyi vestnik* in the 1880's.[25] I will limit myself here to the early stories.

Anna's prose is closely associated with Dostoevsky. When Anna sent her first two stories to him, he reacted with enthusiasm. "Mikhail," the second story, even appeared on the front page of the September 1864 issue of *Epokha*, an unheard-of honor for a novice writer.

Critics have consistently expressed surprise that Dostoevsky could have responded so positively to Anna's work. Marc Slonim finds the first piece, "The Dream," to be marred by "great esthetic failings." [26] Stillman proposes that "to understand the remarkable fervor with which Dostoevsky responded to [Anna's] unremarkable story, one should recall the dismal circumstances of his life at the time he received it." [27] Still others assume that Dostoevsky was conquered not so much by the stories as by the good looks of their author, an absurd assumption since we know for a fact that Dostoevsky and Anna did not meet until after the pieces had been published. A better explanation for Dostoevsky's delight, it seems to me, is the extraordinary correspondence between Anna's prose and Dostoevsky's own literary works. "The Dream" echoes Dostoevsky's early stories. "Mikhail" anticipates the thematic concerns that would shape Dostoevsky's last novel. Thus the great writer recognized parts of himself in Anna's stories, and it is this "shock of recognition," to use Edmund Wilson's phrase, that gives meaning to the literary relationship between the master and the novice.

"The Dream" expresses the hopelessness and despair of a young woman who is condemned to a life of stupid labor. She has recently been taken out of school and must now help to support her family with her sewing. The text has a hushed, fantomesque quality—the members of the girl's family only intermittently appear; other characters only briefly intervene. The main character is Lilenka's own consciousness. Lilenka's authentic life does not take place in the real world, which is characterized by dreary weather, an atmosphere of oppression and silence, but in a fantasy life. In the culminating episode of the story, an epiphanic dream reveals to the heroine an utopian vision of perfect harmony and communion. Thus the story presents a kind of inverted order in which life is in black and white and dreams are in color.

Although the naiveté of Anna's piece is not characteristic of Dostoevsky, "The Dream" bears a distinct resemblance to Dostoevsky's early writing. Like many of his fictions, the piece is set in St. Petersburg, and the weather plays a correspondingly important role. Lilenka also bears a resemblance to Dostoevsky's Netochka Nezvanova. Most important is the dichotomy between inner and outer life. Lilenka's double life is strongly reminiscent of the rich fantasies and humble existence of the young unnamed "dreamer" in *White Nights*. Dostoevsky's definition of the dreamer as "a sort of creature of the neuter gender'' could also apply to Anna's heroine, whose morbid tendencies and undersexed temperament lead her to fall in love with a corpse.[28] Dostoevsky's hero explains lyrically the significance of the dreamer's flights of fancy:

Silence reigns in the little room; solitude and a feeling of indolence enfold his imagination in a sweet embrace. . . . His imagination is once more ready for action, excited, and, in a flash, a new world, a new fascinating life, once more opens up enchanting vistas before him. A new dream, new happiness! A new dose of subtle, voluptuous poison! . . . Look at those magical phantoms which so enchantingly . . . are conjured up before his mind's eye in so magical and thrilling a picture. . . . Look what an amazing sea of adventures, what a never-ending paradise of ecstatic dreams! . . . what is he dreaming of? . . . He is dreaming of everything.[29]

Lilenka's culminating dream seems to follow the lyrical movements described by Dostoevsky's dreamer. In her dream, the dead student is resurrected; a new life with him seems possible. The vocabulary of light and of brightness (her "bright gaze looking up the dark stairway" where the future would be "clear and bright"[30]) contrasts with "the gray Petersburg light."[31]

In the story's tragic outcome, Lilenka dies of that unnamed disease which claimed so many nineteenth century fictional heroines, a disease which is partly physical—tuberculosis or pneumonia—and partly moral—despair. In choosing to live permanently on the side of dream, Lilenka differs from Dostoevsky's hero who survives. The difference in their fates may be due in part to gender. Dostoevsky's male dreamer is a wanderer who feels most at home walking the streets of Petersburg; his literary ambitions give his fantasies a creative outlet. But Lilenka's life is spent sitting on a chair next to a window; she has no outside existence, no prospects beyond years of domestic drudgery. Her death can be seen as a statement of protest, a form of revenge. Indeed, the final image of the story, that of the younger sister forced to take Lilenka's place as the new sacrificial victim, suggests such a possibility.

Anna's second story, "Mikhail," is prophetic of Dostoevsky's *Brothers Karamazov*. It tells the story of a young orphan who enters a monastery and is brought up by his uncle, a monk. A chance meeting with a young girl impels him later to leave the monastery and to enter society. But he grows disillusioned, returns to the monastery and dies. When Sofia Kovalevskaia mentioned to the great master that his Alesha bore a great resemblance to the hero of her sister's work, Dostoevsky struck his forehead with his hand and replied: "Maybe you are right . . . but, believe me, I had forgotten Mikhail when I imagined Alesha. Unless, of course, he appeared to me unconsciously."[32]

The Slavicist Robert Belknap has suggested that Dostoevsky's blindness to Anna's impact on his novel was due to the intervention of an "intermediate source, a work influenced by 'Mikhail' which in turn influenced *The Brothers Karamazov*. . . . This intermediate source is Dostoevsky's own *Idiot*, which he wrote less than four years after publishing 'Mikhail.' "[33] But the numerous parallels between Anna's story and Dostoevsky's novel are important enough to necessitate a whole separate study.

In conclusion, I would like to leave you with the fleeting image of Anna, as a young girl on the brink of womanhood, torn between two life models. On the one hand, her father whose fury when he learned of his daughter's literary success caused him to say: "Now you are selling your stories, but the time will come—mark my words—when you'll sell yourself."[34] On the other hand, Dostoevsky who writes to Anna in December 1864: "Not only can you, but *you must* take your talent *seriously*. You are a poet."[35] That Anna did not take her father's advice seriously was, no doubt, to her credit, but that she did not follow Dostoevsky's exhortations is most definitely our loss.

NOTES

Note on Translation

In the case of Kovalevskaia's *Memoirs* (see *Vospominaniia detstva*, note 18), I have used Beatrice Stillman's translation, *A Russian Childhood* (see note 1), except where the Russian text is indicated (see *Vospominaniia i pis'ma*, note 10), in which case the translations are my own. The passages cited from *Nigilistka* (see note 19) and "Son" (see note 24) ("The Dream") are my own translations.

Note on Transliteration

I have used the Library of Congress transliteration system (without diacritical marks) throughout the article, rather than the International Scholarly system. Exceptionally, in the case of Tolstoy, Dostoevsky, and one or two others, I have adopted the well-established English spelling.

1. See Beatrice Stillman, Introduction to Sofya Kovalevskaya, *A Russian Childhood* (New York: Springer-Verlag, 1978), pp. 15–16; Leonid Grossman, *Dostoevskii* (Moscow: Molodaia gvardiia, 1962), pp. 329–30; Vassili Soukhomline, "Deux femmes russes combattantes de la Commune," *Cahiers internationaux. Revue internationale du monde du travail* II, no. 6 (1950), 61.

2. Sofia Kovalevskaia was in Paris from April 5 to May 12, 1871. Later in her life, she planned to write memoirs of her commune experience. But she did not live to realize this project.

3. This was in great part due to the two novels of the period, Turgenev's *Fathers and Children* (1862) and Chernyshevsky's *What Is to Be Done?* (1863).

4. *Vest'*, no. 46 (1864). Cited in Charles Moser, *Antinihilism in the Russian Novel of the 1860's* (The Hague: Mouton, 1964), p. 44.

5. Sofya Kovalevskaya, *A Russian Childhood*, translated, edited, and introduced by Beatrice Stillman (New York: Springer–Verlag, 1978), 135.

6. Ibid., p. 152.

7. Ibid., pp. 146–47.

8. Beatrice Stillman, "Sofya Kovalevskaya: Growing up in the Sixties," *Russian Literary Triquarterly*, no. 9 (Spring, 1974), 277.

9. Stillman, Introduction to *A Russian Childhood*, pp. 8–9.

10. S. V. Kovalevskaia, *Vospominaniia i pis'ma* (Moscow: Akademiia Nauk, 1951), p. 121.

11. A respected member of the intelligentsia, General Evreinov, father of Anna Evreinova, was famous for saying that he would rather see his daughter in a coffin than in a university. See Soukhomline, "Deux femmes russes combattantes de la Commune," p. 59.

12. Mary G. Mason, "The Other Voice: Autobiographies of Women Writers," in *Autobiography; Essays Theoretical and Critical*, ed. James Olney (Princeton, N.J.: Princeton University Press, 1980), p. 210.

13. Mason, "The Other Voice," p. 210.

14. Kovalevskaya, *A Russian Childhood*, p. 199.

15. Mason, "The Other Voice," p. 232.

16. Franco Venturi, *Roots of Revolution* (New York: Grosset & Dunlap, 1971), p. 503.

17. Ibid., p. 498.

18. Sofia Kovalevskaia, *Vospominaniia detstva; Nigilistka* (Moscow: Gos. Izd. Khud. Lit., 1960), p. 210.

19. Kovalevskaia, *Nigilistka*, p. 222.

20. Cf. Kovalevskaia, "Vstrechi s V. S. Goncharovoi," in *Vospominaniia i pis'ma*, pp. 183–202, 482–84.

21. See, for example, the case of Elizaveta Dmitrieva-Tomanovskaia, in

I. S. Knizhnik-Vetrov, *Russkie deiatel'nitsy Pervogo Internatsionala i Parizhskoi Kommuny: E. L. Dmitrieva, A. V. Zhaklar, E. G. Barteneva* (Moscow/Leningrad: Nauka, 1964).

22. Kovalevskaya, *A Russian Childhood*, p. 210. Emphasis mine.

23. Kovalevskaia, *Vospominaniia i pis'ma*, p. 113.

24. "Son," *Epokha*, August 1864; "Mikhail," *Epokha*, September 1864. (Published under the name Iu. O-v. [Iurii Orbelov was the literary pseudonym of Anna Korvin-Krukovskaia].)

25. "Zapiski spirita," *Severnyi vestnik*, July 1886; "Fel'dsheritsa," *Severnyi vestnik*, March 1887.

26. Marc Slonim, *Les Trois amours de Dostoievsky* (Paris: Correa, 1955), p. 177.

27. Kovalevskyaya, *A Russian Childhood*, p. 206.

28. Fyodor Dostoevsky, *White Nights: Great Short Works of Dostoevsky* (New York: Harper & Row, 1968), p. 161.

29. Dostoevsky, *White Nights*, p. 166.

30. "Son," p. 15.

31. Ibid., p. 16.

32. Kovalevskaia, *Vospominaniia i pis'ma*, p. 97.

33. Robert Belknap, "The Origins of Alesha Karamazov," in *American Contributions to the Sixth International Congress of Slavists, Prague, 1968* (The Hague: Mouton, 1968), 2: 12.

34. Kovalevskaya, *A Russian Childhood*, p. 168.

35. F. M. Dostoevskii, *Pis'ma*, ed. Dolinin, 3 vols. (Moscow/Leningrad: Gos. Izd., 1928), 1: 382. Emphases are in the text.

14

Juliette Adam: She Devil or *Grande Française?*

Jean Scammon Hyland and Daniel H. Thomas

EARLY YEARS AND ADULTHOOD

Juliette Lamber LaMessine Adam was born in Verberie, Picardy, October 4, 1836, and died at the Château de Lagnelles in the Var, at the home of her daughter, Mme Paul Segond, on August 23, 1936, less than two months short of her hundredth birthday. A beloved only child, she spent her early years buffeted between a doting conservative grandmother and an adoring liberal father. Early in life she learned to forge her own way between their two opposing viewpoints. In 1853 she married Alex LaMessine, many years older and of a temperament totally unsuited to hers. For Juliette, the marriage was a disaster, except that it gave her a child, Alice LaMessine, and the opportunity to move into Paris and its literary and political circles.

As early as 1858, Madame LaMessine, then twenty-two years old, aroused public notice by challenging certain ideas that the socialist theorist Pierre Joseph Prudhon espoused in his new work *De la Justice dans la Révolution et dans l'église*.[1] In a book entitled *Idées anti-proudhoniennes sur l'amour, la femme et le mariage*, she attacked the sexist attitudes of the well-known philosopher who claimed the physical, mental and moral inferiority of women, singling out particularly George Sand and Daniel Stern as examples.[2] As she stated in her second volume of *Mémoires*:

I would have been the first to have acknowledged the master qualities of which Prudhon gave evidence in his *Justice dans la Révolution*—his great power of argument, an incomparable style—had it not been for the brutal, the most vulgar insults he showered upon two women whom I admired above all others: George Sand, the author of so many chefs-d'oeuvre, and the Comtesse d'Agoult (Daniel Stern), the universally admired writer of the Revolution of 1848.[3]

The more unconventional ideas that she advocated in her book included: total equality for women, equal accessibility to professions—including especially those of judge and magistrate, equality in marriage contracts and availability and ease of divorce. Particularly interesting in this work are the early signs of a prodigious polemic talent and unusual reasoning power in debate, talents that she would later put to use in her articles on the Belgian defenses on the Meuse. Juliette Adam continued her interest in women's rights, including the English suffrage movement, and met and admired Christobel Pankhurst during the latter's period of refuge in Paris.[4] Several pages were devoted to the *Idées anti-proudhoniennes* in the 1963 work by Edith Thomas, *Les Pétroleuses*, a study of the role of women in France from the beginning of the Second Empire to the end of the Commune.[5]

Because of the *Idées anti-proudhoniennes*, the name of Juliette LaMessine began to be heard. She was invited to participate in the salon of Daniel Stern where she met and cultivated many well-known figures of the day, including Edmond Adam, a millionaire *conseiller d'état*, senator, ardent republican and chief of the Paris police during the 1870 siege of Paris. In 1863 Juliette separated from her husband, LaMessine, who then became involved in various shady dealings in North Africa. When word arrived, in 1867, that he had died, Juliette was free to marry again. Even before her marriage to Edmond Adam, she had set up her own salon in the Rue de Rivoli and had attracted a number of popular political figures. Among her literary friends the most widely known was George Sand who referred to her as *Ma petite Juliette* and *Ma chère mignonne*. Although much older than her protégé, George Sand saw herself in Juliette—her temperament, her love of independence, her ideas on women (after all, both women were virtually divorced at a time when such a thing was simply "not done").[6]

The marriage of Edmond and Juliette Adam was, from all that is known of it, one of love and harmony. Each complemented and supported the other in his or her undertakings. The small salon on the Rue de Rivoli was enlarged at their apartment on the Boulevard Poissonnière and gained in importance. By far the most noteworthy habitué of the salon, and the one who brought it fame, was Léon Gambetta. The relationship between Juliette Adam and Léon Gambetta is still not entirely clear. If one is to believe her *Mémoires* (which are often romanticized and of doubtful veracity), it was she who rescued him from his provincial country bumpkin appearance and turned him into the leading statesman of his time. There is some hint that she was, or would have liked to be, his mistress. Even if these views are highly exaggerated, certainly Juliette Adam did exercise a tremendous influence on Gambetta and helped form his political thinking between 1868 and 1878, after which time they split on ideological grounds. Politically, she had moved steadily from Left to Right—from Gambetta's liberal republicanism to the extreme nationalist *Revanchard* (Revenge) temperament of General Boulanger, Léon Daudet, and company by 1888.

After Edmond Adam's death in 1877, Juliette continued her salon and her political activities but found her voice did not have the same force without a senator as her mate. She tried travel—Italy, Russia, Egypt, Greece—and wrote a number of rather mediocre novels and travel books. None of these activities was sufficient, however, for her energy and fertile mind. She missed being in the political arena; her competitive spirit refused to retire. Finally, in 1879, she decided to take the chance and found a review. Many counselled against it, saying she could never compete with the *Revue des Deux Mondes*. Our author, on the other hand, thought she had something to say and much to contribute. Using part of her personal fortune (left to her by Edmond), she launched the *Nouvelle Revue* in October, 1879 with a threefold purpose, which she explained to the English statesman William E. Gladstone when he asked the goals of the new review: "To oppose Bismarck, to demand the restoration of Alsace-Lorraine, and to encourage our young writers." [7] The restoration of Alsace-Lorraine required *Revanche* and opposition to Bismarck. The encouragement of young writers meant she was to rival both the aforementioned *Revue des Deux Mondes* and the *Journal des Débats*. For twenty years she saw her journal gain steadily in importance and stature. Madame Adam controlled the *Revue*, selected the contributors, and ultimately founded a publishing house in connection with it. Among the many writers published in her review were: Leconte de Lisle, Pierre Loti, Ivan Tourgueneff, Erckmann-Chatrian, François Coppée, Victor Hugo, Guy de Maupassant, Gustave Flaubert, Anatole France, Paul Bourget and

Léon Daudet. The biweekly "Journal de la Quinzaine" and "Lettres sur la Politique Extérieure," which she wrote, were eagerly digested by her followers and, for many, provided one of their few sources of information on both foreign and domestic questions. These articles (six per volume, six volumes a year for twenty years) are a veritable gold mine of information for details on domestic issues. The foreign affairs articles, also thirty-six per year, although too often inaccurate and certainly geared to the Right politically, are extremely helpful in understanding France's position vis-à-vis Germany, Russia, Austria-Hungary, Persia, Britain and others. They are written in the masterful polemic style already evidenced in the *Idées anti-proudhoniennes*, capable of convincing the layman that Juliette Adam was the wisest political analyst of the day, even if her academic credentials for this designation were lacking.

Even before founding the *Revue*, Adam had concluded that France's only hope for the future lay in rapprochement with Imperial Russia, an idea that became reality in the Franco-Russian Alliance negotiated in 1891–94. Like many others, she saw a continuing threat in the increasing militarism on the eastern side of the Rhine. What the Germans had done to France in 1870–71 could be done again. She had lived through the Siege of Paris and could not forget it. She considered Bismarck a ruthless dictator, ready to sacrifice everything for his military machine in preparation for a coming attack on France. For ten years she preached her hatred of Bismarck in diatribes that became more and more virulent as she saw the country drifting away from the policy of *Revanche*. Caught up in the movement of Extreme Nationalism, she naturally moved toward the camp of Georges Boulanger and Charles Maurras. Her writing began to be sprinkled with the well-known ideology of Integral Nationalism—love of the French nation, the common people and Joan of Arc (*la patrie, le peuple et Jeanne d'Arc*), as well as a struggle for the return of the beloved lost provinces of Alsace and Lorraine. Until then an agnostic, almost pantheistic lover of ancient Greece, she returned to the early Catholic teachings of her grandmother, abandoning the enlightened Hellenism taught by her father. Her diatribes against Bismarck came to their natural culmination in the "Meuse Forts Affair," which will be discussed at some length as an illustration of why the appellation "She Devil" (*Diablesse de Femme*) was applied to her by Bismarck.

THE MEUSE FORTS AFFAIR

In the particular polemic we have entitled "The Meuse Forts Affair," Juliette Adam pitted herself against such formidable foes as King Leopold II of the Belgians and Prince Otto von Bismarck. In this instance she tried to prove that Leopold II had agreed to ally himself with Bismarck in any future war with France.

To understand this journalistic campaign a brief background is essential. In many of the wars between the French and the Germans, contending armies avoided the rivers, mountains and forests on their common frontier and attacked through the open central Belgian plain above the Meuse River. In the 1830's, the five great powers—Britain, France, Prussia, Austria and Russia—had sought to make Belgium a barrier rather than a battleground by guaranteeing its neutrality as well as its independence. The small state's plan of defence had been to delay the likely invader—France—until German and British military aid could arrive in fortified Antwerp. When Prussia united the Germans into the more powerful German Empire, Belgian officials feared that it, rather than France, might be the invader in another Franco-German war. In 1887 the Brussels ministers requested appropriations to build forts on the Meuse around Liège, near the German border, and Namur, up the river toward the French border. In addition, an effort was launched to increase funds for an army sufficiently large to deter both France and Germany from attacking across Belgian soil. Most legislators of the Right favored fortifications and opposed a larger army, and most of those on the Left favored a larger army and opposed the new fortifications. The result was a smaller number of forts than some leaders declared essential and an army that some equally regarded leaders declared inadequate for the forts.[8]

In that same year, 1887, and the following year, certain French journals charged that the king of the Belgians intended to permit German troops to occupy the forts upon the outbreak of war. In February of 1888, the Belgian foreign minister labeled such reports absolutely fallacious, and the French government concluded that the forts were being constructed only for Belgian defense.[9] At this time, nevertheless, Juliette Adam opened her campaign against both the Belgian king and Bismarck by publishing an article by Faucault de Mondion, a one-time secret agent of the Quai d'Orsay with whom she had collaborated in writing for the *Revue*. According to the article, "A State Secret" [July-August, 1888], Léopold II and Bismarck's son had signed a "Convention d'Ostende" in 1887, and the king and chancellor were negotiating a secret treaty by which German troops might occupy Belgian forts if a French attack appeared imminent. In subsequent articles ("Belgian Neutrality violated by Germany" [September-October, 1888]; "Belgian Neutrality" [November-December, 1888]; "Belgian Neutrality and Swiss Neutrality" [July-August, 1889]) Adam claimed that an alliance had already been signed, that only Léopold could deny her charges since he had the constitutional right to negotiate secret alliances and that the Swiss, unlike the Belgians, had stood up to Bismarck. She offered ten documents as proof of her accusations.

The Brussels government now had something tangible to investigate. Its probers found that eight of the documents had been stolen from the interior ministry, had been only slightly altered and dealt with labor disputes of little consequence. The other two were forgeries. The investigators were convinced that the theft was by a Belgian, George Nieter, a one-time foreign ministry employee and an acquaintance of Mondion. Mondion admitted to having uncovered the documents that Adam published.[10]

By this time, August 1891, Belgian Premier Auguste Beernaert thought he must respond publicly to the various charges. He explained that Germany and the other guarantors had both the right and the duty to dispatch forces into Belgium, but only if neutrality were violated; his country had been scrupulous in fulfilling its duties and would continue to be.[11]

In the meantime, the able French ambassador, Albert Bourée, also became concerned about the serious charges, partly because he feared that they might damage the existing cordial relations between the French and the Belgian governments and publics. After investigating, he found no evidence to support the charges.[12] As the attacks by Adam and others became sharper, the Quai d'Orsay ordered Bourée to make a deeper probe. He finally came to conclusions that appear to be definitive: Nieter had stolen the documents and had added forgeries to one of them in order to obtain a better price. Mondion offered the latter to the Quai d'Orsay, which turned him down.[13] In all likelihood Mondion then sold to Adam these and other documents, which she published. Upon receiving the results of the ambassador's investigation, the Quai d'Orsay agreed that the charges were a malicious myth.[14]

Berlin conducted a lesser investigation: its ambassador in Paris reported that Mondion was an imposter and had published almost nothing of value;[15] its ambassador in St. Petersburg put the same label of imposter on Nieter.[16] The British foreign office received several reports on the charges from its minister in Brussels who stated that they were pure invention and contained no truth.[17] Bismarck advised the Belgian government to show its contempt by ignoring Adam's charges, just as he was doing.[18]

This brief account of the charges against Belgium illustrates the indifferent criteria many journalists—French in this case—used for judging the evidence for their accusations. The best student of Juliette Adam states that one result of her campaign was to damage the reputation of her journal.[19] Although the French ambassador concluded that she had not harmed Franco-Belgian relations, one wonders why not since she was denounced by various Belgian papers. Certain foreign journalists, of course, thought there must be some fire where so much smoke existed (as in London's *Standard*, July 4, 1888). As late as 1906 the French *Journal* (January 10) reported that some editors had revived her charges, and in 1911 the *New York Daily Tribune* (February 13) repeated her claim that the Ostend Convention existed. It was not unusual for both earlier and later French and German journalists to charge Belgium with unneutral intentions. Occasionally, British editors did the same. But the Adam campaign was exceptionally harsh, and her charges were relatively specific. Even though the documents she was duped into publishing were of little consequence, she was sufficiently clever to convince many readers who were unwary or already suspicious of Léopold II and Bismarck. Discredited as she may have been, there was still some truth in her claim in the *Revue* issue of January-February, 1889 that she had caused doubt about these men, neither of whom was then very popular in the West.

LATER YEARS AND INFLUENCE

In 1899 Juliette Adam was sixty-three years old and tired. She had run the *Nouvelle Revue* almost single-handedly for twenty years and thought she was ready to take a rest. As she said in her retirement article:

The *Nouvelle Revue* has lived so well that it has come of age. Since, outside of its "national" goal and its political faith, it was created for the young, it should, logically, be taken over and continued by the young now that its directress is forced into semi-retirement. . . . I am sure that the *Revue* will fit even better its title of *New* now that two new young directors are taking over from a director whose fatigue from twenty years of excessive work was becoming serious.[20]

The authoress retired to her newly acquired home, the Château de Gif, rebuilt on the grounds of a medieval monastery in the Chevreuse Valley. Even at the age of sixty-three, however, hers was not a temperament to sit and watch. Much as she wanted to remain active, she found that she was being increasingly passed over for younger people. It was at this point that she decided to write her *Mémoires*, a series of seven volumes that would recount her life and the lives of those who had surrounded her from birth in 1836 to the time of writing (1902– 1910). An extremely thorough study of these memoirs was done by Saad Morcos in 1962 as part of a Sorbonne dissertation he published on Juliette Adam.[21] In his study, Morcos points out the many discrepancies, deformations of facts and figures, juxtaposing of events in time and the generally egocentric viewpoint of the author. The scope of the present chapter is not sufficient to treat this subject in depth, but, whether literally true or not, the *Mémoires* are fascinating reading and present a panoramic view of the Paris of 1855–1900. "The Index of Names Appearing in the Seven Volumes," thirty-two pages in length, contains the names of some fifteen hundred people, many of them extremely important figures of the time.[22] As G. P. Gooch has stated: "The student of France in the second half of the nineteenth century can neglect them as little as the journals of Horace de Viel-Castel and the de Goncourt brothers."[23] The seven volumes in chronological order are entitled: (1) *The Romance of My Childhood and Youth*; (2) *My Literary Life*; (3) *Feelings and Our Ideas before 1870*; (4) *My Illusions and Our Sufferings during the Siege of Paris*; (5) *My Anguish and Our Struggles*; (6) *My Political Friends before the Abandonment of a Revanche Policy*; and (7) *After Abandoning Revanche*.[24]

The most entertaining of the volumes is without doubt the highly romanticized story of Juliette's childhood, which includes unlikely episodes such as that of her grandmother "kidnapping" her in the dead of the night to remove her from the insidious liberal influence of her pragmatist father. More important to students of the late nineteenth century, however, are the last four volumes dealing with the Franco-

Prussian War and the years following the formation of the Third Republic. Of particular interest are the many pages on her relationship with Gambetta and the charming descriptions of vacations spent at her country estate, *Bruyères*, at Golfe Juan in the company of many well-known people. After publication of her *Mémoires*, Adam continued to live quietly at the Château de Gif, occasionally receiving friends and family. She lived to see France regain Alsace-Lorraine after the bloodiest war to that time, and she was invited to attend the signing of the Versailles Treaty in the Hall of Mirrors. She also lived to see the rise of Adolph Hitler, far more ruthless than Bismarck, but mercifully died before his humiliating victory over France in 1940.

From the foregoing comments, one might expect that Juliette Adam would be a prominent figure in the annals of nineteenth-century French literary history; yet current scholars pay her scant attention despite a number of studies by previous generations. The most complete and scholarly is the aforementioned biography by Morcos, which itself was published twenty-two years ago in Beirut, Lebanon. Earlier studies include a one-sided nationalistic study by a friend, Anatole Elliot in 1922, an unpublished doctoral dissertation for the University of Bonn in 1933 by Dora Arndt, an extremely complimentary biography in French by Adrienne Blanc-Péridier, written as a tribute to Madame Adam just after her death in 1936 and the one complete work in English devoted to Juliette Adam, a biography by Winifred Stephens, written in 1917.[25] This biography is highly romanticized and draws almost exclusively from the subjective *Mémoires* for its facts. Stephens had the advantage of knowing Adam and talking with her extensively, but one has the impression that it is the work of an English "gentlewoman" who wished to present her friend to the world but had little concern for fact or solid scholarship. A second study in English, a scholarly monograph by Joseph O. Beylen, *Madame Juliette Adam, Gambetta and the Idea of a Franco-Prussian Alliance*, was published in 1960.[26]

Juliette Adam is discussed in Richard Whiteing, *My Harvest*, Léon Daudet, *The Years between the Wars*, G. P. Gooch, *Courts and Cabinets* and Edith Thomas, *Les Pétroleuses*.[27] The *Correspondence* of George Sand contains twenty-four letters to Madame Juliette Adam,[28] and *Lettres de Gambetta* includes thirty-eight letters written by Gambetta to "Ma Chère Madame" between 1874 and 1880.[29] Additional letters to Juliette Adam are found in Julien Viaud's *Lettres de Pierre Loti à Juliette Adam*.[30]

Finally, hundreds of short commentaries about Juliette Adam, her ideas and/or her works were written between 1865 and 1965. At the time of her death almost every Parisian paper carried a lengthy article about her, principally in August, September and October of 1936. Less than a dozen of all these articles are in English, and virtually nothing has appeared since the Morcos biography of 1962.

CONCLUSION

Our intention in this chapter has been threefold. The first aim has been to introduce students of nineteenth-century women writers to this fascinating, if enigmatic, woman who played an extremely important role in French political and literary life for more than fifty years as novelist, journalist, memorialist and friend of many eminent writers and statesmen of the time.

To demonstrate the extent of Juliette Adam's influence, we have chosen, as our second aim, to present one incident of importance to three governments—those of France, Belgium and Germany. From the discussion of the "Meuse Forts Affair" it is clear that Juliette Adam was a woman to be reckoned with and her journal one that received considerable attention even in diplomatic circles. Her writings on the defenses of the Meuse did not change the course of diplomatic history, but her ideas were still being seriously considered as late as 1911 and were taken even more seriously by many of her readers at the time they were formulated.

Our third aim has been to ask a number of questions that have not, to our knowledge, been sufficiently answered. Why has this important spokeswoman been virtually ignored, especially at a time when particular attention is being given to women's liberation and recognition movements? Did her political passions for the restoration of Alsace-Lorraine and the thwarting of Bismarck destroy her objectivity and credulity in political writing as Gambetta suggested and her own government concluded in the Meuse Forts Affair? Are her memoirs, seen through the eyes of an emotional older woman, too subjective, too feminine and too egocentric as Morcos contends? Were her novels, essays and travel books too mediocre to interest twentieth-century scholars? Was she, in fact, an important and influential woman in nineteenth-century France or merely the beautiful, intelligent and spoiled wife of a Paris millionaire? These are all questions which deserve further investigation and more concrete answers if we are to understand fully the role played by Juliette Adam in the Paris of 1855–1925.

Was she, in truth, *La Grande Française*, Bismarck's *"Diablesse de Femme,"* Gambetta's *Madame Intégrale*, George Sand's *Chère Mignonne* or, perhaps, a mixture of all these personalities?

NOTES

1. Pierre Joseph Prudhon, *De la Justice dans la Révolution et dans l'Eglise* (Paris: Garnier Frères, 1858).

2. Juliette LaMessine, *Idées anti-prudhonniennes sur l'amour, la femme et le mariage* (Paris: A. Taride, 1858).

3. Mme Edmond Adam, *My Literary Life* (New York: D. Appleton and Co., 1904), p. 77.

4. Winifred Stephens Whale, "Madame Adam (Juliette Lamber)," *The Contemporary Review*, July-December, 1936, p. 453.

5. Edith Thomas, *Les Pétroleuses* (Paris: Gallimard, 1963), pp. 38–40.

6. George Sand, *Correspondance*, 6 vols. (Paris: Calmann-Lévy, 1882), V: 253.

7. Whale, "Madame Adam," p. 454.

8. *Histoire de la Belgique contemporaine, 1830–1914*, 3 vols (Brussels: De Witt, 1928–30), II: 173–80.

9. Chambre, *Annales parlementaires belges* (Brussels, 1888, February 21, 1888), p. 598.

10. Belgique, *Rapport du Procureur général près de la Cour d'Appel de Bruxelles sur l'instruction relative au vol des documents d'Ursel*. Presented to the Chambre, July 16, 1891, pp. 1–65; Saad Morcos, *Juliette Adam* (Beirut: Dar al-Maaref-Liban, 1962), pp. 288, 293–96, 623–25.

11. Chambre, *Annales parlementaires belges*, August 13, 1891, pp. 1870–72.

12. Bourée to Ribot, February 13, May 20, 1888, Archives, Ministère des Affaires étrangères, Paris, CP, Belgique, 81; and Bourée to Ribot, January 9, February 25, December 20, 1889, 82.

13. Bourée to Ribot, May 5, 1890, ibid., 83.

14. Bourée to Ribot, January 16 and Ribot to Bourée, January 29, 1890, ibid.

15. Münster to Bismarck, February 26, 1890, Johannes Lepsius, Albrecht Mendelssohn-Bartholdy and Friedrich Thimme, ed., *Die grosse Politik der europäischen Kabinette, 1871–1914* 40 vols. in 54 (Berlin: Deutsche Verlagsgesellschaft für Politik und Geschicte 1922–27), V: 348–49.

16. Schweinitz to Bismarck, January 23, 1890, ibid., 349–50.

17. Vivian to Salisbury, December 31, 1887, Public Records Office, FO,

566/84, Ind. 22773; October 3 and 16, 1888, 10/522; and August 28, 1889, 10/541.

18. Greindl to Chimay, October 27, 1888, Service des Archives, Ministère des Affaires étrangères Brussels, CP, Allemagne, 15, no. 92. A broader treatment of the Meuse Forts, the charges of being unneutral and Belgian efforts to counter the latter have appeared since this chapter was written. See Daniel H. Thomas, *The Guarantee of Belgian Independence and Neutrality in European Diplomacy* (Kingston, R.I.: D. H. Thomas Publishing, 1983), pp. 396–419.

19. Morcos, *Adam*, p. 296.

20. Juliette Adam, "Une Lettre de Mme Juliette Adam," *La Nouvelle Revue*, November-December, 1899, pp. 6–7.

21. Morcos, *Adam*.

22. Juliette Adam, "Index des noms contenus dans les sept volumes," *Après l'abandon de la revanche* (Paris: Alphonse Lemerre, n.d.), pp. 462–95.

23. George Peabody Gooch, *Courts and Cabinets* (New York: Knopf, 1946), p. 344.

24. Juliette Adam, *La Roman de mon enfance et de ma jeunesse*; *Mes premières armes littéraires et politiques*; *Mes sentiments et nos idées avant 1870*; *Mes illusions et nos souffrances pendant le siège de Paris*; *Mes angoisses et nos luttes*; *Nos amitiés politiques avant l'abandon de la revanche*; *Après l'abandon de la revanche*.

25. Anatole Elliot, *Madam Adam* (Paris: Plon, 1922); Dora Arndt, "Juliette Adam" (Diss., Bonn, 1933; Wurzburg: Dissertations-druckerei und Verlag Konrad Triltach, 1933); Adrienne Blanc-Péridier, *Une princesse de la Troisième République, Juliette Adam* (Paris: Editions "Education Intégrale," 1936); Winifred Stephens, *Madam Adam* (New York: E. P. Dutton and Co., 1918).

26. Joseph O. Beylen, *Juliette Adam, Gambetta and the Idea of a Franco-Prussian Alliance* (Stillwater: Oklahoma State University, 1960).

27. Richard Whiteing, *My Harvest* (New York: Dodd, Mead, 1915), pp. 140–46; Léon Daudet, *L'Entre-deux-guerres* (Paris: Nouvelle Librairie Nationale, 1915), pp. 230–47; Gooch, *Courts and Cabinets*, pp. 334–65; Thomas, *Les Pétroleuses*, pp. 38–40.

28. Sand, *Correspondance*, vols. V, VI.

29. Daniel Halévy and Emile Pillias, *Lettres de Gambetta (1868–1882)* (Paris: Editions Bernard Grasset, 1938).

30. Julien Viaud, *Lettres de Pierre Loti à Juliette Adam* (Paris: n.p., 1924).

NINETEENTH CENTURY WOMEN WRITERS' INTERNATIONAL CONFERENCE

November
7, 8, 9, 1980

Eliza Acton
Juliette Adam
Bettina von Arnim
Jane Austen
Fredrika Bremer
Charlotte Brontë
Germaine de Staël
Emily Dickinson
Annette von Droste-Hülshoff
George Eliot
Michael Field
Charlotte Forten
Margaret Fuller
Elizabeth Cleghorn Gaskell
Sarah Grimké
Josephine Heard
Mary Jane Holmes
Harriet Jacobs
Anna Korvin-Krukovskaia Jaclard
Sophia Korvin-Krukovskaia Kovalevskaia
George Maldague
Ely Montclerc
Susanna Moodie
Adelaida Muñiz y Mas
Louise Otto
Elizabeth Stuart Phelps
Christina Rossetti
George Sand
Catherine Parr Traill
Flora Tristan
Frances Milton Trollope
Rahel Varnhagen
Catherine Fenimore Woolson

HOFSTRA UNIVERSITY

HEMPSTEAD, NEW YORK 11550

CONFERENCES AT HOFSTRA UNIVERSITY

George Sand Centennial - November 1976   Vol. I - available

Heinrich von Kleist Bicentennial - November 1977   Vol. II - December 1980

The Chinese Woman - December 1977

George Sand: Her Life, Her Works, Her Influence -   Vol. III - 1981
    April 1978

William Cullen Bryant and His America - October 1978   Vol. IV - 1981

The Trotsky-Stalin Conflict and Russia in the 1920's -   Vol. V
    March 1979

Albert Einstein Centennial - November 1979   Vol. VI

Renaissance Venice Symposium - March 1980   Vol. VII

Sean O'Casey - March 1980

Walt Whitman - April 1980   Vol. VIII

Nineteenth Century Women Writers - November 7, 8, 9, 1980   Vol. IX

Fedor Dostoevski - April 9, 10, 11, 1981   Vol. X

Gotthold Ephraim Lessing - November 12, 13, 14, 1981   Vol. XI

Johann Wolfgang von Goethe - April 1, 2, 3, 1982   Vol. XII

Twentieth Century Women Writers - November 5, 6, 7, 1982   Vol. XIII

Jose Ortega y Gasset, 1883-1983 - Centennial Celebration   Vol. XIV
    Spring 1983

Romanticism in the Old and the New World - Celebrating   Vol. XV
    the Bi-Centennials of Washington Irving, Stendhal,
    and Vasilii Andreevich Zhukovskii -- 1783-1983 -
    Fall 1983

"Calls for Papers" -- available upon request

NINETEENTH CENTURY WOMEN WRITERS' INTERNATIONAL CONFERENCE

November 7, 8, 9, 1980

PROGRAM

CONFERENCE DIRECTORS: Avriel Goldberger
                                     Rhoda Nathan

CONFERENCE COORDINATORS: Natalie Datlof
                                     Alexej Ugrinsky

CHAIRMAN OF CONFERENCE COMMITTEE: Robert N. Keane

CONFERENCE COMMITTEE: Joseph G. Astman   Nora McNair
                                     Diana Ben-Merre   Maureen O. Murphy
                                     Edwin L. Dunbaugh   Robert B. Sargent
                                     Arthur Gregor   Wilbur S. Scott
                                     Denis-J. Jean   William S. Shiver
                                     William A. McBrien   Miriam Tulin

COOPERATING INSTITUTIONS: Consulate General of the Federal Republic
                                       of Germany
                                     New York, NY

                                     Country Art Gallery
                                     Locust Valley, NY

                                     Cultural Services of the French Embassy
                                     New York, NY

                                     Goethe House
                                     New York, NY

                                     Nassau County Office of Cultural Development
                                     Roslyn, NY

UNIVERSITY CENTER FOR CULTURAL & INTERCULTURAL STUDIES

HOFSTRA UNIVERSITY
HEMPSTEAD, NEW YORK 11550

Joseph G. Astman, Director
University Center for Cultural & Intercultural Studies

The Conference on Nineteenth Century Women Writers

is dedicated to

GERMAINE BREE

--in grateful admiration of her life's work as master teacher-scholar, inspiring generations of students -- many of whom have become noted teachers and critics in their own right -- with the understanding that literature is central to human experience;

--in grateful recognition of her scholar's discipline and her breadth of imagination which have been applied to the question of literature by women: her skill and her reputation have made a major contribution to the intellectual legitimizing of such studies as well as to our understanding of the writers and works involved;

--in grateful appreciation of her generosity over the years to us at Hofstra in the Department of French and to the whole University community.

In Praise of the Woman Writer

The title of this conference has been formulated to reflect a broad
spectrum of distinctive talents and nationalities. Our purpose is to explore
and pay homage to the creative genius of nineteenth century women writers.
However, in the process of organizing the individual panels, we encounter a
problem inherent in so ambitious an undertaking: will it be possible for the
twentieth century scholar to bring Jane Austen's satire, Emily Dickinson's
wit, George Eliot's intellect and George Sand's passion into a coherent
cultural framework for the purpose of drawing instructive conclusions about
women in the nineteenth century? From the biographies of these writers,
their poems, novels and letters, and the reliable histories which deal with
their contributions, we learn that they were alternately and sometimes
simultaneously encouraged, ignored, relegated to the kitchen and elevated to
the salon. They wrote in secrecy, reigned in public, served some men and
were served by others. Their subjects were personal, social, political and
philosophical. In short, they represented no single point of view, nor shared
any common overriding preoccupation. What characterized nineteenth century
women writers was the intensity of their commitment to their craft and the
excellence of a large proportion of their work. Although the peripatetic
Margaret Fuller, the reclusive Brontë sisters and the sedentary Mrs. Browning
led diverse lives, they shared the qualities of courage, devotion to their
art and persistence. They were, to a woman, high-minded and dedicated,
remarkable as personalities and formidable as writers.

The directors, conference committee and coordinators have gone beyond
the familiar major authors of the period to encourage papers about minor
figures such as Mary Jane Holmes, Continental and Afro-American poets of
distinguished but minor reputation, and even some curiosities, such as two

women writing under a single male <u>nom de plume</u>. Themes central to nineteenth
century domestic life, such as education, marriage and mental health, have been
grouped in panels devoted to questions of culture. Our moderators are professors
and authors of distinction, men and women who have taught and written about the
subjects under discussion. All the events and entertainments and celebrations
of this three-day conference are dedicated to women writers of the nineteenth
century, to their integrity as artists, and to their pioneering role in the
world of letters.

                                        Rhoda Nathan, English Department
                                        Avriel Goldberger, French Department

GREETINGS

All good fortune to your Conference.

> Joseph Jay Deiss
> Positano, Italy

With all good wishes for the success of your program.

> Gordon S. Haight, General Editor
> The Clarendon Edition of the Novels of
> George Eliot
> Woodbridge, CT

Best Wishes to the Women Writers' Conference. I wish I could be with you.

> Julie Harris

Greetings from Higginson Press, especially the Dickinson Studies section, for a successful sesquicentennial conference at Hofstra University. It is a deep satisfaction to know that Dickinson is considered on a par with George Eliot. My two Dickinson journals, after thirteen years, now reach all continents, including Japan, India, Africa, and Australia. Her "letter to the world" is truly taking place.

> Frederick L. Morey, Editor-Publisher
> Higginson Press
> Brentwood, MD

To the Conference on Two of Our Greatest:

When I said I couldn't come, Natalie Datlof and Alexej Ugrinsky, in a joint communiqué, asked me if I'd write a paragraph of greetings, to include some of my "thoughts and feelings about Emily Dickinson and her place and significance as an American woman and poet." (How can one resist a joint communiqué?) The greetings are easy -- and here they are, warm and (because I can't be with you) envious. It should be a memorable occasion.

As to my thoughts and feelings: we're gaining all the time. When I was in college, her name was never even mentioned -- and I majored in English. And now, just a few weeks ago, the Washington Post, no less, called her "the great, arguably the greatest, American poet." (I'll argue for her any time). That's the focus I like. Certainly we must try to understand her position as a woman in her time, though I'd warn against extrapolating late 20th century tensions into the mid-19th. But the overarching aim of all our endeavors is to make her poetry -- and those marvelous poetic letters -- live and breathe (those are her metaphors) for all people who can read English, so that never again will an English major leave his Alma Mater without having at least tasted that immortal wine!

> Richard B. Sewall
> Professor of English, Emeritus
> Yale University
> New Haven, CT

Thursday, November 6, 1980   Hofstra University Library, David Filderman Gallery
                              Department of Special Collections - 9th Floor

Pre-Conference Event   Art Exhibit:

7:30 - 9:30 P.M.   Women Artists of the Berry Region - France

                             Marie Ebbesen - Eguzon, France
                             Christiane Sand - Gargilesse, France

                             Wine and cheese Reception

Friday, November 7, 1980

9:00 - 11:00 A.M.   Registration David Filderman Gallery
                                           Dept. of Special Collections
                                           Hofstra University Library - 9th Floor

11:00 - 12:00   Greetings from the Hofstra University Community

                            Joseph G. Astman, Director
                            University Center for Cultural & Intercultural Studies

                            James M. Shuart
                            President

                            Opening Address: Germaine Greer
                                              Director, The Tulsa Center for the Study
                                              of Women's Literature
                                              University of Tulsa
                                              Tulsa, OK

                            "'Infinite Riches in a Little Room': Suggestions
                            Toward an Alternative Aesthetic."

12:00 - 1:00 P.M.   Opening of Gallery Exhibit and Reception

                            Greetings: Marguerite Regan
                                        Assistant to the Dean of Library Services

                            "Nineteenth Century Literary Women"

1:00 - 2:00   Lunch Main Dining Room, Student Center, North Campus

                            Dining Rooms ABC, Student Center, North Campus

1:30 - 2:00   Film: "The World of Emily Dickinson"
                                     starring Claire Bloom

2:00 - 3:30   PANEL I: EMILY DICKINSON AND T. W. HIGGINSON

                            Moderator: Rhoda Nathan
                                        Dept. of English, Hofstra University

                            "T. W. Higginson and Emily Dickinson in Feminist
                             Perspective."
                            Tilden G. Edelstein, Rutgers University
                            New Brunswick, NJ

Friday, November 7, 1980 (cont'd.) - Dining Rooms ABC, Student Center, North Campus

2:00 - 3:30	"The Soul's Society: Emily Dickinson and Colonel Higginson." Anna Mary Wells Douglass College - Rutgers University New Brunswick, NJ Professor Emerita "A Second Look at 'The Belle.'" Howard N. Meyer Rockville Centre, NY
3:30	Coffee Break
3:45 - 5:15 P.M.	PANEL II: GEORGE ELIOT Moderator: Virginia Tiger, Dept. of English Director of Women Studies Rutgers University-Newark Newark, NJ "Feminism and Positivism in George Eliot's Romola." Nancy L. Paxton, Rutgers University New Brunswick, NJ "George Eliot and Feminism: The Case of Daniel Deronda." Bonnie Zimmerman, San Diego State University San Diego, CA "George Eliot and Barbara Leigh Smith Bodichon: A Friendship." Nancy Pell, University of Michigan Ann Arbor, MI
5:30	Dinner Dining Rooms ABC, Student Center, North Campus $4.25 - Prix fixe (unlimited)
8:00	Evening Program - Student Center Theatre, North Campus Greetings: Robert C. Vogt, Dean Hofstra College of Liberal Arts & Sciences Marcia E. O'Brien, Director Nassau County Office of Cultural Development

---

Margaret Fuller - "Still Beat Noble Hearts."
          Part II - The European Years, 1846-1850

          Laurie James
          Actress and Dramatist

Sponsored by: Hofstra College of Liberal Arts & Sciences
          Robert C. Vogt, Dean

          Nassau County Office of Cultural Development
          Marcia E. O'Brien, Director

**HOFSTRA UNIVERSITY'S
NINETEENTH CENTURY WOMEN WRITERS'
CONFERENCE**

proudly presents

LAURIE JAMES as MARGARET FULLER

in

Still Beat Noble Hearts

Part II

THE
EUROPEAN YEARS
1846 - 1850

A Dramatic Portrait written,
directed, and produced by
Laurie James

FRIDAY, NOVEMBER 7, 1980 8:00 PM
STUDENT CENTER, NORTH CAMPUS

Sponsored by:
Hofstra College of Liberal Arts & Sciences
Robert C. Vogt, Dean

Nassau County Office of Cultural Development
Marcia E. O'Brien, Director

Saturday, November 8, 1980   Dining Rooms ABC - Student Center, North Campus

8:00 - 9:00 A.M.   Continental Breakfast

                        David Filderman Gallery Exhibit
                        "Nineteenth Century Literary Women"

                        Gallery hours: Saturday, Nov. 8 - 9:00-1:00 & 2:15-4:00 p.m.
                                        Sunday, Nov. 9 - 9:30-2:00 p.m.

9:00 - 5:00 P.M.   Book Fair - Student Center Mezzanine

9:00 - 10:30   PANEL III A: EMILY DICKINSON

                        Moderator: Wilbur S. Scott
                                    New College, Hofstra University

                        "The Bride of the White Election: A New Look at
                           Biblical Influence on Emily Dickinson."
                        Peggy Anderson
                        Virginia Beach, VA

                        "The Second Act: Dickinson's Orphan-Child."
                        Vivian R. Pollak, Cheyney State College
                        Cheyney, PA

                        "'Oh, Susie, it is dangerous': Emily Dickinson and
                           the Archetype of the Masculine."
                        Joanne A. Dobson, SUNY - Albany
                        Albany, NY

9:00 - 10:30   PANEL III B: GENERAL EUROPEAN: RUSSIA, SPAIN, & SWEDEN

                        Moderator: Myroslava Znayenko, Dept. of Foreign Langs.
                                    Rutgers University-Newark
                                    Newark, NJ

                        "Fredrika Bremer: Sweden's First Feminist."
                        Doris R. Asmundsson, Queensborough Community College
                        Bayside, NY

                        "Adelaida Muñiz y Mas: Maruja Carmela, a Spanish Parody."
                        Patricia Bentivegna, Saint Francis College
                        Loretto, PA

                        "A Nigilistka and a Communarde: Two Voices of the
                           Nineteenth Century Russian Intelligentka."
                        Isabelle Naginski, Bard College
                        Annandale-on-Hudson, NY

10:30 - 11:00   Coffee Break - Student Center Mezzanine

11:00 - 12:30   PANEL IV A: GENERAL ENGLISH

                        Moderator: Carole Silver, Dept. of English
                                    Stern College - Yeshiva University
                                    New York, NY

                        "Christina Rossetti: A Reconsideration."
                        Robert N. Keane, Hofstra University
                        Hempstead, NY

Saturday, November 8, 1980 (cont'd.)   -   Dining Rooms ABC - Student Center, North Campus

11:00 - 12:30   "The Price of Love -- Eliot and Gaskell."
                             Coral Lansbury, Rutgers University
                             Camden, NJ

                             "'Michael Field' (Edith Cooper and Katherine Bradley)
                                and Their Male Critics."
                             David J. Moriarty, Hofstra University
                             Hempstead, NY

11:00 - 12:30   Special Panel under the Auspices of the Consulate
                                General of the Federal Republic of Germany:

                             PANEL IV B: ANNETTE VON DROSTE - HÜLSHOFF

                             Moderator: Ulrike Woods
                                          Goethe House
                                          New York, NY

                             "Annette von Droste-Hülshoff and Her Critics."
                             Maruta L. Ray, Rider College
                             Lawrenceville, NJ

                             "Inwardness and Creativity: Privacy and Artistic
                                Commitment in Emily Dickinson and Annette von
                                Droste-Hülshoff."
                             Edith Toegel, University of New Hampshire
                             Durham, NH

                             "Feminism and the Feminine in Annette von
                                Droste-Hülshoff."
                             Friedrich Ulfers, New York University
                             New York, NY

12:30 - 1:15   Lunch   Main Dining Room, Student Center, North Campus
                                     A la carte

1:15 - 2:00   Special Presentation:

                             Lucille and Walter Fillin
                             Hofstra Library Associates

                             "Nineteenth Century Women Cook Book Writers."

2:00 - 4:00   PANEL V A: GENERAL NORTH AMERICAN

                             Moderator: Margaret Vanderhaar Allen
                                          Bethlehem, PA

                             "Sisters and Survivors: Catherine Parr Traill
                                (1802-99) and Susanna Moodie (1803-85)."
                             Ann Edwards Boutelle, Suffolk University
                             Boston, MA; Mount Holyoke College, S. Hadley, MA

                             "Nineteenth Century Afro-American Women Poets."
                             Renate Simson, Syracuse University
                             Syracuse, NY; SUNY at Morrisville, Morrisville, NY

Saturday, November 8 1980 (cont'd.)   -   Dining Rooms ABC - Student Center, North Campus

2:00 - 4:00   "Margaret Fuller's Woman in the Nineteenth Century:
                          The Feminist Manifesto."
                       Marie O. Urbanski, University of Maine
                       Orono, ME

2:00 - 4:00   PANEL V B: GENERAL FRENCH

                       Moderator: Erica Abeel, Dept. of Foreign Languages
                                    John Jay College - CUNY
                                    New York, NY

                       "Juliette Adam: She Devil or Grande française."
                       Jean Scammon Hyland, University of Rhode Island
                       Daniel H. Thomas, University of Rhode Island
                       Kingston, RI

                       "Flora Tristan: A Woman's Struggle for Equality
                          and Justice."
                       Mary Lee Morris, Cathedral College
                       Douglaston, NY

                       "George Sand's View of the English."
                       Patricia Thomson, University of Sussex
                       Brighton, England

                       "George Sand and the Puppet Theatre at Nohant."
                       Julia Bloch Frey, University of Colorado
                       Boulder, CO

4:00 - 4:30   Coffee Break and Book Fair - Student Center Mezzanine

                       Student Center Theater, North Campus

4:30 - 6:15   PANEL VI - WOMEN AND EDUCATION

                       Moderator: Vivian Gornick
                                    New York, NY

                       "Education for Wifehood in the Courtesy Book Novels
                          of Mary Jane Holmes."
                       Lucy Brashear, Appalachian State University
                       Boone, NC

                       "Minerva in the Shadows: Women and the American
                          Intellectual Tradition."
                       Berenice A. Carroll, University of Illinois at
                          Urbana-Champaign, Urbana, IL

                       "Lewis Carroll and the Education of Victorian Women."
                       Morton N. Cohen, The Graduate School of CUNY
                       New York, NY

                       "The Career Woman Fiction of Elizabeth Stuart Phelps."
                       Susan Ward, St. Lawrence University
                       Canton, NY

6:30   Conference Banquet - Dining Rooms ABC, Student Center

                       Greetings: James M. Shuart, President
                                    Hofstra University

                       Guest of Honor: Germaine Brée
                                         Wake Forest University
                                         Winston-Salem, NC

                       Keynote Address:

                       "The Unpredicted Double: Nineteenth Century Women
                         Writers as Twentieth Century Mirrors."

                       Award Ceremony:

                                        Avriel Goldberger, French Department
                                        Cultural Counselor of the French Embassy
                                        James M. Shuart, President

                                           PROGRAM

Sonata in F Major   George Philipp Telemann
   Vivace   (1681-1787)
   Largo
   Allegro

Variations on a Theme by Rossini   Frédéric Chopin
                                                               (1810-1849)

Offertoire, Op. 12   Johannes Donjon
                                                             (19th century)

Divertissement No. 2, Op. 68   Friedrich Kuhlau
                                                               (1786-1832)

                                    INTERMISSION

Gigue   Jean-Marie Le Clair
                                                           (1697-1764)
                                                    arr. Georges Barrère

Syrinx   Claude Debussy
                                                             (1862-1918)

Baroque Suite   Ellen Levy
   Allegretto   (1954-   )
   Andante
   Moderato

Concertino, Op. 107   Cécile Chaminade
                                                             (1857-1944)

                          Martha Tunnicliff, Flute
                          Mary Elizabeth LaTorre, Piano

Sunday, November 9, 1980   Dining Rooms ABC - Student Center, North Campus

8:00 - 9:00 A.M.   Continental Breakfast

                                David Filderman Gallery Exhibit - 9:30 - 2:00 p.m.

                                "Nineteenth Century Literary Women"

9:00 - 11:00   PANEL VII - MME DE STAËL AND WOMAN AS ARTIST

                                Moderator: Avriel Goldberger
                                            French Department, Hofstra University

                                "Corinne and the 'Yankee Corinna': Mme de Staël
                                  and Margaret Fuller."
                                Paula Blanchard
                                Lexington, MA

                                "Woman as Mediatrix from Rousseau to Mme de Staël."
                                Madelyn Gutwirth, West Chester State College
                                West Chester, PA

                                "Mme de Staël on the Position of Women in France,
                                  England and Germany."
                                Eve Sourian, The City College of CUNY
                                New York, NY

                                "Henry James and the Woman Novelist: The Double
                                  Standard in the Tales and Essays."
                                Mary P. Edwards, Randolph-Macon College
                                Ashland, VA

11:00   Coffee Break

11:15 - 1:00 P.M.   Special Panel under the Auspices of the Cultural
                                Services of the French Embassy:

                                PANEL VIII - GEORGE SAND AND INTERTEXTUALITY

                                Moderator: Michael Riffaterre, Chairman
                                             French Department
                                             Columbia University
                                             New York, NY

                                "Intertext and Sexuality in George Sand's Lélia."
                                Sherry A. Dranch, Wheaton College
                                Norton, MA

                                "Lélia: An Intertextual Perspective."
                                Shelley Temchin Henze, Tufts University
                                Medford, MA

                                "Intertextuality: George Sand and Flaubert -- An
                                  Exchange of Letters as an 'art poétique.'"
                                Gérard Roubichou, Cultural Attaché
                                Cultural Services of the French Embassy, New York, NY

                                "Alfred de Musset and George Sand: An Intertextual
                                  Literary Liaison."
                                Alex Szogyi, Hunter College/CUNY
                                New York, NY

Sunday, November 9, 1980 (cont'd.) - Dining Rooms ABC, Student Center, North Campus

1:00 - 2:00	Brunch Main Dining Room

1:00 - 2:00   Brunch   Main Dining Room
                                             Prix fixe (unlimited)
                                             $3.95

2:00 - 4:00   PANEL IX A - GENERAL EUROPEAN: FRENCH PANEL

Moderator: Beth Brombert
               Princeton, NJ

"George Sand et Frances Trollope."
Marie-Jacques Hoog, Douglass College-Rutgers University
New Brunswick, NJ - Presently at Université de Tours
Tours, France
Read by Marie M. Collins, Rutgers University-Newark
Newark, NJ

"Regards sur le 19ème siècle - le témoignage au féminin."
Marie-Claire Hoock-Demarle, Sorbonne-Nouvelle
Paris, France

"Les femmes auteurs de romans populaires dans la
  Grande-Presse française à la fin du 19ème siècle."
Evelyne Diebolt, Université de Paris VII
Paris, France

2:00 - 4:00   PANEL IX B - GENERAL EUROPEAN

Moderator: Robert N. Keane, Chairman
               Department of English
               Hofstra University

"The Rediscovery of Nineteenth Century Women Waiters:
  The Contribution of Ellen Moers."
(This talk is in honor of the late Ellen Moers)
Ruth Prigozy, Hofstra University
Hempstead, NY

"Toward a New Freedom: Rahel Varnhagen and the German
  Women Writers Before 1848."
Doris Starr Guilloton, New York University
New York, NY

"An Introduction to the Life and Times of Louise Otto."
Ruth-Ellen Boetcher Joeres, University of Minnesota
Minneapolis, MN

Sunday, November 9, 1980 (cont'd.) - Dining Rooms ABC, Student Center, North Campus

4:00   Coffee Break - Dining Rooms ABC

4:15 - 5:45   PANEL X - GENERAL ENGLISH

                             Moderator: Rachel France, Drama Dept.
                                          Lawrence University
                                          Appleton, WI

                             "Jane Austen's Mediative Voice."
                             Alison G. Sulloway, Virginia Polytechnic Institute &
                               State University
                             Blacksburg, VA

                             "Once More to the Attic: Bertha Rochester and the
                               Pattern of Redemption in Jane Eyre."
                             Gail P. Griffin, Kalamazoo College
                             Kalamazoo, MI

                             "Jane Eyre and Poverty."
                             Barbara Gates, University of Delaware
                             Newark, DE

                             "The Alcoholic Female in the Fiction of George Eliot
                               and Her Contemporaries."
                             Sheila Shaw, Wheaton College
                             Norton, MA

6:00   Wine and Cheese Reception

Nineteenth Century Women Writers Conference
Book Exhibition

Participants

AMS Press
56 East 13th Street
New York, NY 10003

Canadian Women's Studies
Toronto, Canada

Farrer, Straus & Giroux
19 Union Square West
New York, NY 10003

The Feminist Press
Box 334
Old Westbury, NY 11568

Hofstra University Publications
Hempstead, NY 11550
  George Sand Newsletter
  Twentieth Century Literature

Irvington Publishers, Inc.
551 Fifth Avenue
New York, NY 10016

The New American Library, Inc.
1633 Broadway
New York, NY 10019

New Sibylline Books, Inc.
Box 266 - Village Station
New York, NY 10014

Paulette Greene Rare Books
140 Princeton Road
Rockville Centre, NY 11570

Paulette Rose, Ltd.
Fine and Rare Books
3 North Lake Circle
White Plains, NY 10605

Wantagh Rare Book Company
18 East Sunrise Highway
Freeport, NY 11520

Nel Panzeca
Director, Book Exhibition

CREDIT for the success of the Conference goes to more people than can be named on
   this program, but those below deserve a special vote of thanks:

HOFSTRA UNIVERSITY OFFICERS: James M. Shuart, President
                               Harold E. Yuker, Provost
                               Robert C. Vogt, Dean, HCLAS

ARA Slater: Richard Adler

DAVID FILDERMAN GALLERY: Department of Special Collections
                           Marguerite Regan, Assistant to the Dean of Library Services
                           Nancy Herb
                           Anne Rubino

DEPARTMENT OF COMPARATIVE LITERATURE & LANGUAGES: Alice Hayes, Senior Executive Secretary

ENGLISH DEPARTMENT: Barbara Stroh, Senior Executive Secretary
                      Nancy Mumolo, Secretary to the Faculty

FRENCH DEPARTMENT: Colette Bailey, Senior Executive Secretary

HOFSTRA LIBRARY ASSOCIATES: Walter Fillin, President

HOFSTRA UNIVERSITY LIBRARY: Charles R. Andrews, Dean

OFFICE OF THE SECRETARY: Robert D. Noble, Secretary
                           Armand Troncone
                           Doris Brown and Staff

SCHEDULING OFFICE: Margaret Shields

UCCIS: Marilyn Seidman, Conference Secretary
         Conference Assistants: Karin Barnaby
                                  Alexander Lake
                                  Nel Panzeca

UNIVERSITY RELATIONS: Harold Klein, Director
                        Brian Ballweg, Assistant Director

THE WOMEN'S CENTER

STUDENT AIDES: English Department

Index

About the Contributors

DORIS R. ASMUNDSSON is professor of English at Queensborough Community College of the City University of New York. She is the author of *Georg Brandes: Aristocratic Radical*, a biography of the nineteenth-century literary critic, and of articles on Scandinavian literature.

PAULA BLANCHARD, an independent writer and scholar, is the author of *Margaret Fuller: From Transcendentalism to Revolution*. Her latest book, a biography of the Canadian painter and writer Emily Carr, is nearing completion and should be published shortly.

GERMAINE BREE, recently retired as Kenan Professor of Humanities at Wake Forest University, was previously Vilas Professor of French at the Institute for Research in the Humanities at the University of Wisconsin/Madison. She chaired Romance Languages and directed the Graduate School of Arts and Sciences at New York University and was professor of French at Bryn Mawr College. A former president of the Modern Language Association and *chevalier* of the Legion of Honor, she has served on the advisory boards of the American Council of Learned Societies and the National Endowments of Arts and Humanities. Her many books include works on Proust, Gide and Camus; *Crisis and Commitment* and *Women Writers in France*.

JULIA FREY is associate professor of French at the University of Colorado and also taught at Yale and Brown Universities, the University of Paris I and Sarah Lawrence College. She has published *George Sand, the Woman and her World* and the first edition of the recently located Flaubert manuscript *La Lutte du sacerdoce et de l'empire*. She is currently writing a biography of Henri de Toulouse-Lautrec.

DORIS STARR GUILLOTON, professor of German and comparative literature at New York University, is director of German Undergraduate Studies. She has published articles on German Romanticism, the Faust theme and methodology and is author of *Deutsche Literatur von Heute* with A. Domandi and *Der Begriff des Symbols in der deutschen Klassik und Romantik*.

MADELYN GUTWIRTH, professor of French and women's studies at West Chester University, is the author of *Madame de Staël, Novelist: The Emergence of the Artist as Woman*. She is particularly interested in the cultural expression of gender conflict. Her writing includes a major article on Laclos. At present she is concentrating on the art and literature of the French Revolution.

MARIE-CLAIRE HOOCK-DEMARLE is maître de conférence in German literature and civilization at the University of Paris (*Sorbonne Nouvelle*). She has published a number of comparative studies on women and social inquiry at the beginning of urban industrialization. Her main interest is Bettina Brentano-von Arnim, and she has published on this subject.

MARIE-JACQUES HOOG has taught in the Department of French at Rutgers, the State University of New Jersey, for more than twenty-five years, following appointments at Hunter College and Smith College. Fellow of l'Ecole Normale Supérieure, Paris, France, she has concentrated, in the past ten years, her principal research efforts on the reassessment of George Sand as a major writer and on the delineation of the Myth of the Sibyl, which is the subject of the book she is preparing, *La Sibylle Romantique*.

JEAN SCAMMON HYLAND, associate professor of French and co-ordinator of study abroad at the University of Rhode Island, has taught at the College of William and Mary, Christopher Newport College and the University of Kansas. She is the author of *Reading Proficiency in French*, a four-volume work. She has written on the twentieth-century French novel and Robert Brasillach, concentrating since 1980 on Juliette Adam.

RUTH-ELLEN BOETCHER JOERES is professor of German and director of the Center for Advanced Feminist Studies at the University of Minnesota. Primarily interested in the social and literary history of German women in the eighteenth and nineteenth centuries and the development of feminist theory, she has published extensively on Louise Otto and is currently working on a study of feminism and femininity in nineteenth-century Germany.

MARUTA LIETINA-RAY is assistant dean of the college and teaches in the Department of Germanic Languages and Literature at the University of Virginia. Previously, she was associate professor of German at Rider College. Her interests and publications include bilingualism, the methodology of teaching culture, and the works of Annette von Droste-Hülshoff.

ISABELLE NAGINSKI is assistant professor of French and comparative literature at Tufts University. She has also taught at Columbia and Rutgers universities as well as at Bard College. She has published numerous articles on nineteenth-century French and Russian literature and has recently completed a book entitled *Literary Traffic: The Impact of French Fiction on the Russian Novel*. Her new volume on George Sand will shortly be published by Rutgers.

EVE SOURIAN is associate professor of French at the City University of New York and at the Graduate Center of the City University. She is director of the Women's Studies Program at City College. She is the author of *Madame de Staël and Henri Heine: Les deux Allemagnes* and has written frequently on George Sand.

ALEX SZOGYI, professor of French and comparative literature at Hunter College/CUNY, has translated more than forty plays including all of Chekhov. He is the author of *Molière abstrait* and was invited to discuss the playwright on Bernard Pivot's *Apostrophes*. He has published more than a dozen articles on George Sand and is a founding editor of the *Sand Newsletter* at Hofstra University. He has prepared a guide to New York restaurants.

DANIEL H. THOMAS, is professor emeritus of the University of Rhode Island. With Lynn M. Case, he edited the much-used *Guide to the Diplomatic Archives of Western Europe* and *The New Guide*. His most recent work is *The Guarantee of Belgian Independence and Neutrality in European Diplomacy, 1830s–1930s*.

PATRICIA THOMSON is now emeritus reader of the University of Sussex where she held an appointment from 1964. Previously at Aberdeen University, she held a visiting professorship at SUNY/Buffalo in 1966–67. She is the author of *The Victorian Heroine: A Changing Ideal* and *George Sand and the Victorians*.

About the Editor

AVRIEL H. GOLDBERGER is Professor and Chairman of the French Department at Hofstra University. She is the author of *Visions of a New Hero* and has translated and annotated Germaine de Staël's *Corinne: Or, Italy*. She has published papers in *Twentieth Century Literature* and *French American Review*.

Hofstra University's
Cultural and Intercultural Studies
Coordinating Editor, Alexej Ugrinsky

George Sand Papers: Conference Proceedings, 1976
(Editorial Board: Natalie Datlof, Edwin L. Dunbaugh, Frank S. Lambasa,
Gabrielle Savet, William S. Shiver, Alex Szogyi)

George Sand Papers: Conference Proceedings, 1978
(Editorial Board: Natalie Datlof, Edwin L. Dunbaugh, Frank S. Lambasa,
Gabrielle Savet, William S. Shiver, Alex Szogyi)

Heinrich von Kleist Studies
(Editorial Board: Alexej Ugrinsky, Frederick J. Churchill,
Frank S. Lambasa, Robert F. von Berg)

William Cullen Bryant Studies
(Editors: Stanley Brodwin, Michael D'Innocenzo)

*Walt Whitman: Here and Now
(Editor: Joann P. Krieg)

*Harry S. Truman: The Man from Independence
(Editor: William F. Levantrosser)

*Nineteenth-Century Women Writers of the English-Speaking World
(Editor: Rhoda B. Nathan)

*Lessing and the Enlightenment
(Editor: Alexej Ugrinsky)

*Dostoevski and the Human Condition After a Century
(Editors: Alexej Ugrinsky, Frank S. Lambasa, and Valija K. Ozolins)

*The Old and New World Romanticism of Washington Irving
(Editor: Stanley Brodwin)

*Einstein and the Humanities
(Editor: Dennis P. Ryan)

---

* Available from Greenwood Press